Teaching Young Children

Edited by

Tricia David

P·C·P

Paul Chapman
Publishing Ltd

Selection, editorial material and Chapter 1 © Copyright 1999 Tricia David
Chapter 2 © Copyright 1999 Teresa Grainger and Kathy Goouch
Chapter 3 © Copyright 1999 Bryan Hawkins
Chapter 4 © Copyright 1999 Gill Bottle and Claire Alfrey
Chapter 5 © Copyright 1999 Mike Waring
Chapter 6 © Copyright 1999 Peter Dorman
Chapter 7 © Copyright 1999 Eric Parkinson and Caroline Thomas
Chapter 8 © Copyright 1999 Gill Nicholls
Chapter 9 © Copyright 1999 Stephen Scoffham
Chapter 10 © Copyright 1999 Beryl Webber
Chapter 11 © Copyright 1999 Vanessa Young
Chapter 12 © Copyright 1999 Tricia David and Angela Nurse
Chapter 13 © Copyright 1999 Carl Parsons and Carol Precious

First published 1999

 Paul Chapman Publishing Ltd
A SAGE Publications Company
6 Bonhill Street
London EC2A 4PU

SAGE Publications Inc.
2455 Teller Road
Thousand Oaks, California 91320

SAGE Publications India Pvt Ltd
32, M-Block Market
Greater Kailash-I
New Delhi 110 048

British Cataloguing in Publication Data
A catalogue record for this book is available from the British Library

ISBN 1 85396 439 5
ISBN 1 85396 396 8 (pbk)

Library of Congress catalog card number available

Typeset by Anneset, Weston-super-Mare, Somerset
Printed and bound in Great Britain by Athenaeum Press, Gateshead
ABCDEF 32109

Contents

Acknowledgements

As Editor, my first acknowledgement must be to the authors who have contributed to this book and to their families for sustaining them, when they needed space in order to write in an already over-worked life! We all acknowledge the role played by our students and other colleagues at Canterbury Christ Church University College and in the wider world of education, from preschool to university level, for without their debate and challenge our own thinking would be limited. Our publishers, especially Marianne Lagrange, have been ever patient and helpful and Louise Duff invaluable for her secretarial skills.

Canterbury Christ Church University College is a developing, vibrant community of learners, set geographically in a position to influence and be influenced by other learners in this large county of Kent and beyond – for we are a 'quick hop' from mainland Europe. The College has been recognised as a leading teacher training institution and so, as teacher educators, we seek in this and the companion publication, *Young Children Learning*, to share some of our ideas and to encourage the debate and disagreement which are the signs of a strong and healthy democracy. In particular, within that debate, we want parents, educators, teachers, politicians and policy makers to discuss what childhood is for and what education is for, especially in the earliest and the primary school years. When we have decided on some answers to these questions and have explored the meaning of those answers, in terms of the values underpinning our society, we will be clear about the content and processes of the curriculum for children in the earliest stages of their lifelong education.

Tricia David
Canterbury
June 1998

The authors

Claire Alfrey is a Senior Lecturer in Education at Canterbury Christ Church College. Although having taught throughout the primary age range, she specialises in the early years. Claire's interest in young children's understanding and knowledge of mathematics comes from teaching children in reception and observing her own son beginning to tackle and make sense of preschool mathematics.

Gill Bottle is a Senior Lecturer in Education at Canterbury Christ Church College, where her main teaching responsibilities lie in mathematics and science curriculum studies. She has extensive experience as a classroom teacher, specialising in the early years of schooling. Gill has an MA in mathematics curriculum studies and she is currently researching babies' mathematical experiences. Her earlier investigations have included a study of young children learning number, as well as research into children's and adults' aptitude for algebra.

Tricia David is a Professor of Education at Canterbury Christ Church College and Director of the Centre for International Studies in Early Childhood. She is currently leading a comparative research project on children's early literacy, which is funded by the Esmée Fairbairn Foundation. Tricia's many publications have focused largely on the ways in which societies treat and educate their youngest citizens.

As a serving teacher in an area of Educational Priority on Tyneside, **Peter Dorman** came to the use of computing as a possible strategy for differentiating the curriculum for pupils with Special Educational Needs. Working with colleagues in neighbouring schools and HEIs, Peter developed support and training materials for use within school settings. A period with the Advisory Service in Kent enabled him to develop these activities further and to work with colleagues in a range of contexts. Peter's present work at Canterbury Christ Church College, as Primary ICT Coordinator, brings him into contact with the next generation of teachers at a time when the role of Information and

Communication Technologies is about to expand at an ever increasing rate. Peter's current interests are in the areas of multimedia and web authoring.

In her role as a tutor at Christ Church College, **Kathy Goouch** focuses mainly on English teaching and young children's learning. Kathy is a member of the research team currently exploring the meaning of literacy in preschool settings in England and France. Together with a former colleague at the College, she used video to study appropriate ways of teaching reading and this work has been used to help students on initial teacher training courses at Canterbury Christ Church College.

Teresa Grainger works as a Principal Lecturer in Education, mostly in English inservice training, although she still teaches regularly in schools. Teresa is particularly fascinated by young children's artistic, linguistic and imaginative competence, and how educators can enhance this potential.

Bryan Hawkins grew up in South London, where he was massively influenced by a superb art teacher and developed a love of art, ideas and drawings. He attended the Chelsea School of Art in the mid-1970s. Following this, Bryan spent time travelling in China, New Zealand and Australia and on his return he trained as an Early Years teacher. He then spent seven happy years as a primary school teacher, with a particular interest in children with special educational needs and in the potential of art and the arts generally. Bryan is currently employed as a Senior Lecturer in Art at Canterbury Christ Church College. He is active as an artist and his research interests include making art (drawings, paintings, prints) and writing.

Gill Nicholls worked at Canterbury before becoming a Senior Lecturer at the University of Surrey. Gill's research interests lie in transitions from primary to secondary school, Science Education and children's cognitive development.

Angela Nurse has a first degree in history but trained as a teacher. Much of her teaching has been with very young children with special needs, mainly in inner London and Kent. Before coming to Canterbury Christ Church College as a Senior Lecturer, she worked in an advisory capacity with teachers and colleagues in the other statutory services and within the private and voluntary sectors.

Angela has worked extensively with parents, often in their own homes. She now directs the Early Childhood Studies degree programme at Canterbury and is a Registered Nursery Inspector and Vice-Chair of the governing body of her local school. Her new role as a grandmother, however, brings into sharper focus all the work she has done with very young children!

Eric Parkinson is a Senior Lecturer in Primary Education at Canterbury Christ Church College. His research field concerns the development and applications of construction kit activity in the early years. His experience in this area has been supported by class teaching experience and leading of continuing professional development activity in the UK, West Indies and southern Africa, as well as overseas consultancy activity for a number of global agencies and Commonwealth governments.

Carl Parsons is a Professor of Education at Christ Church College. He has long experience of evaluation and quality assurance in education. He has written workshop materials on evaluation for teachers and proposes a model of self-evaluation which is for development rather than accountability. Recent articles he has written are critical of Ofsted because of their punitive orientation. Carl is well known nationally for his work on exclusions at both primary and secondary levels.

Carol Precious was headteacher of an infant school before taking up her post as a Senior Lecturer at Canterbury Christ Church College. Carol is especially interested in literacy in the early years and has undertaken a study of parents and children writing together.

Stephen Scoffham is senior lecturer in primary geography at Canterbury Christ Church College. He has written a wide range of teaching materials including *World Watch Geography* and the *Key Start* atlas programme. He contributes regularly to *Primary Geographer* and currently serves on the governing bodies of the Geographical Association, Canterbury Environment Centre and World Education Development Centre (East Kent).

Caroline Thomas is Deputy Headteacher of Kemsing County Primary School in Kent. Formerly she was a Senior Lecturer at Canterbury Christ Church College, specialising in Science and in Design and Technology Education. She has undertaken international research in Health Education and Health Promotion.

Mike Waring is a Lecturer in the School of Education at Durham University. He has worked as a teacher, researcher and lecturer in Physical Education for the past decade. His main areas of interest are: children and young people's involvement in physical activity; ITT; and the development of qualitative research methodology.

Beryl Webber was a Senior Lecturer at Canterbury Christ Church College before taking up an appointment with the new Medway Authority. She was responsible for the coordination of assessment across the primary phase teacher education courses. Beryl has worked closely with SCAA/QCA in the development of National Baseline Assessment and has a particular interest in children learning mathematics.

Vanessa Young is a senior lecturer in the Department of Education. Apart from her main curriculum area of music, she coordinates primary school-based CPD and staff development for the department. Her previous role was as a Staff Development Coordinator for Kent LEA.

1

Changing minds: teaching young children

Tricia David

Ask anyone (in the UK) to recall what was special about a 'good teacher' who taught them in primary school and most will come up with similar descriptions of a person who was firm but fair, warm but not over-familiar, respectful, had a sense of humour, knew their stuff and made each pupil feel they (and their work) mattered. Embedded in these descriptions is a message about relationships. Research (Huttunen 1992) with older pupils which attempted to tease out what children in Finland valued about the preschools they attended until age seven demonstrated clearly that relationships are the most important and enduring factors. In his fine-grained research Andrew Pollard (1996) demonstrated how the quality of relationships is a crucial element in children's learning processes. The impact of emotional aspects of a school or nursery situation has long been neglected in the UK, as is amply demonstrated by the list of criteria for judging the quality of teaching drawn from Ofsted[1] criteria (Moyles and Suschitzky 1997). Perhaps such aspects are meant to be embedded in phrases like 'manage children well' but they do not really conjure up the kind of emotional well-being involved in the holistic view of early learning researched by Claire Mould (1998).

Relationships take time to develop and classrooms are, like the home, places where relationships are negotiated and refined (Delamont 1990; Edwards and Mercer 1987). Essentially, teaching is about relationships – between the teacher and: the children, their parents or carers, other teachers and staff, other professionals, the wider community. Teaching is also about the relationships between children, about setting up a learning environment, a climate for learning, and this requires knowledge of children generally and the immediate group of children in particular. Working together with parents (the people who know their children best) is a way of ensuring continuity

1

and coherence for children but all have their own histories and assumptions about what and how young children should be taught (Barrett 1986). So teachers' assumptions and knowledge bases should be constantly challenged by both initial and inservice training. To set down a prescribed, fixed knowledge base for teachers which might lead them to conclude there was little more to discover and that some-one somewhere has all the answers, the certainties, is a disservice to teachers and children.

However, in order not to become paralysed by uncertainty, as Lilian Katz has suggested, teachers of young children should be able to teach with 'optimal certainty' in the rightness of their actions and that these should be based on 'robust evidence' (Katz 1996, p. 145) but teachers should also be imbued with a healthy scepticism in order to question their own practice.

In her discussion of the philosophy underpinning the teaching in the celebrated nurseries of Reggio Emilia in Northern Italy, Gunilla Dahlberg (1995) draws attention to the ways in which pedagogical practice is recognised as dependent upon social constructions which are simply the beginning, being based on assumptions and experiences which are not 'neutral and innocent' but rather have the 'potential of being dangerous' (p. 10). In order to be able to critique and reflect on their practice, Reggio teachers maintain rigorous documentation and use this in their weekly sessions of continuous professional development. The documentation is more than a record of work with children, it is a story of a community, a way of exploring one's construction of oneself as a teacher and, as such, can lead to a realisation that rethinking of one's approaches, styles, children's learning and achievement, is necessary. In other words, teaching decisions are made on the basis of evidence and experience that have been analysed – but on the understanding that one must live with uncertainty, one cannot be sure that one's actions in teaching will always have the desired effect. In other words, in an ever changing world in which we are attempting to give children feelings of security and safety within a context where we want them to dare to make mistakes and to learn, we have to be prepared to change our own minds, and to try to change the minds of others in influential positions.

Further, parents' or teachers' actions are imbued with meaning and these meanings may differ from culture to culture and over time. In terms of the responses different actions evoke from children, what seems to be important are the meanings the children attach to particular behaviours on the part of parents and teachers (Katz 1996), so we need to be aware of how we change their minds through our teaching and through the hidden curriculum. Part of that hidden curriculum will be the way we view ourselves as learners:

> In the 'improving' schools teachers were encouraged to be learners themselves. Staff were encouraged to collaborate by learning with and from each other.
>
> > (Harris and Russ 1993, par. 5.3)

However, it is from the children, both individually and collectively, that we can learn most and according to Claxton 'good teachers' in the traditional sense may maximise training procedures which enable pupils to succeed at tests, examinations and in applying 'familiar operations to familiar content' (Claxton 1990, p. 154) but it is the type of teachers whom Claxton calls 'mentors' who equip their pupils to be 'good learners', because these 'good learners' are resourceful, creative and persistent, intelligent in the face of change.

The recent changes of mind concerning the training of teachers here in the UK has been criticised: 'the role of the teacher is being articulated in a way which displaces extended professionalism and replaces this with a version of "performativity" (Ball 1998, p. 5). It is assumed that there is a 'common framework for people with fixed goals ' (Furlong 1992, p. 168) and that all teachers need to know about is skills, task analysis and testing.

> Any alternative view of teaching is neatly marginalised . . . Of course we believe that academically able and effective classroom managers are needed in schools but the act of teaching is much more than this. A professional teacher is one who has a commitment to a professional code of ethics and displays professional integrity. We are concerned that a wider vision of the school teacher is being lost in the process of laying down, in minute detail, what it is that teachers need to know and be able to do . . .'
>
> > (Maguire *et al.* 1998, pp. 6–7).

During the last few years, teachers in the UK do seem to have borne the brunt of criticisms for whatever is wrong with our economy and society – for recessions, unemployment, unemployability, disaffected youth, illiteracy, indiscipline, immorality, export failures – the list appears endless and the brickbats continue. Not only teachers have failed, so the argument goes, so too have those who have educated and trained the teachers. So much so, that a 'national curriculum' for training teachers has been instituted (DfEE 1997 and 1998) and the inspections by Ofsted (Office for Standards in Education) of training establishments have been repeated (presumably because the inspectors themselves were thought to have failed to apply the framework appropriately the first time around), in a bid to ensure new teachers in primary schools achieve the standards delineated in the Government Circular.

In addition, strategies for literacy, piloted in 1997–98 and, although not compulsory, expected to be instituted by almost all primary schools, include patterns of teaching which not only prescribe the content of lessons but modes of 'delivery'. What constitutes 'good mathematics teaching' too is being prescribed.

Yet when the National Curriculum was being implemented and when the *Desirable Outcomes for Children's Learning on Entering Compulsory Education* (guidelines relating to under fives' education) were disseminated (SCAA 1996), it was claimed that teachers were to be the arbiters of the best teaching approaches for the children with whom they worked. In other words *what* children are to learn was dictated centrally but *how* they were to be taught was to be decided 'locally'.

However, as Jim Campbell points out, since 1992 there has been an

'obsession with pedagogy in a sophisticated but rather unsubtle attempt to deflect criticism from the structural problems in the curriculum, and problems of resources and expertise, onto teachers.'

(Campbell 1998, p. 98)

There has been pressure to teach whole-class fashion for significant proportions of the school day, in a style mimicking the Pacific Rim countries whose economies were, until recently, held up as a beacon to the British workforce.

Meanwhile, another development, the setting up of Nursery Partnerships, has been demanded of all local authorities. Nursery Partnerships are groupings of under fives' providers from the maintained, private and voluntary sectors, initiated so that educators from the whole range of settings (for example, maintained and private nursery schools and classes, childminding, playgroups/preschools, reception classes) can come together to provide a coordinated system of nursery education for four year olds (in the first instance). Further, during 1998–99 nursery partnerships must ensure that a qualified teacher is involved in some way with every setting offering a place to a four year old funded out of the public purse. This means that new challenges face the teachers appointed to carry out such work. It is possible that even within one local authority area several different models of teacher involvement may be piloted, for some models will grow out of the history of the links between the statutory and the other sectors. Eventually provision for children under four and care facilities for children up to age 14, outside school hours, must be developed (DoH and DfEE 1998). The ways in which teachers and professionals from other agencies, such as Social Services and the Police, work together is expected to change when the Government's proposals concerning inter-agency cooperation to safeguard children are finalised (DoH 1998a). The Department of Health (1998a) consultation document stresses the implications of existing legislative changes such as the publishing of Children's Services Plans, developed after consultation among all service providers, and the new proposals, while intended to improve the situation for children in distressing circumstances, will place additional responsibilities on schools and teachers.

A further development resulting from Governmental recognition of the burdensome nature of some of the new demands is the proposal to rationalise inspections of early childhood services in the private and voluntary sectors. Such settings are at present inspected by both Social Services and Ofsted registered nursery inspectors but they use different frameworks (see Chapter 13 for further discussion of under fives' inspections).

So both practising teachers and those in initial training for early years and primary work must be prepared for the multi-professional field in which their role and responsibility meshes with that of many other adults, especially children's parents and carers.

Finally, in the belief that literacy and numeracy achievements will be ameliorated, the Secretary of State for Education has freed up legal requirements of schools in the Foundation subjects (Art, Music, PE, History, Geography) from September 1998 until 2000, during the period of the New Labour Government's review of the National Curriculum. This will mean that certain subject coordinators may find the time for their specialism being almost squeezed out. School teams will need to ask themselves searching questions about children's access to different areas of experience and the effect omissions may have. This is not simply a question of some children being denied opportunities to develop talents they may be bringing to schools, which is in itself important. It is a vital question for our society. We need to go right back to the question of what education is for, what different areas of the curriculum, or subjects are 'for', and thus what education and training is needed by our teachers.

Teaching young children: questions of pedagogy

In 1992 the report *Curriculum Organisation and Classroom Practice* (Alexander *et al.* 1992) was published at the request of the then Secretary of State for Education, Kenneth Clarke. This report used research evidence to make recommendations about 'teaching methods and classroom practice . . . particularly in Key Stage 2' (par. 1). In fact, it was ostensibly the upper years of primary schooling about which there was most concern and for which it was claimed subject specialisation by teachers was particularly important. The problem was that the authors of that report seemed to take no account of the fact that any tinkering with what happens in the classes of older children has always involved downward pressure on teachers of younger children. This is not to say that changes should never occur, it is to argue that a consideration of the organic nature of our education system was required. It was already known (David 1993; Sylva *et al.* 1992) that the implementation of the National Curriculum in Key Stage 1 (KS1) had had repercussions for the early years (suddenly this term was being applied only to children between three and five years old, whereas the international definition of early years has traditionally been the phase from birth to eight years). Educators in under fives' settings not trained as early years teachers were anxiously attempting, inappropriately, to 'teach' the National Curriculum contents to children in nurseries and playgroups, and parents were pressurising staff in all under-fives' settings to teach formally, especially in those areas to be tested at the end of KS1, because they concluded formal teaching to be the best 'insurance policy' against their child's failure and subsequent labelling at age seven. More recent research (Sharp and Davis 1997) confirms the trend – that parents are concerned to have their children learn reading and mathematics at an early age. But parents questioned for the 1997 study did want a range of play activities for their young children too, at least the parents of three year olds emphasised this and the parents of four year olds wanted to be sure of a balance between reading and mathematics and play.

Although some researchers argue that play has not actually been proven as the pre-eminent vehicle for young children's learning (e.g. Smith 1986) and there is much debate about what exactly *play* means to many practitioners (free choice or experiential activities structured by an adult), there is strong evidence that children's long term achievements in school are promoted by early learning which is child-directed (Sylva 1998). In fact Ofsted (1993) placed a heavy emphasis on the balance between learning through self-directed play and learning through teacher-directed activities in classrooms for young children. There is a similar emphasis in the Ofsted Nursery Inspection Framework (Ofsted 1997 and 1998), with requirements that children are enabled to take the initiative in some of their activities. In fact the Welsh version of the Desirable Outcomes relating to the framework for learning in the early years (Curriculum and Assessment Authority for Wales 1996) stresses *play* as the main mode of 'delivery' of such outcomes.

However, it can be difficult to teach through a play-based curriculum in the face of pressure for formal reading, writing and arithmetic, baseline assessment which may reflect badly on preschool provision, and fears that the earlier one starts, the better the child will be in literacy and numeracy, in spite of claims to the contrary (see Chapter 12 for a fuller discussion). It is not content that is necessarily the problem – as Bruner pointed out (1966) an accomplished teacher can teach more or less anything to a learner no matter what their age – it is *how* they teach it that is the question and the appropriateness or otherwise of their chosen approaches. So in fact, pedagogy is about both what is to be taught, the pupils' development and learning, as well as about teaching strategies.

The haste to formalise is sometimes attributed to the lack of child development courses in recent teacher education, partly because it was pushed out by other content in the teacher training curriculum, partly perhaps because of the claim that 'teaching is not applied child development' in the 1992 report (Alexander *et al.* 1992). While this is being remedied by Circular 4/98 (early years teachers will have to cover this in their training and teachers wishing to take up posts linking preschool providers involved in the Nursery Partnerships must have taken such courses), it should not be a simple matter of teaching Child Development as it was taught in the past. Developmental psychologists themselves are questioning their own specialism and its relevance, because it was founded on the methods of natural science which took no account of the cultural context in which the children studied (or used as 'norms') were developing, nor the shared meanings and co-constructions of reality. Such methods also meant that the definition of 'objectivity' adopted demanded distance between the researcher and the child observed – yet those of us who are parents and grandparents and who have extensive experience working with young children know that most children in this age group behave very differently in the presence of a stranger, particularly one who may themselves seem to exhibit strange behaviour as far as the children are concerned. So some of the laboratory-based child development 'norms', most derived from experiments with white middle class children in the USA, tell us simply about that situation.

In their research publication *Common Knowledge*, Edwards and Mercer (1987) demonstrate how children and teachers together develop the culture of the environment they share. This culture is, of course, set within the culture of the school, whose ethos and underpinning values will permeate life in that shared environment. When all the teachers in a school team have an agreed set of principles and have come to a common set of value statements, children can move from one class to another with ease. Similarly, such teachers are clear about their goals and purposes, about how their class fits into the whole that is the school, set within the community, within the local area, within the national scene.

Thus it is also important for teachers to be clear about the place of children in society. So often in the past, discussion of teaching young children has failed to take account of the context at a number of different levels. Firstly, how are children, especially preschool children, seen globally? In spite of many years of work by organisations like UNICEF, Save the Children, and others, young children are still vulnerable to the ravages of disease, hunger and war. The severely malnourished could, we are told, be fed by a fraction of what is spent on armaments or by half the money Europeans spend on smoking. At a national level, the infant mortality rate in certain groups in our society is linked to the proportions living in relative poverty; fathers in Britain work the longest hours in the European Community but we also have the second highest proportion of unemployed fathers (of children under nine years old); the decline in reading standards relates to the rapid increase in relative deprivation over the last twenty years; a child aged under one year is four times more likely to be the victim of homicide than a person in any other age group. In other words, we appear to have paid insufficient attention to the needs of very young children (David 1996).

Thankfully, as we approach the millennium in the UK, the place of young children seems to be one of greater visibility than ever before and they are beginning to be seen as learners from the moment of birth, the foundation phase of lifelong learning. So early years and primary teachers need to know about babies and toddlers, for it is in these years that attitudes to and styles of learning are laid. We need to develop our own 'bank' of observations of what children can do, at what ages, in what kind of setting, under what circumstances and to create our own theories about child development, comparing them with the 'grand theories' of the published experts. For children seem to 'live up or down' to the expectations of those around them – those they wish to please.

Similarly, we need the Government to recognise the sound advice provided by Professors Jim Campbell (1998) and Robin Alexander (1998) that schools be freed from too much curricular prescription, that debate commence as to which aspects of potential learning areas, or subjects, are vital to members of our future society and should therefore form the core curriculum (rather than whole subjects being 'in' or 'out').

According to international comparisons, high standards in the '3Rs' are achieved in countries where the curriculum is broad and balanced, where children have access to a wide range of subjects, so narrowing the curriculum down to little more than literacy and numeracy does not guarantee high standards (Le Métais and Tabberer 1997). As Alexander says, 'the debate now is about values first, structures and content second' (1998, p. 67). He points out that the SCAA's,[2] discussion of *Values in Education and the Community* failed to examine the values already reflected in the existing curriculum – and this would also apply to the *Desirable Outcomes* (SCAA 1996). Certainly an analysis of the *Desirable Outcomes* for Wales (Welsh Office 1996) demonstrates different values from the English document (SCAA 1996). And as Robin Alexander stresses, it would be pointless for 'a grand statement of educational purposes for the next century' (1998, p. 67) to be made, if the curriculum did not reflect them. The present emphasis seems to be instrumental – about teaching children what is needed for them to be future workers, in other words, the education service is in the service of the economy.

However, the extent to which children's learning is viewed **only** in terms of the future of the economy and not in other important respects means that some aspects of the role of teachers may still be underdeveloped. For example, Professor Michael Bassey (1995), in *Creating Education through Research*, argues that

> Country by country the formal education systems of the world deserve the focused intelligence of researchers striving to improve theory, policy and practice. Globally the world has a need for empirical, reflective and creative research into learning how to prevent famine, war, environmental pollution, resource depletion, extinction of wild-life species, and disruption of ecological systems.
>
> Creating education through research is . . . an imperative for democratic societies in free world.
>
> (Bassey 1995, p. 142)

Again, we are brought back to a discussion of values.

Teachers as weavers

The early years curriculum in New Zealand is based on the concept of a woven mat – a metaphor which is very appropriate in a society where the indigenous population are renowned for the beauty and complexity of their weaving. The strands the teacher must take comprise all the talents and dispositions of young children together with the areas of learning considered important by their society. For some children certain strands will be stronger, because of particular gifts or because of family encouragement, and in some communities certain strands will be more important than in others, but it is up to each community to decide on the 'width' of that strand.

In order to qualify to teach in primary schools and nurseries in all the other OECD (Organisation for Economic and Social Cooperation) and EC (European Community) countries, it is planned that degree level qualifications will be required in future (in some this is already the case). As a result of our history, we have one of the most diverse preschool systems in the world, with maintained, private and voluntary sectors providing for children under five and previously with very little coordination and cooperation, except where there has been local policy and encouragement to do so. What this has meant is that we also have a diverse range of training opportunities, some of which mesh together to form a 'climbing frame' of qualifications, but some do not mesh and are dead-end routes. Now the Government is demanding a coordinated service, developed by the Nursery Partnerships in each local authority. One of the problems to be addressed is indeed that of professionalism and qualifications. There are many very experienced preschool providers who have learnt on the job, who have great expertise with young children and their families, yet who do not wish to go through the rigmarole of gaining a qualification and, in any case, cannot afford to do so unfunded. There are others who claim to wish to stay as they are perhaps because they believe that while unqualified they are not so accountable. However, presumably anyone who takes up the role of educator of another person's children must be accountable: it is the role, not the qualification which demands the accountability.

In their research about nursery teachers and nursery nurses, Moyles and Suschitzky (1997) provided a list of the criteria for quality in teaching, derived from Ofsted's Schedule 5.1. (Ofsted 1995). They suggest (p. 8) that teachers should:

- have secure knowledge/understanding of subjects/areas
- set high expectations/clear objectives

- challenge pupils
- deepen children's knowledge and understanding
- plan effectively
- match methods to curriculum objectives
- match methods to needs of children
- manage children well
- use resources effectively
- assess children's work thoroughly and constructively
- use assessment to inform teaching
- ask relevant questions
- gather resources children will need
- differentiate
- use exposition/explanation that is lively and well-structured
- probe children's knowledge and understanding
- offer purposeful practical activity (i.e. play)
- allow children to think about what they have learned
- meet SEN Code of Practice requirements
- plan effectively
- provide continuity and progression
- create effective systems for for assessing children which are used to inform curriculum planning
- ensure sound record-keeping systems.

In the conclusions to their research, they add that where teachers are being replaced by practitioners (even Nursery Nurses, who have considerable expertise and knowledge), who do not have equivalent levels of training to the specialised teachers, and where they are required to adopt a greater teaching role, additional training is vital for the role. That role requires the ability to be a weaver of the complex tapestry which is each child's curriculum.

In her review of a number of research projects which explored children's achievements following engagement with different types of early years curricula, Kathy Sylva (1998) demonstrates the importance of teaching which allows children themselves to direct and make decisions about their learning foci, teaching which is effected through what to the children is play. However, both Penny Munn's research (1994) and that by Bennett *et al.* (1996) indicate that early years teachers and other early childhood educators need continuing professional development which encourages discussions based on observations of children's play, and their own provision and assessment of this, in order to ensure achievement and progression in the children's learning. The models of inservice support which these research projects advocate, therefore, are in line with the Goldsmiths' *Principles into practice project* (Blenkin *et al.* 1995) and with the model developed in the celebrated nurseries of Reggio Emilia in Northern Italy (see Edwards *et al.* 1998). It is not that these models are based on the notion of teaching as applied child development but that they demand a clear view of what children are doing, what is being offered as their learning environment, equipment, teaching plans and interactions, peer interactions, the context and community. However, what such approaches also do, as I explained earlier, is to establish the habit of critical thinking about one's own assumptions and practice, within a collegial network of other professionals engaging in the same quest for appropriate pedagogical principles and knowledge – not a universal pedagogical 'formula'.

The search for pedagogical principles and knowledge: changing minds through research and reflection

The chapters of this book are written by experienced teacher educators and researchers, all of whom have worked in primary and/or nursery schools. What they seek to do for readers is to engage with a topic in such a way as to promote an understanding of the weaving together of what we know about children's development and learning with what we know about the curriculum, or particular subjects/areas of learning. Such weaving is not without its challenges and dilemmas. Each chapter confronts the issues involved, demonstrating that teaching young children is a complex, exciting task.

In the nurseries of Reggio Emilia (where the children are educated from birth to age six), they speak of the 'hundred languages of children' and by this they mean all the different ways in which children can express themselves and communicate with each other and with the adults who share their lives. They are not expected to spend time in formal literacy and numeracy instruction, their exuberance and curiosity are used as the keys to learning and although it is the processes of exploration, experimentation, discovery, representation, transformation, interpretation, creation and evaluation which are central, their products achieve critical acclaim worldwide. (As those who attended the British Association for Early Childhood Education exhibition about the Reggio Emilia nurseries, at the Bethnal Green Museum of Childhood, London 1997, will attest.) In a sense, this book is an expression of fellow-feeling for the Reggio educators, albeit confined as we are by our national culture and the legal constraints of recent years. However, policies, laws and practices grow out of assumptions and understandings. Perhaps we can at least offer a challenge to some of the more limiting of those assumptions – we seek to be part of the exciting process of changing minds.

The chapters by Teresa Grainger and Bryan Hawkins deliciously celebrate the subversive nature of young children's being, the ways in which language and art can be used by them to express original and provocative ideas. Gill Bottle and Claire Alfrey stress the creative potential (so often ignored) of mathematics, its beauty and power are all around in the things which interest young children, from snails' shells to the stars. As the recent television documentary *Too much too soon* (Channel 4, 1998) argued, we may be wasting children's precious learning time and destroying their self-confidence by asking them to 'jump through formal hoops' and to use abstract symbolisation too early. Recent research from the USA (Sylva 1998) shows that children there who do not attend nurseries but who share many everyday mathematical experiences with their carers, such as sorting out socks or arranging the groceries, later outperform their peers who did attend nursery where they were expected to engage in school-type, planned maths activities.

In proposing a framework for primary physical education, Mike Waring's chapter should cause us to reflect on the gross and fine motor play in which children gain experience in a nursery or playgroup, or at tumble tots. Each society decides what physical skills it wishes to emphasise and develop – research indicating the decline in the length of breaks (playtime as it used to be called) should worry all who believe children need to move, to spend some time on self-chosen pursuits and to mix with other age groups. Compared with earlier periods in our history, there is very little time for children to engage in 'children's culture' (David and Nutbrown 1992; Hillman *et al.* 1990).

However, one area children may make their own is information technology – because they are so much more adept than adults in this area of learning. Peter Dorman asks: who controls children's experience and learning in IT – should it be the child? In the light of the new ICT (Information and Communications Technology) documentation for teacher training, which must be welcomed as of good intent, it has even been described as 'radical and imaginative' (Maguire *et al.* 1998, p. 35). However, philosophical and pedagogical concerns should exercise us, since the document (DfEE 1998) itself fails to address many of the issues, such as equal opportunities (especially gender), access and resourcing.

Creativity in both Science and in Design and Technology is an important aspect for teachers to consider, as chapters 7 and 8 suggest. In both these areas children are able to engage in ways which can be planned according to Janet Moyles' play spiral (Moyles 1989) and use Corinne Hutt's (Hutt *et al.* 1989) ideas about epistemic and ludic play – in the first, allowing children to explore, to metaphorically ask 'What does this do?' and then, creatively, in the ludic phase, using the knowledge they have gained through structured play/experiential learning 'What can I do with this?'

In his chapter about young children's perceptions of the world, Stephen Scoffham draws on his own and others' research, including that of Canterbury students. Stephen concludes that children today seem to hold much more sophisticated ideas about places, and at an earlier age than their counterparts of a generation or two ago, perhaps due to the impact of greater exposure to these ideas, possibly through television and travel. However, in relation to racism, comparisons from the research of twenty years ago with that carried out today should lead us to ask if we are now doing enough in our schools to prevent racist attitudes towards members of minority communities in the UK and to the Majority World in the global context.

With Baseline Assessment becoming universally applied in September 1998, Beryl Webber's chapter encourages readers to recognise that conscious and systematic assessment processes can help children's development and learning – and need not become a straitjacket. Here there are echoes of Mike Radford's chapter, *Co-constructing the world*, in the companion book *Young Children Learning*, for Beryl argues that the child internalises the explanations, clarifications, and language provided by an adult in one context and applies them to another at a future time. All the more reason for teachers and parents to work closely together, to truly understand the child's perceptions of a learning situation, because the child may have applied something understood at home and with which connections seem to help that child make sense.

Vanessa Young discusses the problems associated with a prescribed curriculum – the apparent loss of teachers' autonomy. As more and more is dictated by outside bodies, the teacher's work becomes merely functional. Vanessa suggests that in order to retain a professional orientation, teachers must use inservice not to be told how to implement the latest dictum but to develop 'organisational habits and structures that make continuous learning a valued and endemic part of the culture of schools and teaching' (Fullan 1991). The Teacher Training Agency has proclaimed its intention that teaching should be a research-based profession, both using the research findings of others appropriately and carrying out research. Coming together in local, national and international networks to share research can be empowering and subversive, for what one learns from and about other education systems can often challenge the thinking of policy-makers as much as that of practitioners.

Finally, the last two chapters examine aspects of evaluation of practice. The first, by Angela Nurse and myself, considers how the inspection systems operating in under fives' settings are impacting on the terminology used to describe children's learning activities and provision for young children with special educational needs. The second, by Carl Parsons and Carol Precious, suggests a way forward – self-evaluation – to pre-empt the pain of 'outsiders' telling us what is 'wrong', to know our strengths and weaknesses and plan how we will move forward.

Circular 4/98 (DfEE 1998) is a positive step in the recognition of early years teaching as a complex and demanding professional task. The curriculum for teacher education contained in Circular 4/98 has been criticised by some as overly prescriptive. It seems like the culmination of almost twenty years of a process of centralisation and, during that time, the re-articulation of 'the teacher'. However, if centralisation is the continued goal, in some senses there may be a contradiction in the Teacher Training Agency's (TTA) current intention to develop teaching as a research-based profession, since this signals a move away from the model of teaching as an applied science to a new 'clinically based' model, which implies local solutions for local problems. Such a model could also indicate a change in the values underpinning teacher training (back to 'teacher education'?). In order to engage in a research-based, transformational model of teacher education, Sally Lubeck (1996, p. 163) suggests there is a requirement for:

> a situated knowledge base, observational fluency, reflection, and interactive routines . . . collaborative inquiry, social constructionism, ethnography, and a disposition toward educational possibility . . . the use of literature . . . and humanistic understandings that come from other ways of knowing.

Issues

1. In what ways is teaching young children (aged between birth and eight years) different from teaching older pupils?
2. In what ways is teaching young children similar to teaching older pupils?
3. Write down the assumptions and expectations you hold about children aged five. What do you expect them to know and to be able to do? Where have these assumptions come from? Do you think you need to change your mind about some of these assumptions and expectations – why/why not?

Notes

1. Office for Standards in Education.
2. SCAA: now the Qualifications and Curriculum Authority (QCA) formerly The School Curriculum and Assessment Authority.

References

Alexander, R., Rose, J. and Woodhead, C. (1992) *Curriculum organisation and classroom practice* London: DES.

Alexander, R. (1998) Basics, cores and choices: towards a new primary curriculum *Education 3–13* Vol 26 (2) pp. 60–69.

Ball, S. (1998) Performativity and fragmentation in 'Postmodern Schooling', in J. Carter (ed.) *Postmodernity and Fragmentation of Welfare.* London: Routledge.

Barrett, G. (1986) *Starting school: an evaluation of the experience* London:AMMA

Bassey, M. (1995) *Creating education through research* Newark: Kirklington Moor Press.

Bennett, N., Wood, L. and Rogers, S. (1996) *Teaching through play: teachers' theories and classroom practice* Buckingham: Open University Press.

Blenkin, G., Hurst, V., Whitehead, M. and Yue, N.Y.L.(1995) *Principles into practice: improving the quality of children's learning* London: Goldsmiths College.

Bruner, J. (1966) *The process of education* Cambridge Mass.: Harvard.

Campbell, R.J. (1998) Broader thinking about the primary school curriculum, in N. Tester (ed) *Take Care, Mr Blunkett* London: ATL pp. 96–101.

Channel 4 (1998) *Dispatches: Too much too soon* London: Channel 4 Television, January 1998.

Claxton, G. (1990) *Teaching to learn* London: Cassell.

Curriculum and Assessment Authority for Wales (1996) *Desirable outcomes for children's learning before compulsory school age* (Consultation document) Cardiff: ASESU Cymru.

Dahlberg, G. (1995) Everything is a beginning and everything is dangerous:

some reflections on the Reggio Emilia experience Paper presented at the International Seminar in honour of Loris Malaguzzi, 16–17 October 1995, University of Milan.

David, T. (ed) (1993) *Educating our youngest children: European Perspectives* London: Paul Chapman Publishing.

David, T. (1996) *Changing minds: young children and society* Canterbury: Inaugural lecture, Canterbury Christ Church College, 30 October 1996.

David, T. and Nutbrown, C. (eds) (1992) *The Universal and the National in Preschool Education* Paris: UNESCO.

Delamont, S. (1990) *Interaction in the classroom* London: Routledge.

DfEE (1997) *Teaching: high status, high standards* Circular 10/97 London: DfEE.

DfEE (1998) *Teaching: high status, high standards* (Revised requirements) Circular 4/98 London: DfEE.

DoH and DfEE (1998) *Consultation Paper on the Regulation of Early Education and Day Care* London: DoH/DfEE.

DoH (1998a) *Working together to safeguard children. (Consultation Paper)* London: Department of Health.

Edwards, C., Gandini, L. and Foreman, G. (1998) *The hundred languages of children* (2nd ed.) Norwood, New Jersey: Ablex.

Edwards, D. and Mercer, N. (1987) *Common knowledge* London: Methuen.

Furlong, J. (1992) Reconstructing professionalism: ideological struggle in initial teacher education in M. Arnot and L. Barton (eds) *Voicing concerns: sociological perspectives on contemporary education reforms* Oxford: Triangle Books p. 163–185.

Great Britain (1998) *Meeting the childcare challenge* (Green Paper) London: DoH/DfEE.

Harris, A. and Russ, J. (1993) *Pathways to school improvement* London: DfE.

Hillman, M., Adams, J. and Whitelegg, J. (1990) *One False Move* London: Policy Studies Institute.

Hutt, S.J., Tyler, S., Hutt, C. and Christopherson, H. (1989) *Play, exploration and learning* London: Routledge.

Huttunen, E. (1992) Children's experiences in early childhood programmes *International Journal of Early Childhood* Vol 24 (2) pp. 3–11.

Katz, L. (1996) Child development knowledge and teacher preparation: confronting assumptions *Early Childhood Research Quarterly* 11 pp. 135–146.

LeMétais, J. and Tabberer, R. (1997) *International review of curriculum and assessment frameworks* Slough: NFER.

Lubeck, S. (1996) Deconstructing "child development knowledge" and "teacher preparation" *Early Childhood Research Quarterly* 11 pp. 147–167.

Maguire, M., Dillon, J. and Quintrell, M. (1998) *Finding virtue, not finding fault: stealing the wind of destructive reforms* London: ATL.

Moyles, J. (1989) *Just playing?* Milton Keynes: Open University Press.

Mould, C. (1998) The influence of researcher-teacher collaboration on the effectiveness of the early learning of four year olds in schools in England *European Early Childhood Research Journal* Vol. 6 (1) p. 19–36.

Moyles, J. and Suschitzky, W. (1997) *The buck stops here. Nursery teachers and nursery nurses working together* Leicester: Leicester University School of Education.

Munn, P. (1994) Perceptions of teaching and learning in preschool centres. in M. Hughes (ed) *Perceptions of teaching and learning* Clevedon: Multilingual Matters p. 6–17.

Ofsted (1993) *First Class* London: HMSO.

Ofsted (1995) *Guidance on the inspection of nursery and primary schools* London: HMSO.

Ofsted (1997; 1998) *Guidance on the inspection of nursery education provision in the private, voluntary and independent sectors* London: The Stationery Office.

Pollard, A. with Filer, A. (1996) *The social world of children's learning* London: Cassell.

SCAA (1996) *Desirable outcomes for children's learning on entering compulsory education* London: SCAA.

Sharp, C. and Davis, C. (1997) *Parents' views of pre-school* Slough: NFER.

Smith, P.K. (ed) (1986) *Children's play: research, development and practical applications* New York: Gordon and Breach.

Sylva, K. (1998) *Too formal too soon?* Keynote address presented at the Islington Early Years Conference, Building on Best Practice in the Early Years, 9 July 1998.

Sylva, K., Siraj-Blatchford, I. and Johnson, S. (1992) The impact of the National Curriculum on preschool practice *International Journal of Early Childhood* Vol. 24 (2) p. 41–51.

2

Young children and playful language

Teresa Grainger and Kathy Goouch

In their early years of life young children first encounter language in predominantly playful and highly emotive contexts. Through their relationships with caregivers, siblings and peers in preschool settings, children learn to use language for themselves and indeed very early on they learn to use it subversively. Such subversion takes many forms and includes playing with social conventions in ludic behaviour (Hutt *et al.* 1989) as well as playing with language conventions (Chukovsky 1963). Their pleasure in nonsense and word play is closely linked to the non-conformist practices of early childhood, through which children experience the emotional charge and power of their own words to overturn the status quo and to explore boundaries. Through deliberately manipulating and upending meanings, forms and words, children can achieve their desires, shape their agendas and establish their identity. 'The nature of the possible is what children learn when they discover how to use language for subversion, for re-ordering things in their heads if not in fact' (Meek 1985, p. 49).

The playful irreverence and inventiveness of the early years are energetic forces in their language and as such deserve further recognition, exploration and development. This chapter seeks to explore the nature of such early linguistic discoveries and the contribution they can make to the development of literacy. It also examines the implications of these insights in relation to classroom practice.

Transforming language

The pre-sleep monologues recorded by Ruth Weir (1962) demonstrate the very young child's capacity to experiment with linguistic rules, perhaps as Meek (1985) has noted Anthony Weir was breaking these rules to explore 'the boundaries of his feelings'. Chukovsky (1963) in

19

his seminal work *From Two to Five*, suggests that children have strong desires to discover the laws and rules of being, in order to violate the established order and thus verify their knowledge and understanding. He argues the key to understanding the role of topsy turvies, for example, becomes playing with ideas consciously and demonstrating their knowledge of sense through delighting in nonsense. Evidence of word play is not hard to find in childhood: Patrick, aged four years old, was vigorously rocking a blonde doll from side to side when he announced 'This is baby Jesus' and proceed to sing:

> 'Away in a manger
> No crib for a bed
> Be little Bored Besus
> Baid bown his Beet Belix'

'Beet Belix! No not his Beet Belix' his sister Lucy, aged three, declared delightedly. Both children were reduced to semi-hysterical laughter as the phrase 'Beet Belix' was repeated at will almost endlessly over the morning. It became an in-house joke between them, verbal proof that they understood 'his sweet head' had been replaced by 'his Beet Belix', and that somehow this transformation was delicious. Their shared pleasure in this early parody was twofold, partly in the awareness that the words were nonsense in themselves, 'Be little Bored Besus', but also perhaps in the deliberate substitution of the non-rhyming word 'Belix'. A similar reworking of another known verse was developed a few days later when they were reading *Over in the Meadow* by Louise Voce (1994) with their mother. This traditional counting rhyme, captured as a picture book, has a repeating pattern frame which is both accessible and overtly rhythmic in nature.

> 'Over in the meadow in the sand in the sun,
> Sat an old mother turtle,
> and her little turtle ONE,
> "Dig" said their mother,
> "I dig" said the one
> So he dug all day in the sand in the sun.'

The animals' noises were appropriately given for two ducks, three owls and four mice, until the verse:

> 'Over in the meadow
> In a snug bee hive
> Lived an old mother bee
> And her little bees FIVE'

Then Lucy, looking directly at the picture of bees, chimed with impish delight:

"Woof", said their mother
"We woof" said the five
So they woofed all day
Round their snug bee hive'.

Their mother joined in the ensuing laughter and tickled the delighted toddler whose brother, keen to achieve the same effect, turned the page quickly and urged his mother to read on. The remainder of the text was then given similar treatment, with bizarre noises attached to each animal 'Moo said the squirrels, Meow said the frogs, Neigh said the pigs' and so on. The children took evident pleasure in this rejection of the norm, keenly aware that they had deliberately reworked the text to humorous effect. On each occasion their eyes looked to their mother for evidence of her enjoyment and in anticipation of her tickling response. This physicality was also a seductive source of subversion, an upending of their conventional listening position and a pleasurable invasion of their own space. Their new topsy turvy rhymes overturned the established order of things and showed how they were using the chisel of conceptual incongruity to sculpt and affirm their knowledge of conceptual congruity. Indeed it is possible to see older children behave in a similar way when subverting the text of advertising jingles, traditional or pop songs and substituting their own risqué versions, with friends or siblings, whilst looking to each other for response and support.

Exerting power

The boisterous good humour and physical engagement shown in these examples was also prevalent in other linguistic encounters in which the toddlers transformed the known and reshaped their language. When she found the toddlers early one morning devouring rice crispies and coco pops out of the packet and surrounded by loose cereal spread liberally over the furniture, their mother unsurprisingly expressed her anger. Patrick's immediate oppositional response was to chant 'Mummy is a poo, Mummy is a poo, Mummy a poo'. Delighted in their own daring, they danced around her, repeating the same phrase with crescendo. As Claxton (1984) acknowledges, to be creative is to dare to be different, to take risks with words and actions. Eventually their mother's unequivocal displeasure was expressed, at which point the chant switched, although the ritual dancing remained the same, to 'Mummy is a Mummy, Mummy is a Mummy, Mummy is a Mummy' amidst much hilarity and intense pleasure. This carnivalesque play (Bakhtin 1968) served to challenge their mother's authority since, although their words had changed, the rhythm and meaning had not. The children took obvious delight in this, knowing that their new words were somehow untouchable. Their phrase also served to express their solidarity, as they spoke with one voice united in their words and movements. The audacity of the words seemed to represent an affective, almost physical attraction; they needed to be said, demanded to be chanted and promised gratification through

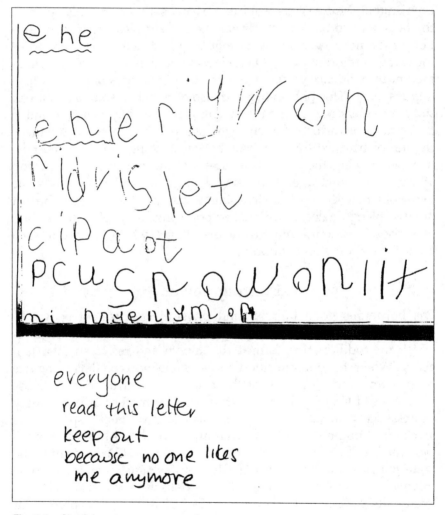

Fig. 2.1 Charlie's note

their repetition, implicit meaning and power. Another child, Charlie, nearly five, had 'disagreed' with his mother. He ran to his bedroom and sometime later sellotaped a note to the door. It said 'everyone read this letter keep out because no one likes me anymore'. There are many significant issues involved in this particular example, for instance his use of the written word to express his feelings of the moment; his understanding that 'everyone' was able to read his message; his ability to make clear his meaning; and of course his knowledge of the system of sounds and marks that support the construction of written language. Of particular interest though is the fact that Charlie understood enough about the system to know the effect of written language; he had used it to vent his anger and assert his power. A colleague reports that her daughter, slightly older and a member of the Brownie pack, was so angry at being thwarted that she constructed with her sister a list of rules for the 'Blackies'! The rules were most subversive and involved restricting rather than aiding the progress of elderly people and dreadful fates for boy scouts! Such examples are not childish acts of rebellion but show children using language as a tool for resistance and opposition, as Walkerdine (1981) has noted of taboo rhymes and rhythms on the playground.

Nonsense is also employed by the young to demonstrate their power and is used as a defiant response by Patrick and Lucy when told off for various misdemeanours. They either blurt gibberish back to their parents or mutter gobbledygook under their breath, almost as if they were telling themselves their version of events and commenting on the perceived injustice of the situation. Enquiries as to what they are saying are met with further nonsense, utilised in this context to subvert the adult agenda. A version perhaps of Halliday's (1978) 'anti-language' which he describes as 'the language a subculture uses to set itself apart from the established society by creating an alternative reality' (p. 179). Their language, albeit nonsense, is expertly used in these situations both to protect themselves and to bait the authority figure. Is this perhaps a post Weir monologue in which the young learners are investigating the boundary applications of nonsense and seeking to seize some power in the discourse by subverting the normal conversational convention of talking sense? In some of their imaginative play too this pair of siblings create make believe worlds which enable them to effectively block out the need to respond to the mundane demands of authority. They do not answer to their names eventually declaring themselves to be 'beelies' or 'boogy wosgars'. These imaginary worlds, and words, provide ammunition for resistance to conformity since they are imaginatively owned by the young players and inaccessible to the adults concerned. It is this inaccessibility which increases the children's power in these contexts.

Humour and carnival

Another of the features of linguistic subversion, besides the playful irreverence, risk taking and power already mentioned, is the intense humour which often accompanies its use. Children love to laugh, their early free wheeling language is packed with laughter and infectious giggles and amused titters pervade their interchanges with one another. Developing a sense of humour is important to help increase children's sense of perspective and tolerance of others' views (Rothbart 1977). When siblings or friends play together in preschool contexts a sense of the festive often becomes part of their subculture and their behaviour takes on carnivalesque overtones of change and renewal. Young children use such laughter effectively to overcome fears or disquiet, for laughter knows no inhibitions. So in the earlier examples, not only is their mother's power made less awesome through the accompanying laughter but also the emotional satisfaction of being subversive is heightened.

Playfulness is very much in evidence in children's ability to subvert, particularly in relation to language and literacy, and the creation of an 'adult free' subculture frees children from the conventions to which we have introduced them. Bakhtin's notion of carnival celebrating 'temporary liberation from the prevailing truth and from the established order' (Bakhtin 1968, p. 135) relates clearly to children's ability to withdraw from formal texts and make language their own. Indeed the Opies, from their observations of children out of school, tell of a 'tribal culture rich in the language arts of song, dance, parody, taunt, vulgarity and subversion' (Whitehead 1995, p. 46). The emotional charge of such contexts represents another highly significant element in subversive encounters. Children's emotive attitude to words and sounds may well be reinforced through such early experiences; however, these need to be built on since as Chukovsky (1963, p. 17) warns us:

> If we repress the child's free expression of his feelings and ideas and do not leave room for his emotional and mental groupings we risk fading the colour of the child's speech, making it anaemic and devitalized, killing its wonderful childishness and inflicting a permanent harm.

Caregivers, educators and writers need to offer children opportunities full of somatic affective possibility and celebrate their language free from inhibition and rich in celebration, humour and feeling.

Impropriety

As well as playing with language conventions and creating their own words to transform the agenda, children also use language deliberately to play with social conventions and voice publicly unacceptable words. For Patrick and Lucy, as for many children, the term 'bottom', whether whispered or declaimed loudly, prompts peals of laughter and acts as an early swear word in their vocabulary. It is liberally applied to the rear end of any animal, doll, toy or human and is also used without physical reference to prompt pleasure, engagement and response. The Disney film *Fantasia* has affirmed their delight in this word and its connotations of delicious impropriety. One animated extract, set to Beethoven's Pastoral Symphony, depicts bare bottomed cherubs as intrepid cupids creating love matches in the world of the centaurs. Initially enchanted, the children named these cherubs 'plum or peach bottomed babies' and have ever since imitated their 'cheeky' behaviour in escalating situations. The desire to be 'peach bottomed babies' often overcomes them; clothing is removed, bottoms are bared and wiggled for all to see, amid much laughter and joyful revelry. This behaviour, which is on the edge of what will be tolerated in their home, is employed by them with extreme delight and daring. The sexual licence, rudeness and sense of 'time off' from good behaviour which 'doing plum bottoms' implies, relates again to the carnivalesque (Bakhtin 1968) and in vignette form demonstrates young children's tendency to upend conventions, resist conformity and control and push boundaries. Does the nation's concern over the introduction to television of the Teletubbies reflect our need to restrict children to formality and adult conventions? Yet gathering evidence of how young children oppose conformity is relatively easy in out of school situations, for example – Peter, nearly four, refused to make a choice from a menu and announced to the world at large that 'we can eat bottoms and willies'. Such key words and alternative declarations instigate laughter, appeal to children's sense of the playful and demonstrate how socially appropriate behaviour is also upended with pleasure and purpose.

In school

As teachers working with young literacy practitioners we must surely become more acutely aware of the existing understanding of young children in terms of their language and literacy use and seek to exploit this knowledge to construct a worthwhile curriculum for them. If, as Hilton (1996) suggests, cognition is 'encultured' then our responsibility must be to acknowledge and use both cultural displays of language and literacy and their transformative and subversive competence. Many popular texts in early years classrooms appeal to children's incipient humour and enable them to savour the flavour of subversion in words and pictures. *Do You Dare* by Paul and Emma Rogers (1992), *Little Rabbit Foo Foo* by Michael Rosen (1990), and *The Rascally Cake* by Jeanne Willis and Korky Paul (1994), are just three examples of somewhat anti-establishment texts, (although the moral order is eventually upheld in every case). Through real and vicarious experience children learn to dare in words and deeds and also begin to realise that illustrators and writers share their love of the risqué, as Meek (1991, p. 122) has observed, 'The young have powerful allies in a host of gifted artists and writers to help them subvert the world of their elders'. It is, however, hard to conceive of Biff and Chip burping, talking nonsense or using the word 'bottom'! If Ashton-Warner's (1980) persuasive argument about key vocabulary is correct then pleasant or respectable words will not do, for the 'captions of dynamic life' need to be available to children to enable them to bridge their knowing and affirm their pleasure in the irreverent. Without such captions, Dannequin (1977) contends, the linguistic environment of the early years classrooms will be impoverished. In the carnival culture of the Middle Ages comic verbal compositions were prevalent in both Latin and the vernacular (Morris 1994). Were such parodies and travesties the antecedents of the work of the Ahlbergs, Rosen, Ross, and others who continue to create popular and alternative carols, hymns, jokes and stories? It would seem that the features of subversion such as humour, risk taking, nonsense, oppositional perspectives and an emotional engagement are revisited and celebrated in the words and pictures of countless children's books. Children need access to such significant texts in particular to satisfy their desire to encounter, master and employ language creatively in non-conformist and transforming contexts.

Another classroom context which provides space for emotional involvement and possible subversion is the imaginary world of the role play area. This adult free zone can be a 'haven' which allows children to re-enact personal experience, trial performances in language and literacy and play their own way forward. Messages, signs, love and hate letters and verbal expressions of feeling surface on a daily basis when time from National Curriculum agendas is allowed. This opportunity resembles in part the outside play that many adults remember experiencing as children, when they indulged in gangs and clubs, in sheds, garages or under the garden hedge, making their own rules, restricting membership and exploring autonomy, perhaps influenced in part by the contentious works of Enid Blyton? In play then, from self set agendas, children find significance in literacy and can liberally apply their semantic knowledge and develop their understanding of how meaning making operates through demonstrating their capacity for playful language learning to become competent and confident literacy practitioners. That is, if we, as controlling adults, can disentangle ourselves from the spurious requirements for continuous conformity and performance in the classroom. Hilton (1996) echoes this when she makes comparisons from the early part of this century and describes schools then, as now in some cases, as supplying a 'generation of clerks', children who, in Vygotsky's terms merely learn 'hand and finger habits' (1978) and are not empowered by their ability to narrate experience and express emotion.

In addition to the classroom consequences in terms of literature and role play, if teachers want to build upon children's early subversive encounters and retain the vitality, emotional engagement and active involvement in learning which they provoke, then attention will need to be given to the subculture of the playground. In schools which develop the lore and language of the playground, the socialising songs and rhymes of the young are still played, replayed and reworked. These practices extend the linguistic transformations encountered in preschool contexts and are consequently undertaken with particular energy and delight. There are zones on the playground which tend to attract games and songs which are outside adult definitions of acceptability (Davies 1982). Indeed such zones offer a literary space, without adults, in which the children can explore those things which adults never address directly. The secret domain of rude singing rhymes, as Grugeon (1988) notes, are mediated by children and for children, as a language of resistance, a verbal art form which to some extent needs to maintain its own territory in order to fulfil its own purposes. Providing children with the opportunity to extend their early delight in utterance can also be offered through celebrating the world of humour, jokes, puns, riddles and funny stories in the classroom as well as by taking an experimental approach to rhythm, rhyme and language. So oral literature can and should be exploited in the classroom to ensure that children's humour, vitality and early energy expressed in words and actions is retained. Even later when word play reduces, a 'glorious irresponsibility' with words still lingers, which Meek (1991) argues is sanctioned for adults through art, TV and comedy. In sum, teachers need, without intruding into this 'tribal culture' or hijacking children's play, to capitalise on children's highly motivated and playful use of language in their early years teaching and to learn to both celebrate it and use it as a tool for learning. The way forward seems to be through sensitive use of observations and records collected over time from informal, non-conventional and perhaps subversive contexts to inform our understanding of individual children's potential as literacy practitioners. Space needs to be found for the electric, oppositional and subversive elements in young children's language to be developed. Irreverence is a quality of early childhood and one parents and educators need to consider, acknowledge, cherish and celebrate in the young.

Issues

1. How can the many languages of childhood be encouraged and 'owned' by children in the early years? What teaching strategies could be used to help children use spoken language to express the meanings of these other languages?
2. What can preschool educators and reception class teachers do together to observe and encourage creative and subversive uses of language and literacy?
3. How can the Literacy Hour be used to stimulate children's language related to text in ways which are playful and allow them to direct their own learning?

References:

Ashton-Warner, S. (1980), *Teacher* London: Virago.

Bakhtin, M. (1968) *Rabelais and His World* Cambridge, Mass.: Harvard University Press.

Chukovsky, K. (1963) *From Two to Five* Berkeley: University of California Press.

Claxton, G. (1984) *Live and Learn* London: Harper and Row.

Davies, B. (1982) *Life in the Classroom and Playground* London: Routledge.

Dannequin, C. (1977) *Les Enfants Baillonne's* Paris: CEDIC/Diffusion Nathan.

Grugeon, E. (1988) The Singing Game: An Untapped Competence, in M.

Meek and C. Mills (eds) *Language and Literacy in the Primary School* Hove: Falmer Press.

Halliday, M.A.K. (1978) *Language as a Social Semiotic* London: Arnold.

Hilton, U. (1996) *Potent Fictions* London: Routledge.

Hutt, S. J., Tyler, S., Hutt, C. and Christopherson, H. (1989) *Play, Exploration and Learning* London: Routledge.

Meek, M. (1991) *On Being Literate* London: Bodley Head.

Morris, P. (ed) (1994) The Bakhtin Reader: *Selected Writings of Bakhtin, Medvedev and Vologhino* London: Arnold.

Rothbart, M.K. (1977) A Psychological approach to the study of humour, in A. Chapman and H. Foot (eds) *It's a Funny Thing Humour* Oxford: Pergamon.

Voce, L. (1994) *Over in the Meadow: A Counting Rhyme* London: Walker.

Walkerdine, V. (1983) A psychosemiotic approach to abstract thought, in Beveridge, M. (ed) *Children Thinking Through Language* London: Arnold.

Weir, R. (1962) *Language in the Crib* The Hague: Mouton.

Whitehead, M. (1995) Nonsense, Rhyme and Word Play in Young Children, in R. Beard (ed) *Rhyme: Reading Handwriting* London: Hodder and Stoughton.

Vygotsky, L. S. (1978) *Mind in Society*, Cambridge, Mass.: Harvard University Press.

3

The imagination, play and the arts

Bryan Hawkins

Imagination should have a history, indeed its very construction is as much a cultural invention as it is the natural basis for a description of a psychic phenomenon..

Maclagan (1989, p. 35)

It is only in playing that the individual can be creative and only in being creative that the individual can discover the self.

Winnicott (1972, p. 63)

More than the will, more than the vital impulse, imagination is the very force of psychic production.

Bachelard (1962, p. 19)

Imagination is our means of interpreting the world, and it is also our means of forming images in the mind.

Warnock (1976, p. 194)

A practical context

An understanding of the nature of the imagination is as essential to an understanding of the arts as it is to an understanding of the young child and education. A consideration of the imagination can unite in a very significant manner elements of theory and models of human thought that are of great significance within the educational context. There are, however, real problems in attempting to engage with the complexity, richness and power of the lived experience that constitute the essence of the imaginative and creative processes of the arts and play.

In order to ground this chapter in the activities it seeks to reflect upon I want to start by outlining something like a context of activity that the chapter can develop. I have chosen just a few of the many, remarkable and mundane, touching and joyous contexts in which the imagination, acting through the arts and play, has touched my experience. Of course such a selection can never be neutral, the choices imply both the values and connections which underlie my analysis. The examples are from both pre-school and primary school situations. They are from in school and out of school contexts. In other words they mark the transition that is the period of early years provision.

Two children play in a garden, sticks, sun-hats, tea-towels have been transformed into costumes. A large cardboard box becomes a castle; a construction kit makes a cannon. The children negotiate and discuss how they will 'play' the 'game' they are building and working upon. They are watched, occasionally helped and looked after, by a parent who is both working in the kitchen and keeping an eye on the children.

A class in a primary school is developing a dance based upon the topic of growth. They have grown plants and observed stages of development. The music has been chosen with care and 'grows' as the children explore through movement growth from curled prone positions on the floor of the hall. The music and the class 'grow' with control,

Fig. 3.1 Children in 'costumes'

sensitivity and grace. One child remains absolutely still. The music continues, the class is now standing waving gently to the music. Suddenly the boy throws out one arm in a violent gesture, then another, after a pause he jumps to his feet – thrusting his limbs in different directions. He opens his eyes, previously closed in concentration. He appears rather surprised by the waving movements of his peers.

A goldfish (called Mintoe) kept in a classroom dies. The class decide with their teacher to make a commemorative book for themselves. The book is filled with poems and pictures. Amongst the poems are these four.

> I remember him swimming in the water
> and lying in the water. He looked peaceful
> Almost smiling he liked to swim
> He never floated till he was dead
> We should get another fish and forget about Mintoe

> Mintoe was a special Goldfish
> He would swim in the water
> He was beautiful, he liked
> The class but he liked
> Robert the best

> Mintoe was a quiet Goldfish
> and peaceful it never got on my nerves
> It was good to me and the class
> (Robert)

> Mintoe was a very
> special goldfish it was quiet and peaceful but
> it was only a goldfish
> but it was sad to see him dead.

A child who has looked at abstract paintings and engaged with a project on Anger involving poetry dance and drama makes an image during lunch time called The Bully.

The theoretical context

Many writers have contributed to the ways in which consideration of the human imagination and the arts can inform and influence educational provision. Mary Warnock (1976) in her tremendously significant book *Imagination* has made a strong case for the relevance of philosophical and aesthetic theory from Kant and Coleridge through to Sartre and C.S. Lewis in relation to the imagination. Warnock has

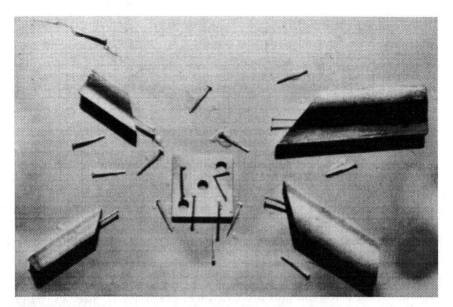

Fig. 3.2 The Bully

highlighted the contribution an understanding of imagination can make to our understanding of the role of the arts and education. More recent examples of this project are the work of Peter Abbs (1987), Peter Fuller (1980) and Richard Kearney (1994) who have sought to bring together a range of psychological, aesthetic and philosophical positions in order to illuminate our understanding of the potential of the arts and their relationship with the imagination.

This project can never be complete. It is not, I believe, a question of finding a definitive answer. Times and the educational climate and environment change. Indeed as Maclagan (1989) has cogently and significantly argued the imagination is not only a human characteristic and in this sense fixed but a way of thinking about ourselves that evolves and changes and is in this sense a product of the cultural activity that the term in part explains. The 'cultural' imagination is changing and mutable. Imagination is the subject of debate as well as the object of our studies. In other words how we think of the imagination changes and how we employ these understandings in education changes. These concerns also connect us with educational debate and broader cultural and political issues.

There is, however, a broad consensus – and it is important to remember this in the midst of more specialised debate – in relation to the value of imagination as attribute, vital commodity and necessary focus of educational concern. This chapter will seek to build on this consensus through the development of the position outlined by Warnock. This development will occur through the selective and partisan deployment of elements of psychology, aesthetics and hermeneutics. This chapter will enthusiastically advocate the importance of the arts, the imagination and the value of play which is understood as a common factor in the processes of the arts and the imagination and the common and uniting element within the theory which I will attempt to synthesise.

This focus upon play towards which my argument travels is essentially compatible with the traditional and particular emphasis and significance placed upon play within early years provision. This focus is also, I hope, a further contribution to the argument for play to be seen as central to educational provision; a contribution to how play is understood within the early years of education and a contribution to the debate which will shape the nature of future provision.

Warnock's position involves a re-engagement with the Romantic aesthetic and historical and philosophical positions in order to re-figure and re-appraise the nature of the imagination in the light of more contemporary theory. Her strategy is not so much nostalgic as historical, recognising the cultural determinants of how we think of the imagination. Without the arts and artists themselves a history of the imagination is impossible and without the writings of poets and artists our understandings of the imagination are impoverished. However, one of the characteristics of recent developments in art education has been the focus upon models of the adult artist as being enormously significant to educational provision (I refer to the National Curriculum structure in the arts). Whilst this has undoubtedly been of value it represents, particularly in terms of early years provision, a 'top-down' model which risks obscuring the importance of our understandings of the nature of the young child and of processes such as play and learning which have traditionally underpinned provision and theory. There are those such as Milner and Winnicott historically, and Fuller and Kuspit more recently who have, I believe, important contributions to make in this area in re-asserting the significance of our understandings of the early years and the processes of play and the arts. Play here is understood as an activity which develops from its basis in the early years of development towards the connection between the individual and culture and beyond to an engagement with the arts. This emphasis is another justification for the strategy that I will adopt of firstly reviewing Warnock's contribution and then of augmenting this on the grounds of reviewing contemporary literature and responding to current theory.

For Warnock the imagination has a centrality and significance which echoes the centrality of Kant within her writing. The imagination is within Warnock's work valued as essential within perception as it is implicated in any situation in which we make sense of the world around us. Imagination is thus understood as the process by which various sense impressions are made coherent as they are internalised, schematised or symbolised. The enormous significance of Hume and Kant within our understandings of the human imagination (Kearney 1994) rest in very large part upon this implication of the imagination in our perception of the world around us. This engagement with imagination at the most fundamental levels of human perception and consciousness is a vital element of Warnock's argument for the importance of the imagination and is profoundly at odds with those views which see the imagination as some kind of alternative or addition to our normal, everyday or rational perception of the world.

In the examples given we see children dealing with perception and understanding of the world through the making of images, the use of words and through movement. The experiences with which they engage are inevitably part perceptual – how a castle looks, how a plant grows, how a dead goldfish compares with a live one, but extends also into other areas: into understandings of music, mortality, feelings and moral behaviour. In particular the boy dancing is, I believe, an example of the giving of form to an important reality in relation to perceptions of growth, a reality which is thought in the act of the dance itself what we may call the thought *within* the imaginative act (the dance) not the thought *about* imaginative act (Podro 1987). Things grow slowly, but things closely observed may appear to grow in spurts. Classroom plants in other words play dead during class time, but during the long nights make leaps so that when we look again they have 'suddenly' grown. At least this is the way I have chosen to interpret the thought contained within the boy's original, different, but valid dance. It is an imaginative thought contained within the language and form of dance. The arts and play constitute such thoughts made in the forms of paint, sound, movement, speech etc. They are manifestations of thought as are all the examples I have chosen.

Kearney (1994) in speaking of Kant's concept of the 'transcendental imagination' states powerfully 'The transcendental imagination is that which grounds the objectivity of the object within the subjectivity of the subject' (p. 167). There is a tendency to think of the most fundamental perception of the world as being an encounter with 'unproblematic' physical phenomena – 'the world out there' – and that this encounter is a matter of 'pure' perception, scientific method and rationality precluding the role of the imagination. Kant's argument for the implication of the individual's imagination in the understanding of the world beyond the individual was philosophical, cultural and aesthetic dynamite. It provided the basis for the philosophical basis to the Romantic aesthetic and beyond that the celebration and valuation of the human imagination characteristic of the twentieth century in general and particularly of Modernism in the arts. As Kearney (1994) again argues in relation to the significance of Kant and the Romantics, upon whom Warnock so fully draws.

> The free 'play' of imagination ceases to be denounced. Indeed from Kant onwards this notion of free play was to become one of the pivotal concepts of modern theories of art. (p. 174)

Such a view of the imagination as growing from in part a playful approach to phenomena is supported by writers such as Storr (1972; 1989) who have explored the creativity of both artists and scientists.

What this implies is of enormous significance and is recognised by Warnock in her statements on the importance of the imagination within education. The imagination is essential to the making of connections between ourselves as individuals and the world of objects and experiences. For the young child this task of understanding the world in its most directly sensuous and concrete forms is thus the task of the imagination but of course, to any individual involved as child-carer under the influence of early years theory and practice in recent years, this task of learning implicates play.

This is a theme to which I will return but its appearance of play so early in our consideration of theoretical perspectives is evidence of the unique sensitivity towards the possibilities of play and the imagination that potentially lie in the traditions and very nature of early years provision.

Warnock argues:

> Imagination is our means of interpreting the world and it is also our means of forming images in the mind. The images are not separate from interpretations of the world. We see the forms in our mind's eye and we see these very forms in the world. . . . The two abilities are joined in our ability to understand that the forms have a certain meaning that they are always significant of other things beyond themselves.
> (Warnock 1976, p. 194)

In other words the death of a goldfish must always be more than an isolated event. Intelligence is the manipulation and organisation of connections in the service of understanding. The issue of mortality is raised. Scientific observation of a dead fish can lead to scientific analysis of the problem. However, the identification of the fact of floating – 'he never floated till he died' – seems poetic in that its tragic-comic potency opens up new and even revelatory meanings. The observation is a poignant isolation of a phenomenon bathed in emotional significance and which I remember reading as a revelation. It was something I sort of knew but its expression in this form seemed packed with 'poetic' reverberations and potential.

The educational context

In Warnock's analysis perception forms the basis for further complex interactions and connections. Warnock is evoking a further and secondary function of the imagination, not secondary in the sense of status as it is intricately and deeply linked with its counterpart but secondary in that it is of a different and complementary nature. It is the imagination of the image and symbol. It is the imagination that we may recognise as being the imagination linked to the arts and creative play of the young child as witnessed in the play corner, play ground and the important spaces of childhood in which play occurs. Play here represents the imagination in action. This play is a symbolic activity in which things stand for other things, in which the rules of 'as if' and imagination function. It is an activity that links directly with learning and most importantly with the world of feelings and emotions and the maintenance of emotional growth and health. A goldfish is experienced, in part 'as if' it were a human and through it human loss and love are explored.

What I want to particularly draw from Warnock's analysis and then develop is her emphasis upon the centrality of imagination to education. For Warnock the image and symbol forming imagination are vital in both education and the arts. Writing as she did in 1976 it seems, in retrospect, somewhat surprising that her interest did not lead her into connection with the body of work that has grown from the discoveries of Freud and which deals with the formation of character and personality through the vehicle of the symbol as well as providing the basis for the exploration of the imagination and artistic production. Perhaps Warnock's resistance to this avenue of exploration was in part the result of the ambivalence and occasional apparent hostility towards the artistic imagination and creative production that can be identified in relation to Freud's writings. Warnock's work is of course an extension of an ethical and moral stance in relation to the imagination which equates the imagination with value.

For Freud the artistic imagination (parallel and similar to the imagination possessed by all human beings) was a process mainly of com-
pensation and wish-fulfilment. That is to say the imagination acted
mainly to achieve for the individual artist that which he or she was
unable to achieve in reality. This tended to place the artist and the artistic imagination in the realms of neurosis. More simply put Freud tended
to link artistic activity with illness. This is clearly not the best basis
upon which to build a comprehensive theory of the role of the imagination and the arts in education. The Freudian imagination, neurotic
in nature, situated at the most basic levels of the human psyche and
by nature somewhat uncivilised, stands in contrast to the view of
Warnock and the sources she articulates which place the imagination
in relation to emotional health, achievement and civilisation.

In other words the child's image of bullying would tend to be seen
retrospectively and diagnostically and not as an act of insight or
understanding. As Kuspit (1993) has described, Freud uses the scientific method he associated with psychoanalysis to 'dismiss' with
'destructive contempt art and religion' (p. 318) This contempt was in
Kuspit's view something of a pre-emptive strike attack on the areas of
cultural experience vital to the 'struggle for power' of psychoanalysis. However, in particular contemporaneous contributions and in the
more recent history of the tradition growing from Freud's work we
can detect and identify less aggressive positions and indeed positions
which are of very considerable value to a fuller understanding of the
imagination in the arts and education.

Firstly we may identify a less critical stance in relation to Freud's
approach to the creative imagination than that adopted by Kuspit.
Arnheim (1962), for example, argues that Freud's work tends towards
producing a form of reconciliation of the rational and irrational
aspects of human behaviour as evident in the sciences and the arts
and advocates the creative imagination to the extent that it is seen as
rationally understandable.

It was Freud's trust in the 'ultimate rationality of the apparently
irrational' that led him to describe concretely some of the mechanisms
of creativity for the first time.

Freud in his attempt to explain human behaviour in terms of universal qualities instituted what Arnheim described as a 'democratisa-
tion of the arts'. As the creative imagination is understood to be
similar in the contexts of both the creative genius and the ordinary
person so the value implicit in creativity becomes associated with all
humanity as well as the few. As Arnheim puts it:

Creativity came to be thought of as the possession and privilege of every human being and modern education became a technique for developing this most precious common property.

(Arnheim 1962, p. 11)

The child as an artist, poet and dancer is involved through common processes with their adult counterparts, furthermore the issues of art – the nature of being in the world, issues of desire and mortality – are the issues that all art addresses and that the child engages with through play and within the arts. This position is in line with Warnock's valuation of the imagination even though it draws upon different sources.

In addition, many who have developed Freud's understandings have shifted the trajectory of the operation of the imagination from the maladaptive, the retrospective and the historical to the healthy, the future and the future-oriented and to the potential of the imagination to initiate becoming and growth. In this the psychodynamic tradition reinstates and develops the description and exploration by those such as Kant, Hume, Schiller and Coleridge (sources upon whom Warnock draws) of the imagination as central to human affairs and importantly to the development of 'self'. Thus even in the apparently bleak expression of difficult experience (the child who made the Bully was himself a victim) there is a significance and dignity which is vital to human experience. As Tillich (1996, p. 182) argues 'The creative power which is able to grasp the negativity of the content by the positivity of form is a triumph of humanity'.

The subjects of play and the arts are not always nice but the trajectory is towards good. In these moves away from the problems inherent in Freud's approach the work of the English Object Relations School has been of considerable value and importance. Contemporaneous figures such as Marion Milner, D.W. Winnicott and Anton Ehrenzweig have all made important contributions. Contributions which in many ways have only in the last few years begun to be fully recognised and drawn into the debate surrounding the arts. For Marion Milner in her remarkable book *On Not Being Able to Paint* (1957) the 'illusions' of art are understood as an essential element in the construction of the 'self'. Art represents an illusion in the service of adaptation and health. In important ways the arts take over from the sense of wholeness present in the relationship between mother and child in the earliest months and years of life. The parent in the early years creates the vital 'illusion' that the needs of the infant and the phenomenal world are in harmony. This illusion depends upon the parent's ability to meet, attend to and even predict the needs of the infant. As maturity develops the child is able to adapt to the realisation that needs and world (inner and external dimensions of reality) are not in perfect harmony and also to survive the disillusion this entails.

The creation of the illusion that the mother is part of the child and the child part of the mother precedes a sense of self. This illusion far from being destructive is essential to the development of the human being. Thus for Milner illusion precedes consciousness of self and the nurturing of an other remains a vital element in healthy development. Milner's work is paralleled in the contemporaneous work of D.W. Winnicott. The nurturing of the infant is characteristic of what Winnicott terms 'Good-Enough' aspects of parenting and these largely intuitive acts form the basis for the emergence of a sense of self in the infant.

Winnicott defines a 'transitional space' existing between the inner and outer worlds of the individual. The parent in the course of 'Good-Enough' parenting assists the child in moving from the illusions of infancy to accept the world beyond the child, the complex contradicted world of external experience. The interplay of the inner world of the child developing through the nurturing of the parent and in relation to the world beyond the child is a fundamental requirement. The teacher extends this role and the learning it produces as the arts extend the role of play into adult life.

The child playing castles may well be exploring complex issues and relationships. This exploration is occurring within a space that we can understand as neither internal (the world of dream and our most private thoughts) nor as external (the world of reality and experience), but importantly in a third area of experience (the world of play and culture) which brings these worlds together.

For Freud the language of the unconscious is the symbol and the symbol is to be understood as fixed, defined and retrospective. The symbol is the unconscious speaking, in the case of the artist as of the patient, of past events and fixed forms. Jung's famous break with Freud involved a radical redefinition of the symbol. Jung's approach is essentially expansive as are Milner's and Winnicott's. The imagination and the unconscious are seen as cognitive, future oriented and transforming. The imagination is capable of bringing about new meanings, new understandings and as a result new knowledge and growth. Within recent writings on the arts and education Peter Abbs has consistently sought to value the power of the imagination and to place it at the centre of arts education.

In the work of Abbs (1987) and others there is a value placed upon the importance of the active imagination and the role of play; there is nevertheless no justification of a *laissez-faire* attitude to the arts and education in these approaches. Rather a model emerges of the sensitive interplay of imagination and reflection. This model embraces the autonomy of the creator, the importance of the creative act and the nurturing of creativity but also the interacting importance of reflection, self-awareness and analysis. The role of learning is accepted by Milner (1957) who highlighted the skills, concepts and knowledge of the arts but very importantly put them in the service of the imagination. In speaking of the imagination she states:

> The poet and artist in us, by their unreason, by their seeing as a unity things in which objective reality are not the same, by their basic capacity for seeing the world in terms of metaphor do in fact create the world for the scientist in us to be curious about and understand. . .

> they (the arts) provide a half-way house to external reality, that function of the creative arts by which they carry on throughout our lives, the role that in our infancy has to be filled by a person, their function in providing a perpetual well for the renewal and expansion of our psychic powers.

(Milner 1957, p. 79)

The arts grow from the earliest relationships and from play. The arts understood in part as play for adults are understood as vital experience. Failure to play for the child is the equivalent of failure to engage in the arts for the adult. The arts take the biological roots of identity and awareness and project this vital energy into the realms of culture and language.

The arts as illusion in this context do not act to cloak anxiety and hold back rational analysis. The arts are illusion to the extent that a cohesive sense of self is the product of illusion, to the extent that a secure nurturing childhood is the product of illusion and to the extent that the belief that the individual is capable of finding meaning and worth in experience is illusion. It is illusion in the service of and at the basis of culture. The invention of the self and the humanist projects of the arts are amongst its greatest achievements. Milner's analysis is an example of contributions from within the psychodynamic tradition which far from disempowering the teacher act to create a place and role for the teacher within a model of the artistic imagination and creative processes. The link with the emergence of the human consciousness from infancy made by Milner and codified by Winnicott links the artistic imagination to the necessity of a nurturing environment from the earliest years of life.

The imagination, whilst not being taught in the sense so apparent in recent definitions of curriculum content, is nevertheless dependent upon a nurturing and sensitively aware other – a role that extends the 'Good-Enough' parenting of Winnicott towards the role of the teacher. In this the teacher's role is not one of didact or instructor but of guardian and facilitator extending the commitment, indulgences and love that form the basis of psychic growth. The teacher takes on the role of sympathetic and sensitive co-ordinator and co-explorer of children's art and the world of artistic production and endeavour – the world of culture.

There is clearly a contrast between the terms here being used to describe the teachers' engagements with young children and much recent educational rhetoric. The terms commitment, indulgence and nurture underline the emergence of the arts from the vital, sensitive interactions of the child and parent from which they stem. The insights they provide set the tone for an emergent sense not only of the role of the imagination within education but for the kinds of provision and strategy which will encourage the development of the artistic imagination. They place the emergence of a vital human attribute firmly within an ethical and moral as well as pedagogical context.

Within writings on the imagination it is possible to identify an alternative to the separation of the imagination from other areas of experience. Abbs's work has involved a rejection of Freud's reductionism and an opening up to the value of the symbol as expansive and future oriented. The unconscious and the creative imagination are seen as cognitive and potentially transforming in their potential for growth. The imagination is capable of bringing about new meanings and new understandings. In this sense the imagination shifts from being seen as a fixed system of meaning, a kind of picture writing in the case of the visual artistic imagination, and becomes capable of expressing something previously unknown and potentially revelatory. Thus the imagination and creative process tend to create metaphors with new meaning structured from the fixed cultural symbols of the arts and language which they inherit. This cognitive function of the unconscious acting through the imagination marks a radical break with Freud's understandings. Jung developed these ideas and advocated them within his work on the active imagination, a strategy which encouraged the extension of the freedom, exploration and spontaneity of play into adult life and in the service of emotional and mental growth.

There are many parallels between Jung's model of the 'active imagination' and Milner's writings and her particular attempts to use image-making to understand the operation of the human psyche. In

Milner's explorations we see a process in which neither play nor reflection is allowed to dominate and where imagination is understood as being responsible for the creation of form which in order to be fully completed needs active conscious consideration.

The American artist Philip Guston is an interesting case in point. Deeply involved in the American avant-garde of the 1950s and 1960s his work moved from abstraction back to the figurative. The roughness and spontaneity of his imagery is itself reflective of the complex links between adult and child characteristic of twentieth century art. The subject of Guston's later work can be associated with the nature of the imagination and his writings record the act of painting in terms which recall the unconscious and yet describe how this material is actively and thoughtfully the object of reflection. In relation to the potential for meaning created by his paintings Guston has remarked:

> Yes I too puzzle over meanings – I mean the linkage of images when they are together in a certain way and then how all changes when they are in different combination. But that is the potency of images it is as if we are dense- swamped – image – ridden – we teem with meanings constantly. So the what is never settled.
>
> (Storr 1989, p. 109).

In these quotations we experience painting as a dynamic part unconscious and part conscious act. In the revision of Freud's work and the implicit attack on authoritarian, rigid and didactic teaching there is no justification of a *laissez-faire* attitude to creative activity or the teaching of the arts. Rather a model of sensitive interplay and reflection is being formed. A model that embraces the autonomy of the creator, the importance of the creative act and of the nurturing of the role of the imagination and the uniqueness of the individual. Within this developing model the role of conceptual and skill learning is far from being excluded. Both the child artist and adult artist are involved in learning in the arts. Milner highlights the skills and concepts inherent in the arts but puts them in the service of the imagination. In speaking of the artist she argues:

> He has to accept some public artistic convention, such as the outline of a musical scale or the grammar and vocabulary of a particular language, something that a particular time and place in history make available for him to use in conveying his private idea. Of course he may contribute to this convention himself, enrich and enlarge it, but he cannot start off without it, he cannot jump off from nothing.
>
> (Milner 1957, p. 134)

Our examples are engagements with the skills and language of art, dance and poetry. They do not and should not, however, have these skills as their goal. These skills support the energetic engagements of individuals with the world. Bachelard (1981), a writer for whom the exploration of the nature of the creative process became his central project, has emphasised the role of the imagination in changing and manipulating realised forms and meanings and understandings. He argues:

> Imagination is always considered to be the faculty of forming images, it is however the faculty of deforming the images offered by perception, of freeing ourselves from the immediate images; it is especially the faculty of changing images . . . The fundamental word corresponding to imagination is not image but imaginary. The value of an image is measured by the extent of its imaginary radiance. Thanks to the imaginary the imagination is essentially open, evasive. In the human psyche it is the very experience of opening and openness. More than any other power it determines the human psyche.
>
> (Bachelard 1971, p. 19)

The given language needs to be articulated. To be properly used it should be subjected to change. Engagement with language is not a matter of passive acquisition but of active use. The motor is the desire to make form to give meaning that originates in play.

What is emerging here is a complex and vital model of the imagination drawing in reflection and skills but nevertheless placing the imagination as human value and cognitive motor at the centre of the creative act. It is not imagination which contributes to learning in the arts but learning in the arts which contributes to the efficacy of the imagination. The trajectory of so much recent work in the arts is here, I believe, being fundamentally reversed. There is a need for a reversal of the dominance of the taught elements of the arts over the action of the imagination. Skills, concepts and information are not a goal in themselves, but a means to an end. The goal is the fostering of the imagination in its individual and cultural manifestations. As an individual manifestation it has to do with the active participation of the individual in life and growth and with psychic health and as a cultural manifestation it has to do with the health of the arts and of the health of the cultures in which they flourish.

For Winnicott the essential location of the activities of the imagination through play and culture is neither above nor below as in the respective positions of Warnock and Freud. For Winnicott the imagination and creative processes are located 'in between' in an area of experience that is neither fully internal (in terms of psychology and mental process) or external (in terms of experience or reality) but exists in a third area of experience, a space that constitutes for the child the space in which play occurs and which for adults is the space in which the world of culture and reality and the emergent self interact.

This location of the imagination is of great significance. As Kuspit (1993, p. 89) has identified in consideration of the use of Winnicottian approaches to the arts: 'Art originates in transitional experience, but even more fundamentally it originates in primal expression . . . art as transitional experience carries this expression into social space.'

This model of the creative imagination as a mediation between inner and outer and through its identification of the project of primal material into socially mediated space provides, I believe, a vigorous and rich alternative to the mutual antagonism of depth psychology and critical theory and linguistics. In other words psychology leads us to that place where a study of humanity enters culture and where notions of language and the nature of society in their turn influence who we are. Winnicott's model again proves valuable in that it provides a context which allows for the mediation of social and linguistic structures and processes within the activity of the imagination understood as universal human attribute.

Within the arts the feelings and expressions of self are projected into a social space in which they can be shared, valued, discussed, appreciated. Simply put poems are to be read, performed and broadcast. Dance is a social and cultural act. Paintings have a life beyond the moment of their production.

A contemporary context

The projection of meaning-making into social space recognised as a result of the imagination opens up connections which can be identified within a linguistic context. This emphasis on language as a focus for exploration of the arts and creative process is a characteristic of what has been termed post-modernism. Additionally this 'linguistic turn' (Kearney 1993) has resulted in a dissatisfaction and animosity towards theories of the imagination and creative process which are grounded solely in explanations of isolated individuals' achievement. Language seen as the object of study usurps the individual subject understood as the individual acting as creator. The 'myth' of the artist has been exposed as a lie which both obscures the role of culture and language and aggrandises the creative genius through magical stories of inspiration and insight.

In educational contexts this emphasis has tended to lead to a re-focus upon the arts as languages and as cultural activities based upon skills and conventions and involving the 'reading' of art objects as much as the 'writing' of art. There have undoubtedly been advantages and gains with this re-emphasis. But alongside this has been a contingent lack of emphasis, even hostility, to the arts as activities driven by the imagination and based in individual experience.

This crisis of the imagination in its most extreme forms as identified by Kearney (1993) leads to a kind of death of the imagination at the level of the arts and culture. However, the emergence of new perceptions of the workings of the imagination from within theory derived from linguistic considerations can offer a great deal to a consideration of the imagination in the context of early years education.

Kearney identifies a Hermeneutic Imagination (a perception of the imagination which emphasises the role of imagination in meaning-making) as a developing dimension of our understandings of the imagination. Elements of the writings of Paul Ricoeur are, I believe, of considerable importance in this respect. For Ricoeur the central linguistic process relevant to an understanding of the imagination is the metaphor. This focus provides particular possibilities for new insights. Ricoeur (1991) writes:

> What new access is offered to the phenomenon of the imagination by the theory of metaphor? What it offers is, first of all, a new way of putting the problem. Instead of approaching the problem through perception and asking how one passes from perception to images, the theory of metaphor invites us to relate imagination to a certain use of language, more precisely to see in it an aspect of semantic innovation characteristic of the metaphorical use of language.
>
> (p. 171)

The young children at play utilise a sense of 'likeness' in their use of costumes and base their play upon an 'as-if-ness' that is essential to play and to metaphor. Our two forms of dance are two different metaphorical structures for the understanding of growth. The poems metaphorise, amongst other things, mortality. The image of The Bully creates a metaphor for a complex act in wood and nails.

Here we have a development of Warnock's position and one which through the centrality of meaning-making can act as a bridge between the insights based upon psychology and those growing from more linguistically based approaches. The importance of the metaphor in relation to children's artwork and emotional development has recently been explored by Hawkins (1991) and Greenhalgh (1994). The sense in which play and the arts provide opportunities for the exploration of meanings through symbols, whether in the movement and action of play or in the arts through mark-making, manipulation of materials, voice, movement, sound or other form, provides opportunities for metaphor to function.

Eco (1979) has written of the 'detonating' energy of the metaphor and has linked the creative imagination, as indeed does Warnock, with James Joyce's theory of the epiphany – the everyday yet transforming discoveries of significance in experience. The metaphor, within this view, has enormous potential as it reveals new meanings through articulations of the symbolic components of language, and the arts seen linguistically, whilst renewing the language on which it draws through the opening up of new connections and through the changing system of relationships upon which the language depends. There are for me small epiphanies within the goldfish poems. My own experience of the arts is punctuated by moments of acute and powerful feelings and insights. The tradition of insight and transformation is central to writings on the arts from earlier centuries to the present day and to conceptions of therapy and therapeutic insight and value.

A child playing in a new way or exploring ideas through the arts creates forms which allow the world to be seen in new ways. As Warnock identified in relation to Sartre's view of the imagination there can be no decision-making, no morality and no deliberate action without the individual's ability to imagine that the world might be otherwise. The arts and play provide this experience through the activity of play and play's extension into the arts. Through the arts and play, then, we are able to imagine the world as other than we know it and through this artifice to begin to explore the possibilities of experience, the possibilities of change and our individual and collective potential.

As Ricoeur argues 'all symbols of art and language have the same referential claim to re-make reality' (1991, p. 176). This re-making is a vital function of play and the arts. It is cognition in action and importantly provides opportunities for recognition, discussion and further activity. In other words children involved in puppet plays and paintings and drawings are having important, real and sometimes very significant thoughts about themselves and the world and most importantly for teachers these thoughts can be re-visited, extended and reflected upon through discussion, comment, reinforcement, sharing and extension. In total utilising the range of strategies that constitute communicative activity in early years education to support learning that occurs through the imagination.

Ricoeur also states, 'It is through the anticipatory imagination of acting that I try out different possible courses of action and that I play in the precise sense of the word, with possible practices' (1991, p. 178). That such events occur in early years education should not be doubted. That their full educational potential is developed is another matter.

Bakhtin (1986) has identified this renewing and regenerative process characteristic of the imagination with the novel itself. Indeed Bakhtin argues that the characteristics of subversion and renewal are exactly those that characterise the novel in its unfolding historical manifestations. We recognise the novel as the novel through its role as 'supergenre', in other words through its ability to supersede previous forms and to renew language itself. The novel thus renews the literate culture and language acting through the imagination. Just as a metaphor, initially strange, settles and becomes commonplace it loses its radical and immediate power as it embeds itself in our experience and understandings of the world. At the same time a radical work becomes part of a cultural tradition and heritage, part of our shared experiences and understandings.

The standard, valuable yet normative understandings of growth shared within the dance stand in contrast to the more radical metaphor of the lone dancer. There is a place for both in learning in relation to the arts.

As with the visual arts, music and drama so with literature. The arts can be seen as the 'super genres' of the 'languages' of the arts; both subverting and renewing the culture and the languages upon which they draw. This process reverses the dynamic by which the learning of language and skills facilitates the imagination as it suggests the imagination creates and renews language. This I would argue is as true for the individual child as it is for the culture. The child's imagination is the dynamic by which language is acquired and learnt. This is so because the imagination is an appetitive interest in the making of form (and thus meaning). The imagination is a desire which underpins and provides the origins of learning. The imagination is the process at the core of the appetitive interest in language and form that so clearly distinguishes the motivated and successful learner. This appetitive interest grows from the nurturing of the child by the parent, the teacher, the environment and most importantly from the opportunity to play with form.

The consideration of these processes in relation to the individual and the individual's systems of understanding goes some way to explaining the enormous significance and personal response so often felt in the presence of works of art. The re-casting and re-forming of our patterns of understanding set in place by the imagination acting through the metaphor and the arts and acting as a dynamic of change links with the power of art and with the intuitive understandings of so many practising teachers, individuals who have seen and felt the effects of the arts upon individuals.

In this process it is the imagination which is the dynamic for the arts and play which are both activities that give form to ideas that we recognise after the event of production and encounter. The joy in subversion, delight in pure form, and play with pattern, repetition and disruption characteristic of phenomena as diverse as Nonsense Poetry, the Nursery Rhyme, and children's songs are also characteristic of play in the arts. Play in this sense is a vital element of the creative process of the arts (and sciences (Storr 1972)). Too much attention can be placed upon significance and meaning. Or rather by over-emphasising quick, immediate or superficial or simplistic meaning we can be acting against the meaning-making process of the individual. By searching out significance, by attempting to over-value causal links, we may limit the value of the 'play' of the imagination. The balance between nonsense and sense is a delicate one. Too much chasing of meaning can be counterproductive. Final meanings in the arts do not exist, rather it is the process of meaning which is at stake and is the location of value in the arts. We cannot value the imagination without valuing Nonsense and play too. This has been intuitively understood by many involved in early years education. In an education system dominated by sense, causal relationships, rationality and results this may seem problematic – even scandalous. It is a tall order but it is vital to the child and to art education.

Kuspit, drawing upon the work of Winnicott and, I believe, in support of the values advocated by Warnock, has argued for the recognition of the 'Good-enough Artist', that is artists who find their basis for art-making in the need for meaning-making and the joy of form rather than in the cynical self-consciousness of the post-modern art world. The child is often just such an artist. So in my experience is the teacher. Yet so much of art pedagogy is driven by the model of the successful artist/entrepreneur rather than by an understanding of the child and the nature of the creative process and imagination.

In contemporary education as in contemporary art the imagination has tended to lose its integrity, becoming linked with ideas that from within a particular view of current culture are criticised as naive.

The imagination along with expression appear as areas of experience made docile and turned into pastiches of themselves by the 'knowing' and self-conscious use of their traditions by adult artists.

However, the conception of the imagination as a primary shaping force constantly at play, rebuking and scandalising meaning and language and yet acting in the service of language and the interests of meaning gives new vitality to the imagination and to arts teaching. Part of the rehabilitation of the imagination in education should be an active commitment to the imagination as both a vital human attribute and a vital cultural invention.

The basis of this nurturing of the imagination in the early years of education could be the 'good-enough' teacher. This teacher would have a working understanding of the importance of the nurturing environment and of the importance of play, the arts and the imagination as life-enhancing and as an essential human value, attribute and goal.

Issues

It has been argued that play (for children) shares characteristics with the arts (for adults).

1. Consider the child at play and an adult involved in the arts (watching a play or even TV if you like). What similarities and differences can you identify?
2. Consider a child's or children's work of art drawn from your teaching experience (a drawing, painting, story, poem, video of a dance or play). What ideas are being dealt with in the work? What particular discoveries and thoughts *might* be occurring? How could these ideas be further extended into another art form?
3. Consider an adult work of art (painting, sculpture story, poem, dance or play) – what ideas are being dealt with in the work?
4. What themes, issues and ideas could valuably be explored through the arts within your work context? How could these be organised to fit in with your current provision?
5. How can the loop of cognition and recognition that occurs within the arts be further developed in your work context – i.e. how can the value of the arts work you undertake with children be further expanded by using it as the basis for discussion and further activity?

References

Abbs, P. (1987) *Living Powers* Hove, Falmer Press.
Arnheim, R. (1962) *The Genesis of a Painting; Picasso's Guernica* San Francisco,

University of California Press.

Bachelard, G. in Gaudin, C. (1981) *On Poetic Imagination and Reverie* Spring Publications.

Bakhtin (1986) *Rabelais and his World* London, Routledge.

Eco, U. (1979) *The Role of the Reader* Oxford, Basil Blackwell.

Fuller, P. (1980) *Art and Psychoanalysis* London, Hogarth Press.

Fuller, P. (1985) *Images of God* London: Chatto & Windus.

Greenhalgh, P. (1994) *Emotional Growth and Learning.* London, Routledge.

Hawkins, B. (1991) in *Maladjustment and Therapeutic Education* Volume 9 No. 2.

Kearney, R. (1994) *The Wake of Imagination* London, Routledge.

Kearney, R (1991) *Poetics of Imagining* London, HarperCollins.

Kuspit, D. (1993) *Signs of Psyche in Modern and Post-Modern Art* Cambridge, Cambridge University Press.

Maclagan, D. (1989) *Fantasy and the Figurative,* in A. Gilroy (ed) *Pictures at an Exhibition* London, Tavistock-Routledge.

Milner, M. (1957) *On Not Being Able to Paint* London, Heinemann Educational.

Podro, M. (1987) Depiction and the Golden Calf, in N. Bryson (ed) *Visual Theory* Oxford, Polity Press.

Ricoeur, P. (1991) *From Text to Action* London, Athlone Press.

Storr, A. (1972) *Dynamics of Creation* London, Fontana/Collins.

Storr, A. (1989) *Churchill's Black Dog and Other Phenomena of the Mind* London, William Collins.

Tillich, P. (1996) in K. Stiles (ed) *Contemporary Art* San Francisco, University of California Press.

Warnock, M. (1976) *Imagination* Oxford, Blackwell.

Winnicott, D. (1971) *Playing and Reality* Harmondsworth, Penguin.

4

Making sense of early mathematics

Gill Bottle and Claire Alfrey

Introduction

Mathematics for the ordinary person in the modern world is becoming ever more complex and there is a need to use it in many contexts. The media use charts and graphs increasingly as an illustration tool. A knowledge of statistics is necessary, for example, to work out which school performs best in league tables, especially if we are to take into account the 'value added' (the increase in children's scores over a period of time in school, effected through that school's teaching). It is becoming increasingly important to develop the power to think mathematically in order to be able to understand new situations. In today's transient job market life-long learning is crucial. The increasing use of computers means that today's adults may encounter mathematics never encountered in their school life such as the use of spread sheets and data-handling packages.

The ability to manipulate numbers and symbols in the abstract is an important part of being competent in mathematics, but in the day to day world there is also a need to be able to apply mathematical knowledge to actual situations. Every day we meet problems which need translation into appropriate mathematical operations (Hughes 1986).

Anyone who has experience of preschool children, either as a parent, carer or teacher, will appreciate that children from birth onwards are trying to make sense of their world, to understand why and how things happen. Anyone involved with young children will be continually amazed at their perceptions of the world – part of this world must be mathematics. Every day children are bombarded with new surprising and exciting experiences whilst attempting to make sense of previous ones. Through this 'sense-making' process children can become quite competent mathematicians long before they even enter school.

The following example illustrates the sort of knowledge that a young child may develop quite naturally while at play. A child aged 11 months was playing with large wooden building cubes. There were six bricks in each of four colours. First she arranged the yellow and green cubes alternately in a circular pattern around her. Then she spent some minutes looking at the pattern that she had made. Next she collected all of the green cubes and put them together on a chair and finally she collected all of the yellow ones together and put them to one side on the floor.

The child had demonstrated that she was able to make and recognise a pattern and sort blocks into sets using colour as a criterion. She was already pattern spotting and looking for rules, something which is fundamental to the development of mathematical understanding.

Children are surrounded by mathematics. Number, measure, shape and space concepts are not the sole domain of school and the National Curriculum. Our number system is one children will soon grow familiar with, whether it be through interaction with number in the environment, counting up and down stairs, singing number rhymes or being told how many sweets they can have. The environment in which children develop is number rich.

The following conversation took place in a changing area in a large shop between a mother and her child, aged almost three; each cubicle was numbered 1 to 15. The mother had a ticket saying what number cubicle she should go to:

C: Where are we going?

M: To number 11, it tells me where on my ticket.

C: A one and a one (looking at ticket) look it's got that there, (pointing at the number 11 cubicle), they've all got numbers, look. (The child then starts to count all in order.) Does the lady have tickets for all the numbers?

M: Yes, to tell people which cubicle to go to.

The obliging shop assistant at this point showed the child some of the other tickets and the child went to match them above the cubicles allowing the mother to try on clothes in peace! The child was demonstrating a good awareness of number knowledge in that he was able to match the numbers on the tickets to the numbers on the cubicles. He realised that they were in ascending numerical order, an exciting discovery which reinforced the child's recognition of ordinal number.

Young children seem to have an innate interest in number and will spontaneously count in their effort to try to order their thoughts and make sense of a group of objects. They demonstrate a desire to understand mathematical concepts and to explore them in their quest for comprehension. It is the logic and intelligence demonstrated in this process which is impressive and can often be under-estimated.

Meanwhile, school mathematics is often 'context free' (Hughes 1986, p. 45) and although the mathematics involved can be applied to a variety of situations that make 'human sense' (Donaldson 1978) to the child, all too frequently this is not the case. For example, the sum, 2 − 1 = 1, could be put in context by asking 'If I have 2 sweets and I eat 1, how many have I got left?' The character of school mathematics, however, is that it is a code with no context, written in symbols, which becomes increasingly difficult. What starts in a simple concrete form preschool, becomes something much more complex, available only to those who have learnt to crack the code. Hughes (1986) and Atkinson (1992) emphasise differences between informal preschool mathematics and abstract, decontextualised, formal school mathematics.

It is important that children come to grips with the formal mathematics. However, it would be wrong to think that informal mathematics necessarily has less value than school mathematics. Many cultures have systems of what is recognisably mathematics but is totally unlike school mathematics as we know it, yet these systems serve the needs of the cultures in which they exist (Ascher 1991; Zaslavsky 1973).

Many current educational developments in the area of mathematics are a reaction to the idea that English primary schools are not stretching and challenging pupils. Current teaching methods have been criticised because they lack pace and rigour. It is important that we realise that while the notion of a less demanding school programme might have appeared to gain some respectability from the 'bottom-up' rather than the 'top-down' approach advocated by Cockcroft (1982) in recent years, this approach in the early years does not excuse low expectations of any child. Piagetian notions that children cannot be educated beyond their own level of development does not warrant failing to provide them with the challenge that moves their development on and cross-cultural and other research provides challenges to Piagetian ideas of immutable stages in cognitive development.

Attempts to improve the efficiency of primary education include the National Literacy and the National Numeracy Projects. The Numeracy

Project gives a framework for planning the mathematics curriculum on a termly and weekly basis and also gives guidance for running effective lessons. These clearly are very positive aims and they might be an instrument for leading the teacher to make better use of technical knowledge. On the other hand one of the reasons why some teachers do not teach effectively is their tendency not to think in broad and critical terms about their teaching but simply to get on with what they see as the 'job in hand'. There is a danger that such teachers might come to see the task no longer as progressing unimaginatively through a published mathematics scheme but as progressing unimaginatively through the termly objectives of the National Numeracy Project. Since these objectives are, quite rightly, expressed in formal terms the result could be yet further neglect of children's pre-existing understanding (National Literacy and Numeracy Project 1997).

In the light of recent research that explores the notion that the classroom may be unsuccessful in pacing children's learning it is worth asking whether parents at home might be more successful. An important issue to explore is that of whether many parents might be able to give their children a better mathematical education during the early years than can be provided by early childhood educators in the range of preschool provision. There is some anecdotal evidence that nurseries are in certain cases producing non-contextual worksheets of an abstract nature, modelled on the least imaginative practice in primary schools and definitely not of a standard that TTA (Teacher Training Agency) and Ofsted (Office for Standards in Education) would find acceptable. This can only add to the problems of the 'gap' between home and school mathematics.

This chapter looks at two aspects of the relationship between home and school in early mathematics education. One is the acknowledged weakness in the failure of some schools to make good use of the contribution that the home has made to preschool learning. A further issue concerns the ways in which schools might breach the gap between the informal mathematics experience of home and preschool and the requirements of the formal mathematics curriculum in ways which will make sense to such young learners. Finally we question whether recent initiatives, such as the *Desirable Outcomes* (SCAA 1996), baseline assessment and the Numeracy Project, will be beneficial in addressing those two key issues.

Preschool mathematics

Evidence abounds that very young children may have extensive mathematical understanding, usually of an informal kind. Hughes (1986 esp. pp. 24-36) gives many examples of preschool mathematical abilities. In one experiment 83 per cent of his sample were able to solve small-number addition and subtraction problems connected with cubes being placed in or removed from a box in front of them. Atkinson (1992) reports on the successful classroom application of insights given by Hughes. When Hughes asked children exactly the same small-number addition and subtraction problems but without any practical context, the success rate fell from 83 percent to 15 per cent.

Children will often show a willingness to go beyond informal practical skills and may attempt to fathom out the intricacies of our number system. For example a child aged 3.1 years who would usually count correctly from 1 to 10 counted on 'eleven, twelve, thirteen, fourteen, FIVETEEN, sixteen, seventeen, eighteen, nineteen, ZEROTEEN'.

The child has clearly spotted some pattern in the numbers and is trying to extend it. Unsurprisingly he has failed to guess how we cope with the number written as 20 but it shows that he does have a good grasp of many mathematical ideas.

By the time children reach school formal abilities may be well developed. Aubrey (1993 and 1994) reports on studies of children in the reception class (usually aged four and five years) and concludes among other things that 'The high attaining children were well towards mastery of level 1 of the National Curriculum Mathematics Attainment Target 2 for Number on school entry. The low attaining children brought into school a range of informal competencies and a less stable conventional knowledge' (1993, p. 39). In other words, some children enter school already ahead of expectations, while others are a long way behind, presumably largely as a result of their different preschool experiences.

Early years school mathematics differs not only from the mathematics of home but also from mathematics that the child will encounter later in education and in adult life. In our society formal school mathematics is definitely important; but this does not necessarily mean that infant school mathematics has an intrinsic value of its own. Tall (1991, esp. p. 20) stresses that the mathematics of higher education is quite a different thing from the mathematics of the secondary school. The mathematics of the secondary school clearly has few similarities with the mathematics of the early years class.

An important question is how well the early years classroom enables children to take what they will need from secondary and higher education in order to meet the demands of society. Girling

(1977) and Plunkett (1979) drew attention to the informality of mathematics actually used in society and questioned whether the formalities of school were useful preparation for everyday life. During the intervening 20 years this debate has made little headway in political and public circles. Any loss of complacency about the ways in which early mathematics is taught in school should not lead us into deeper complacency about what is taught and whether this is the best or the only route.

It is generally accepted that school mathematics fails to build upon the children's prior understanding. It is therefore worth taking a serious look at whether the contribution of the home may be more useful than that of the classroom.

The early beginnings of number recognition and sequence develop in the first few years of life to a position where children, now familiar with the number sequence and their properties, may play with numbers to try to solve problems. In the following example a child aged four years was engaged in a conversation with his grandmother at a family gathering. They were discussing birthdays:

G: How old are you?

C: I am four and I will be five next, and after that I will be six and then seven.

G: What will you be after that?

C: I don't know. I know I'll count one, two, three, four, five, six, seven, eight. Yes eight.

G: And then?

C: Nine, then ten. I will be big then.

G: What will you be after ten?

C: I'll count (counts to eleven) Eleven I will be eleven. And after eleven what will I be then?

G: Don't you know?

C: No, you tell me.

G: Perhaps you will be 42?

C: No that's too big. I'll count (counts to twelve).

To join in this conversation the child needed to have gained a good grasp of many mathematical concepts. He needed an understanding of logic, rules, ordinal nature of number (he knew that 42 was too big), pattern of number, ascending order of number and magnitude. He had developed the ability to think about number in the abstract, to engage in mental manipulation, and to recognise something about larger numbers being in a fixed order.

Given such evidence that young children can come to grips with the foundations of number, it is important to harness this early mathematical development and use it to develop the higher cognitive skills necessary for the mathematics of the classroom. A number of research studies suggest that children do not transfer the knowledge that they have learned informally to their school mathematics learning (Atkinson 1992; Hughes 1986; Nunes and Bryant 1996). The link between home and school mathematics may not be made by many children unless specific help is given to perceive such connections.

A child (3 years 10 months) and her mother are playing with a toy garage, there are four spaces for cars:

M: You've got two cars in your garage, how many more can you put in?

C: Two.

Despite being able to understand and answer this addition problem in a concrete context the child may have problems converting this understanding to the formal symbolism of addition. Aubrey (1997, p. 20) amongst others document this 'gap'. But why does the 'gap' occur?

Mathematical knowledge – the 'gap' between home and school

The first issue is that of identifying the link between what children know and what we are trying to teach. This can be a problem both for the children and their teachers. In fact in a recent study it was noted that 'teachers seemed quite unaware of the rich, informal knowledge brought into school' (Aubrey *et al.* 1997, p. 85). Hughes (1986) emphasises that it is important for teachers to help children towards this link by using examples of 'mathematical metaphors' (p. 173) from the child's experience to underpin mathematical ideas. Basing mathematics on children's previous experience seems to make sense, but it is necessary to keep in mind the long term mathematical learning outcomes. However, such informal mathematics may not be compatible with the extended development of mathematical understanding and it is important to appreciate that not all mathematically related preschool experiences are necessarily beneficial for children in their later 'school mathematician' days.

Many incompatibilities are centred around the issue of language.

Walkerdine (1988, pp. 19–27) suggests that not all of the mathematics a child hears and uses at preschool is useful or correct. She discusses how words such as 'more' have meanings in the home, especially in relation to the consumption of food, which are important in themselves but which are quite unrelated to the use of 'more' required in school mathematics. For example if a child asks for more chips, they will probably be given less than they were given the first time.

Another example of this would be the notion of a 'half', which is often used in everyday situations to tell a child to cut an object into two rather than into two equal parts. As Hughes (1986) and Atkinson (1992) suggest, much of the language children hear used by adults is an informal usage of mathematical terms, for example 'wait a minute' does not really mean a minute, more a short space of time. Another problem specific to preschool and school mathematics is that of the technical language. Many words such as relation, odd and table all have mathematical meanings totally unrelated to the children's experience of them prior to school maths. This 'mathematical usage which is very specific . . . needs to be made clear to pupils' (Orton 1992, p. 130).

A further issue which may contribute to the 'gap' is that of problem solving. It seems inexplicable that while children's early mathematics is about problem solving, later on problem solving becomes a difficulty in itself. It may be that children lose the ability to do this, that for some reason they do not progress in this field, that the problems that we set them do not make sense to them, that the language of mathematics in school is unfamiliar, or a combination of these. The problem may be that the children are unable to match up formal notation with informal working out. Children often have difficulty working out what the formal notation of a problem might be. For example a child engaged in a problem may ask things such as 'Is it add?' or 'Which one of these numbers do I take away?' It would appear then important for teachers to think about how such questions should be answered and what action they need to take.

Published mathematics schemes are used in many schools today and they can be useful in supplying a structure for learning mathematics. Teachers, however, should not allow the amount of material published to determine the amount of time a child spends on each topic as this may stifle a child's development and slow down progress. An over-reliance on published maths schemes means that skills are often practised in isolation. Hughes discovered that: 'Written calculations often formed the main element in mathematics work and in some schools the sole aim seemed to be for the children to reach a standard of efficiency in abstract calculations' (Hughes 1986, p. 90).

As long ago as the early 1980s, H.M. Inspectors pointed out that most first schools concentrated on basic skills but no time was spent in one to one situations where teachers and children could engage in high quality discussion and the analysis of the children's thought processes (Cockcroft 1982). Teaching was often limited to what the child needs to know to complete the given page of the scheme rather than whether they understand the concepts involved. There is a danger that mathematics in school can emphasise only the facts to be learned and the skills to be practised. Hughes believes that 'proficiency in basic number is not enough' (Hughes 1986, p. 10). Over-practising of skills can lead to mathematical mystery and the relationship between those skills taught and the ability to use them to solve problems may be lost. There is therefore a definite need to teach children in a way that both questions their ideas and encourages them to apply their mathematics in a way that is meaningful to them such as in a data collection task or working out ingredients for cooking.

Possible solutions for filling the 'gap'

The possible problems that children may encounter in their early schooling are many and complex and we have only just scratched the surface of some of them. In this section we will draw on that which has been discussed above and to try to analyse how some of the problems in our teaching may be addressed practically in the classroom.

It is widely known that Britain is not keeping up with other countries in improving the standard of mathematics education for our young people. Not surprisingly therefore, there has been a backlash to the 'new methods' of the 1960s and 1970s, with the Government and many parents now feeling that traditional is best. However, the question is will the drive for 'back to basics' approach, that is teaching rigid methods of calculation, meet children's needs in today's world? After all, as discussed above, one of things that has been blamed for children's lack of progress is the over-practising of basic skills.

If we look back we discover that neither 'back to basics' nor 'progressivism' have been entirely successful in the past. It is therefore important that we analyse both methods in order to utilise the successful attributes of each.

Neither the 'back to basics' fundamentalists nor the 'play way' progressives were able through their method alone to generate the sorts of mathematical thinking in children that would offer confidence and understanding. Research now suggests that to be effective the teacher should utilise the ways children themselves impose pattern and structure on what they learn.

(Fisher 1990, p. 212)

The argument between 'Back to basics' and the importance of concrete experience needs to be seriously considered. Is it sensible to look at these two arguments in opposition? On their own neither gives the full picture. Both seem to be important and it could be argued that one supports the other. It is obviously desirable for children to be freed from the need to use concrete apparatus in order to develop the higher cognitive skills necessary for future development. However, it seems that concrete experiences and mathematics put into meaningful contexts underpin much mathematical understanding and lay the foundations on which to build. Meaningful experiences should not only be confined to the early mathematical experiences of children, as they also appear to form the 'scaffolding' that holds later concepts together. Practical experience, should therefore not be ignored as the children progress from them into the use of more abstract symbolism and formal notation. Although this aspect of learning is crucial so too is a sound basic understanding of taught number facts.

In their discussion about primary school practice, Alexander *et al.* suggested, 'there is a persistent and damaging belief that pupils should never be told things, only asked questions' (Alexander, Rose and Woodhead 1992, p. 31). Mathematics is about communication and the symbolic representation of ideas. This being the case, children need to understand the symbols which can be directly taught in the same way as spelling and letter formation.

Successful mathematics teaching needs to be interactive and to involve the children in thinking and doing so that they are not merely passive onlookers but are enthusiastic participants. The work presented to the children must allow them to question ideas. 'Research evidence demonstrates very clearly that the level of cognitive challenge provided by the teacher is a significant factor in performance' (Alexander, Rose and Woodhead 1992, p. 21).

Getting the children to analyse their own thinking and intuitive methods of calculation is one way to challenge their thinking. So although they may write $32 - 27 = 5$, examples of the method of calculating the answer in their head may vary. They might think that 32 is twelve more than 20 therefore $12 - 7 = 5$ or they might count on to 32 on fingers = 5. Alternatively they may think that 32 is $30 + 2$, 27 is $25 + 2$ the difference between 25 and 30 is 5 therefore the answer is 5.

Discussion with the teacher can help the children to develop the investigational and problem solving skills that they come to school with. As a result of her research evidence, Nunes believes that 'Children's understanding of mathematical concepts is generative . . . children do not need to learn every single bit of mathematics that they will need to know' (Nunes and Bryant 1996, p. 234). It is therefore important to help children to develop mathematical creativity so that they are not reliant on taught algorithms for solving mathematical questions.

Even at the earliest stage pupils can begin to develop their cognitive skills through investigation and problem solving activities and they can begin to generalise their findings into some kind of simplistic statement. For example, when looking at the number pattern 2, 4, 6, the child will be able to predict that the next number in the sequence will be 8 then 10 'because each number is 2 more than the last'. 'Through investigations with concrete materials, students develop conceptual understanding while discerning patterns and making generalisations. Such experiences contribute to the development of higher cognitive skills and a sense of accomplishment in mathematics' (Berman and Friederwitzer 1989, p. 21). One long term aim may be that the children work towards an understanding of the 'structure of knowledge'. To do this, they need to be encouraged to identify pattern and mathematical rules. They need to be invited to look for the patterns that are all around them in their everyday world because pattern spotting and looking for rules is fundamental and at the heart of mathematics.

Mathematics can be perceived as one of the languages that children can be helped to acquire. To achieve this they need, as with any other language, opportunities to explore it creatively, for example, manipulating a given number of objects to find out the mathematical possibilities within the task. The way that a teacher approaches mathematics with her pupils in the early stages can have a fundamental effect on the cognitive development of the children. It is therefore important to develop the children's ability to be as creative in their mathematics as in other subjects.

Will baseline assessment and desirable outcomes help overcome this gap?

As has already been identified, even though children may begin their primary school careers with quite a sound understanding of various mathematical concepts, their formative years of schooling do not always appear to build on these. So can the application of *Desirable*

Outcomes (SCAA 1997a) and baseline assessment provide a solution to eradicate this 'gap'?

The *Desirable Outcomes for Children's Learning on Entering Compulsory Education* (SCAA 1996) focuses on six areas of learning, one of which is mathematics. The desirable outcomes set for this area of learning on entering school reception class are topics such as being familiar with 'number rhymes, songs, stories counting games and activities. [Children] compare, sort, match, order, sequence and count using everyday objects.' (SCAA 1996, p. 11) These appear perfectly reasonable and within the grasp of the preschool children discussed earlier. Further SCAA suggests that 'through practical activities children. . . begin to show an awareness of number operations such as addition and subtraction, and begin to use the language involved' (SCAA 1996, p. 11). Again many preschool children will be able, in practical situations, to demonstrate such an understanding.

In SCAA's (1997a,) proposals for baseline assessment in mathematics much of the suggested assessment material does draw upon and use practical concrete situations. There is little use of 'formal mathematics' except for one activity to assess mathematical language, more specifically to assess whether or not a child 'can explain an addition sum' (SCAA 1997a, p. 38) such as $3 + 2 = 5$. It is suggested that the teacher 'use whatever words the child is likely to understand and encourage the child to talk about the sheet.' (SCAA 1997, p. 39). The process is indeed one that is familiar to children, but how many would be able to explain it, even with the help of the pictures of buttons, when faced with a formal 'sum'? Although some children who have a secure base developed with the use of concrete and practical activities may well understand this algorithm and be able to interpret it, many will not at this stage.

Whilst recognising that the notion of 'value-added' (the increase in children's scores over a period of time in school, effected through that school's teaching) is important the hope is that, firstly, preschool providers or parents will not be pressurised into starting formal mathematics algorithms too early at the expense of the crucial stage of practical work alongside language development in order for their children to be able to cope with the baseline assessment and to get a high total on the Baseline Assessment Scale. Additionally, care will need to be taken so that very young children are not put off mathematics. One four year old child who attends a private nursery had obviously been carrying out work on formal algorithms and had also been to assembly in the main school. In his attempt to make sense of his experiences, he asked his mother later that day 'Why does God make us do sums? I don't like them.'

Conclusion

Preschool children become quite competent mathematicians before school because they use and learn mathematics in a context. We as educators need to be aware of the 'gap' between home and school mathematics and find a way to eliminate the fear of mathematics and make it accessible to all. Explicit teaching is necessary to advance children's mathematical development. Indeed, how else will the children come to understand and utilise the complex number system and notation that is conventional in our culture? Nevertheless, there could be a danger in this formalisation in that children may be introduced to abstract symbolism too early and this could endanger the spontaneous, curiosity-driven learning of preschool which is so vital if children are to become competent mathematicians. Educators need to think long and hard about the changing nature of the mathematics curriculum and the methods employed to teach it effectively. There are two possible responses to the current situation. First, we can recognise that the new initiatives do at least challenge any complacency that educational professionals might feel concerning the methodology of the early years classroom. Secondly, we can encourage a strengthening of effective mathematics education by ensuring early years teaching takes full account of what the home experience has to offer.

Issues

1. What can be done about the perceived home school 'gap' and how could the education of children in the early years be organised to address such a problem?
2. What is the purpose of school mathematics? Is it purely for equipping children for everyday life or is it important that all children are given the opportunity to develop higher mathematical concepts?
3. It is widely recognised that there is a need to raise standards. Is there a danger, however, of dismissing all of our current practice, even that which is good, in favour of a new and as yet largely unresearched alternative?

References

Ascher, M. (1991) *Ethnomathematics: a multicultural view of mathematical ideas* Belmonte: Brookes/Cole.

Atkinson, S. (Editor) (1992) *Mathematics with Reason* London: Hodder and Stoughton.

Aubrey, C. (1993) An Investigation of the Mathematical Knowledge and Competencies which Young Children Bring into School *British Educational Research Journal* Vol. 19 No. 1 pp. 27–42.

Aubrey, C. (1994) An Investigation of Children's Knowledge of Mathematics at School Entry and the Knowledge their Teachers Hold about Teaching and Learning Mathematics, about Young Learners and Mathematical Subject Knowledge *British Educational Research Journal* Vol. 20 No. 1 pp. 105–121.

Aubrey, C. (1997) Children's Learning of Number in School and Out, in I. Thompson, *Teaching and Learning Early Number.* Buckingham: Open University Press.

Cockcroft, W. (Chairman) (1982) *Mathematics Counts: Report of the Committee of Inquiry into the Teaching of Mathematics in Schools* London: HMSO.

Berman B. and Friederwitzer F. (1989) Algebra can be Elementary – When Its Concrete *Arithmetic Teacher* Vol. 36 No. 8 p. 21–24.

Donaldson, M. (1978) *Children's Minds* Glasgow: Fontana Press.

Fisher, R. (1990) *Teaching Children to Think* Oxford: Basil Blackwell.

Girling, M. (1977) Towards a definition of basic numeracy *Mathematics Teaching* No. 81 December pp. 4–5.

Hughes, M. (1986) *Children and Number* Oxford: Blackwell.

National Literacy and Numeracy Project (1977) *Framework for Numeracy: Termly Planning for Years 1 to 6 (Draft March 1997)* London: DfEE.

Nunes T. and Bryant P. (1996) *Children Doing Mathematics* Oxford: Blackwell.

Orton A. (1992) *Learning Mathematics* (2nd edition) London: Cassell.

Plunkett, O. (1979) Decompostion and all that rot *Mathematics in School* Vol. 8 No. 3 pp. 2–5.

School Curriculum and Assessment Authority (1996) *Desirable Outcomes for Children's Learning on Entering Compulsory Education* London: SCAA.

School Curriculum and Assessment Authority (1997a) *Baseline Assessment Scales* London: SCAA.

Suggate J., Aubrey C. and Pettitt D. (1997) The number knowledge of four to five year olds at school entry and at the end of their first year *The European Early Childhood Education Research Journal* Vol. 5 No. 2 pp. 85–101.

Tall, D. (ed.) (1991) *Advanced Mathematical Thinking*, Dordrecht: Kluwer.

Walkerdine, V. (1988) *The Mastery of Reason* London: Routledge.

Zaslavsky, C. (1973) *Africa Counts* London: Prindle, Weber and Schmidt.

5

Developing a framework for primary PE

Mike Waring

The responsibility for developing healthy and informed children is all too often inappropriately laid solely at the door of the school, and especially the physical education curriculum. Therefore, the challenging ambition of this chapter is to outline a framework for the provision of physical education (PE) in the primary school that identifies not only the essence and structure of the content associated with each activity area, but the essential shared understanding and collaboration between the key agents (family, children and schools) in the provision of a progressive and cohesive education for children. A curriculum which is created in partnership with these key agents will help to lead children in their search to be informed independent people into life-long participation in physical activity.

The family, and in particular the parents, have a major influence on a child's quality of experience in physical activity (Brustad, Wiggins and Wyatt 1995; Brannen et al. 1994; Hendry et al. 1993). It is evident from a great deal of research that in collaboration with the parents, the school and in particular its PE curriculum play a prominent role in constructing attitudes towards habitual forms of physical activity (Kremer et al. 1997). This is true whether at recreational, competitive or elite level (Ogle and Kelly 1994; Telema, Kannas and Tynjala 1995). The compulsory status of PE in the National Curriculum (NC) has to date guaranteed some form of PE for every child during each phase of their school career. Despite this, a major cause for concern is the constant erosion of time for PE within school, especially primary schools. This is in part due to the ever increasing demands on time from other curricular areas. However, there is also the issue of the necessary expert PE knowledge of some primary teachers to consider (Wetton 1997; Evans, Penny and Davies 1993; Wright 1991).

The movement towards and development of a critical and

autonomous child (in and through the realm of PE) demands a broad, balanced and relevant curriculum. This requires differentiation of content and approach to suit individual cognitive and physical needs (Green 1995; Shultz et al. 1985). Unfortunately, all too often translation of this into the primary school PE and extended curriculum is misguided. This is due to the variety of contrasting perspectives and agenda brought by an array of those agents influencing provision in schools. These agents range from the government, to charities, parents, teachers, administrators and the children themselves. To compound this potential conflict, there is the necessity to initially establish and then co-ordinate coherence of philosophy and content across the entire PE curriculum, which should also encapsulate progression within, as well as across, its constituent and adjoining Key Stages (KS).

It can be argued that the promotion of life-long physical activity through the formulation of a pyramid of 'individual' and especially 'team' activities is the dominant hegemony. This has been reinforced by the ideology of the previous and present government with regards to sport. Unfortunately, such a position offers only a very limited understanding of the essence, fundamental principles and processes that should be promoted through PE in the primary school. This has created and perpetuated a culture of acceptance that for children is far from 'healthy', from not only a physiological (Armstrong and Welsman 1997) but a pedagogical point of view (Almond 1997). Parents and teachers have to be able to appreciate and co-ordinate their collaborative roles in the provision of a child's *physical education*. This will certainly involve each child participating physically in a range of activities. However, it will also involve the formulation of strategies and principles that the child can implement in a variety of contexts. In so doing they can successfully interpret and manipulate different situations and movements to enhance their learning and understanding now and in the future. In addition, this reinforces the notion that such learning and understanding extend beyond PE into all aspects of the school curriculum and beyond. A framework around which parents, teachers, local providers and policy makers can construct and develop a coherent, co-ordinated and complementary learning experience, facilitating this 'right of passage' for children, therefore becomes essential.

The framework

In essence PE in school should strive to expand and develop each child's cognitive and physical understanding of themselves – in so doing facilitating critical thinkers, enhancing imagination and creativity and resulting in healthier, more autonomous and informed citizens in what is today's culturally diverse society: which is possibly the fundamental objective of every parent through the experiences they promote.

Barrow (1990) suggests that most of our problems arise not from ignorance of how to achieve what we want, but from a failure to properly conceptualise what we want. One might disagree, in PE it has been a combination of both of these factors. Figure 5.1 is an outline of a framework designed to facilitate that which we should be striving to achieve in primary PE. After a general overview of the framework and fundamental principles associated with the structure, more specific content related to KS1 will be addressed.

Clay's (1996) vision of the future of PE, supported by Almond (1997) and Harris and Elbourn (1997), emphasises the importance of partnership between parents, schools and local providers. It is only through such partnership that informed life-long participation and involvement in physical activity for all children will be achieved and sustained. Such collaboration is a central principle of the framework presented in Figure 5.1 and the consequences of such interaction impact at every stage. It is important that all agents are allowed to understand, facilitate and experience the notion of an 'active community' relative to their particular context (Harris and Elbourn, 1997). The foundation for this is a well balanced and equally well taught PE curricular that establishes equality of opportunity for all.

Most people would agree that, in an ideal situation, PE contributes to the physical, emotional, social, moral and intellectual aspects of development of all pupils. However, they might similarly admit that the increasingly limited amount of time provided to facilitate such developments might only allow one or two aspects to be satisfactorily addressed in the majority of situations. This discussion could then conceivably become more open regarding the selection of these components and the best time to emphasise each one. During KS1 the main emphasis is quite rightly on the mastery of fundamental motor skills (Smith *et al.* 1991). However, one cannot neglect or ignore the psycho-social domain and its development. A child not only needs to be able to perform fundamental motor skills, but needs to understand the context in which to apply them. As children become 'able to' they should be made aware of the significance of an activity (i.e. with regard to its application to a given context), it is logical to presume that they will be more likely to voluntarily participate in it. It similarly follows that it also needs to be a fun and engrossing activity (Goudas and Biddle, 1993; Weiss 1993).

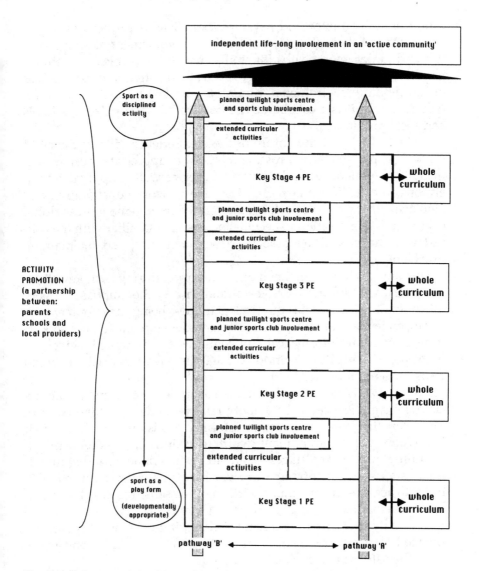

Fig. 5.1 A framework for the provision of physical education

Building on a foundation in KS1 that emphasises play within a developmental framework of fundamental motor skills and psychosocial aspects should be the opportunity to reinforce experiences within the extended school content through extra-curricular activities. A number of factors reinforce this, not least the amount of time that is available to participate in an activity during main curriculum PE time. Establishing extra-curricular clubs and activities allows children to practise what they have learnt and in so doing enhance their application of skills (motor and psycho-social). This is further developed and extended through 'planned twilight' involvement at sports centres and junior sports clubs for similar reasons. However, two things become important here. The first is that the content and experiences of the child are co-ordinated, progressive and associated with the PE NC. Secondly, it is a collaborative initiative between parents, schools and local providers.

It is essential that the nature of these experiences allows the child (as well as parents/local providers/NGBs) to appreciate those fundamental components a child needs to master, as well as apply in a variety of contexts. These key agencies have to work collaboratively to help achieve the child's prolonged informed involvement. In so doing everyone is in a position to become increasingly familiar with the context and the procedures associated with initiating and maintaining involvement.

This approach is maintained and built upon during each key stage. In the Early Years (under 5 years) and in KS1 the emphasis is very much on the notion of physical activities being developmentally appropriate play forms. These evolve and develop into a more sophisticated repertoire of physical and cognitive skills applied to increasingly varied contexts. It is important that there is an increasingly broad range of situations that highlight games/physical activities as more disciplined activity, as pupils will then be in the best position to appreciate the significance of the activity relative to their cultural context. They can therefore, make more informed decisions regarding their involvement and commitment to different kinds of physical activity.

Throughout the key stages identified in the Framework (Figure 5.1) there is a developmental and progressive structure and approach. In order to achieve this the framework has to be sensitive to a child's natural development; it has to have a general broad base, becoming increasingly specialised; it generates increasing responsibility for self-directed learning; it enhances school to community links; and maintains the safety of each child throughout.

Pathways of involvement

The Framework may at first appear relatively inflexible with regard to its structure. However, this should certainly not be the case. It has been organised such that it can address a range of involvement in physical activity within and between each KS. For example, ideally each child would be in a position to experience all components of this framework. However, due to an array of environmental, psychological, developmental, social and cultural factors interrelating to act upon the opportunities and participation (Sallis 1994), a variety of 'pathways to involvement' will arise. Fundamentally every child will experience PE at school as their 'minimum' entitlement. This is identified on Figure 5.1 by pathway 'A'. At the other end of what can be considered an 'experience continuum' is that the child is involved in a number of activities, in a number of contexts. This would be in addition to their involvement in the school's main PE curriculum. This child's experiences are represented in Figure 5.1 by pathway 'B'. The child and parents in this instance are open to experience **all** opportunities at all Key Stages. Of course, this is a somewhat simplistic illustration. In reality the 'pathway of involvement' for each child and their collaborating agents will inevitably be far from linear, due to the great number of variables acting upon the child's involvement. What remains significant, however, is that there is a consistency in the framework for activities to be covered in PE. With this in place it enables the child to maximise their involvement relative to their particular context, regardless of the variables acting upon them at any given time.

Looking at one end of the continuum (i.e. child only involved in physical activity during PE at school), such involvement in PE should still enable a child to positively experience, as well as appreciate, the most appropriate context for continued involvement in the physical activity now and in the future. Parents too need to understand the most appropriate context and mechanisms for access to activities if they are to collaborate with other agents (schools, local providers) to work towards their child's life-long participation in physical activity and indirectly the achievement of a truly active community. With this philosophy and structure in mind, we need to explore more specifically the content of KS1.

Manners and Carroll (1995, p. 3) suggest six principles on which the teaching of PE between 3–7 years depends:

- physical education builds on what the child can already do;
- children should be as active as possible during physical education;
- lessons should be regarded as learning situations with clear, structured outcomes identified;
- there should be a range of activities and sufficient time given to the subject;
- in order to achieve a balanced programme there should be sufficient equipment and adequate facilities;
- all children are entitled to the best physical education programme possible.

CATEGORIES OF MOVEMENT & FUNDAMENTAL MOTOR SKILLS:

(1) LOCOMOTORS

Walk, run, leap, hop, jump (horizontal, vertical, from height), skip, slide, gallop.

(2) STABILITY

Axial Movements (bend (flexion), stretch (extension), twist, turn, reach, lift, fall.);
Springing Movements (vertical jump, headspring, handspring);
Upright Supports - static and dynamic balance (individual stunts, partner stunts);
Inverted Supports (tripod, headstand, forward/backward roll, cartwheel, roundoff.)

(3) MANIPULATIVE

Throw, catch, kick, trap, dribble, roll ball, strike horizontal, volley.

MOVEMENT CONCEPTS:

(1) BODY

Parts (head, neck, trunk, hands, legs, feet)
Actions (support, lead, transfer weight)
Shapes (wide, narrow, round, twisted, symmetrical, asymmetrical)

(2) SPACE

General
Personal (direction, level, pathways, range)
Limited

(3) EFFORT

Time (fast, slow, medium; accelerate, decelerate)
Force (strong, light, medium)
Flow (free, bound)

(4) RELATIONSHIPS

Body (unison, succession, opposition)
Objects (over/under, front/behind, in/out, near/far)
Individuals (mirror, shadow)

Fig. 5.2 A developmental PE curriculum for five and six year olds
Source: Smith, Carlise and Cole 1991

The NC for PE, designed around a process model, is very much concerned with the education of the young child. It has a clear definition of the importance of physical development (active health) and psycho-motor learning (with the stress on performance) (Jones 1996). However, one needs to make more specific reference to the NC regarding the activity areas at KS1 (games, gymnastic activities and dance) in order to further appreciate and fully facilitate the Framework presented in Figure 5.1. Smith *et al.* (1991) present an outline of a developmental PE curriculum for five and six year old primary school children (Figure 5.2). This is a useful guide to help elaborate on the nature of the content at KS1.

Wetton (1997) offers an informed and very useful text which can be adapted to identify similarities between the three activity areas (see Figure 5.3). It is the interrelationship and coherence between and within each activity area that is the significant factor, as it will impact upon the content and nature of provision. Reid (1995) also recognises that 'movement competency has the sharpest focus in gym and dance, but integration and transfer of work between them and games at KS1 is productive. Movement competency refers to the person becoming more agile and athletic, exploring their developing skills in different activities' (Reid, 1995, p. 6). One must cater for and highlight both within and outside of the PE curriculum, given the collaborative nature of the provision and time constraints associated with participation. By looking at each of the three activity areas in more detail we can highlight the coherence, progression and interrelationship between them to enhance provision in the curricula, extra-curricula and local community.

Games

There is a consensus of opinion amongst physical educationalists that games are an important area of activity within the PE NC, and in particular KS1.

> There are two good reasons for including games in a PE programme for early years children. One is based on child development and the concept of play, and the other going back to prehistory.
>
> (Manners and Carroll 1995, p. 34)

However, some ambiguity remains over the nature of these games. This is reinforced by the contrasting nature of the application of games within the NC for PE. Unfortunately, the importance placed on sport in schools by government publications and policy, is too easily misin-

GAMES	GYMNASTIC ACTIVITIES	DANCE
Travelling skills: - running & stopping on a signal - running and jumping - hopping and skipping - running, stopping and turning - dodging Sending skills: - rolling a ball to hit a target - throwing a ball underarm & across the space Travelling skills with equipment: - dribbling a ball to hit a target - bouncing a ball whilst travelling forwards - running around obstacles whilst carrying different shaped balls Receiving skills: - receive a rolling ball or quoit - receive a large ball which has bounced a few times - receive a large ball which has bounced once - bounce and catch a large ball - throw a ball in the air underarm, let it bounce, and catch - stop large ball with feet or hands - catch a large ball coming from the air, thrown by self.	- holding the body still in different parts - hopping and skipping - rocking and rolling - travelling on hands and feet - travelling on different parts of the body - stretching and curling the body - travelling using hands and feet - rolling and sliding - swinging, climbing, spinning and turning - balancing - jumping and landing.	Awareness of the body: - whole body movements (opening, closing, twisting, raising and falling) focus on use of head and spine - walk into space, run lightly in the space, stop and turn around - walk in time to the music - awareness of parts of the body - symmetrical movements - leading movements with specific parts of the body. The body in stillness and motion: - basic locomotor movements; walking, skipping, running, hopping - basic locomotor movements finishing in complete stillness - twisting, curling, stretching, holding finished position still - dance created with moments of action and moments of stillness Travelling and jumping: - basic locomotor movements on various pathways (straight, curved and circular) - jumping on to two feet - marching to music - leaping from one foot to another - bouncing on spot until music stops, then hold the position - leap in any direction and hold the shape in stillness. Shape of the body: - angular and stretched shapes (symmetric and asymmetic), curled shapes - moving from one shape to another Movement quality

Fig 5.3 Outline of content for KS1
Source: Adapted from Wetton 1997

terpreted as 'sport = games = PE'. This must not be allowed to happen. A broad and balanced curriculum should be supported by sport,
but certainly not replaced by it (Clay 1996). Therefore, there is a need
to explore the notion of sports and its relationship within PE and the
Framework presented in Figure 5. 1, as this philosophy will impact on
the practicalities.

The notion of 'Sport Education' presented by Siedentop (1994) and
developed by Almond (1997) is useful in that it highlights the essence

of sport and its role within PE – that is, to help to create competent, literate and enthusiastic participants in sport. Almond (1997, p. 35) further suggests that the task of teachers, when presenting sport to young people, is threefold:

1. to initiate young people into a range of sporting activities that illustrate their significance as important aspects of cultural life;
2. to demonstrate how engagement in sporting activities can enrich people's lives and improve its quality; and
3. to provide opportunities for students to engage in making decisions about involvement and commitment to sport.

Acknowledging this, one can now consider Reid's (1995) work outlining the nature of content and its progression through each KS in relation to games. Of course the types of games selected as learning experiences in lessons should parallel the development of skilfulness. It is the game that gives the skill its context and therefore its significance. Figure 5.4 encapsulates how this might be plotted taking account of the pupils' motivation and readiness to learn, and the PE NC End of Key Stage Descriptions (EKSD) and programmes of study (PoS) for games.

Gymnastic activities

Gymnastics can offer exciting and demanding opportunities for every child. Enabling them to challenge themselves while developing their movement repertoire. The adoption of a simple mapping procedure for this activity area and its programmes of study identifies the necessary progression of content across all KS (see Figure 5.5). This is essential in that it will be from this foundation that teachers (and subsequently parents and local providers) will begin to orchestrate each child's gymnastic education.

Figure 5.5 identifies the increase in the range of involvement in a child's movement vocabulary from KS1 to KS2. This is supported by similar experiences in other activity areas. During KS1 children will develop their basic repertoire of actions (as outlined in Figure 5.2) in an environment which allows them to work independently, as well as co-operatively, within a shared space and using shared equipment (Williams 1995).

The NC is about content, not delivery. Therefore, even though progression can be identified in the NC structure there remains that essential but somewhat 'double edged sword' of professional judgement regarding how best to transmit the content within any given con-

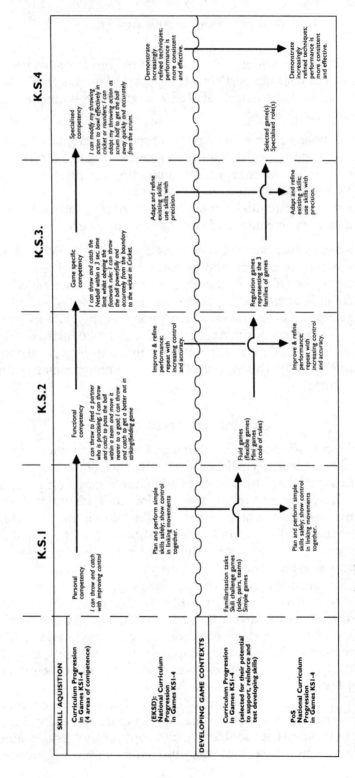

Fig. 5.4 Progressions in games for KS 1 to 4
Source: Adapted from Reid 1995

KEY STAGE 1	KEY STAGE 2	KEY STAGE 3 (Unit B italicised)	KEY STAGE 4
different ways of performing basic actions: travel using hands & feet	different means of travelling using hands and feet	refine and increase range of travelling by stepping	increasingly advanced techniques and how to improve performance
		refine and increase range of travelling by rolling	
different ways of performing basic actions: turn	different means of turning	refine and increase range of actions involving twisting and turning	plan and implement a training schedule relevant to the gym. activities undertaken
different ways of performing basic actions: jump	different means of jumping		apply the principles, rules and criteria for evaluating performance
different ways of performing basic actions: balance	different means of balancing	refine and increase range of actions involving flight. refine and increase range of balancing skills including moving fluently into and out of balance.	
different ways of performing basic actions: swing	different means of swinging	*refine range of advanced actions involving sliding, spinning and wheeling.*	
different ways of performing basic actions: climb	different means of climbing	*refine range of advanced actions involving swinging, circling, lifting and lowering the body*	
above on floor and apparatus	above on floor and apparatus		
link a series of actions	practise, refine and repeat a longer series of actions	*develop, refine and evaluate a series of actions with or without contact with others*	
how to repeat actions	make increasingly complex movement sequences using floor and apparatus	refine series of actions in increasingly complex sequences using floor & apparatus, including variety contrast and repetition	
		complex sequences alone and with others	
	emphases change of shape		
	emphases change of speed		
	emphases change of speed	refine actions involving extension, body tension, and clarity of body shape.	

Fig. 5.5. Progression in gymnastic activities across KS 1 to 4
Source: Williams 1995

text. This is something which applies to all NC activity areas, not just gymnastic activities.

> The task of the teacher then, is to select from the gymnastic material available, a range of activities, skills and challenges which cover the content outlined in the programmes of study in a way which will foster progression and which enable every child to be challenged but to be successful.
>
> (Williams 1995, p. 15)

Differentiation of content in gymnastics (and all other activity areas for that matter) is essential to ensure that all children are given a choice of tasks and are suitably challenged relative to their personal range of ability. In so doing the child is likely to achieve success. This helps to nuture a feeling of security and confidence within a gymnastic context which is vital to enhancing expression and experimentation. However, while innovation and experimentation are to be encouraged, so should the quality of movement. Not only is it a matter of creating imaginative and versatile children who can respond to a variety of movement demands in any given context, it is also a matter of using quality movement to do so. Once again it is the notion of the child adapting their knowledge and performance to a variable context and its demands. This is a principle that can be traced throughout each activity area in each KS. In order to facilitate this movement towards greater independence on behalf of the learner, the teacher must have a broad conception of teaching methodology. It is not simply a matter of selecting a teaching style and sticking with it regardless of the tasks or subject. The teacher should be prepared to move along a continuum of teaching styles and approaches which are most appropriate to the diversity of the content. All of these points should similarly be transferred and applied to dance, as well as other areas of activity.

Dance

> If pupils are to experience and understand dance fully they need to be continuously engaged in composing (planning) and appreciating (evaluating) dances alongside performing them.
>
> (Buckle 1995, p. 16)

Taking this into account, Buckle has developed dance specific statements which link with progression in EKSD (see Figure 5.6). This allows the three processes of composing, performing and appreciating to be clearly identified within a framework that teachers can use to plan learning activities. It similarly provides parents and local providers with a 'blueprint' to inform their facilitation of a child's experience. Significantly it is the balance of experience between these three interrelated processes that should be maintained in order to satisfactorily develop the knowledge, skills and understanding of dance for every child.

One of the main points emphasized in this chapter is that the progression and coherence identified in and between each of the activity areas has to be appreciated by all of the key agents who collaboratively help structure a child's physical education. This once again supports the need for sustained, well informed teaching in school, as well

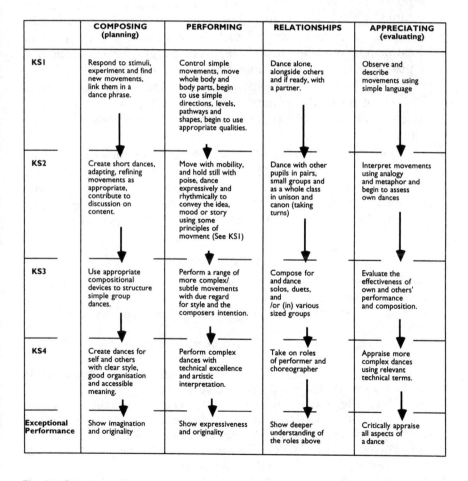

	COMPOSING (planning)	PERFORMING	RELATIONSHIPS	APPRECIATING (evaluating)
KS1	Respond to stimuli, experiment and find new movements, link them in a dance phrase.	Control simple movements, move whole body and body parts, begin to use simple directions, levels, pathways and shapes, begin to use appropriate qualities.	Dance alone, alongside others and if ready, with a partner.	Observe and describe movements using simple language
KS2	Create short dances, adapting, refining movements as appropriate, contribute to discussion on content.	Move with mobility, and hold still with poise, dance expressively and rhythmically to convey the idea, mood or story using some principles of movment (See KS1)	Dance with other pupils in pairs, small groups and as a whole class in unison and canon (taking turns)	Interpret movements using analogy and metaphor and begin to assess own dances
KS3	Use appropriate compositional devices to structure simple group dances.	Perform a range of more complex/ subtle movements with due regard for style and the composers intention.	Compose for and dance solos, duets, and /or (in) various sized groups	Evaluate the effectiveness of own and others' performance and composition.
KS4	Create dances for self and others with clear style, good organisation and accessible meaning.	Perform complex dances with technical excellence and artistic interpretation.	Take on roles of performer and choreographer	Appraise more complex dances using relevant technical terms.
Exceptional Performance	Show imagination and originality	Show expressiveness and originality	Show deeper understanding of the roles above	Critically appraise all aspects of a dance

Fig. 5.6 Dance specific statements which link with progression in EKSD
Source: Buckley 1995

as collaborative and coherent experiences facilitated by parents and local providers both at home and in the community.

If all pupils are to receive their PE entitlement, the curriculum needs to offer equality of opportunity through differentiated programmes which have a clear line of progression. This is a tall order for the non-specialist Key Stage (1 *and*) 2 teacher and partnerships with outside agencies, sensitively handled, have considerable potential for enhancing the curriculum experience of this age group.

(Williams 1996, p. 72).

Issues

1. Who should have control of Physical Education? Policy implemented by the Conservative government, outlined in *Sport: Raising the Game* and perpetuated in Labour's comparable and sympathetic document *Labour's Sporting Nation*, has generally been welcomed as a positive attempt to enhance the provision of sport in schools. However, does this merely perpetuate an inadequate definition of PE, taking away the education from the physical? At what age, when and how should sport be introduced to children in primary schools?
2. The National Curriculum is about content and not delivery. It therefore facilitates professional judgement regarding how best to transmit content within the context of any given school. What do you consider to be the fundamental components and principles underpinning the delivery of any activity area in KS1 (and beyond)?

References

Almond, L. (Ed.) (1997). *Physical Education in Schools.* (Second Edition) London, Kogan Page.

Armstrong, N. and Welsman, J. (1997). *Young People and Physical Activity.* Oxford, Oxford University Press.

Barrow, R. (1990). *Understanding skills: thinking feeling and caring.* Ontario Canada, The Althouse Press.

Brannen, J., Dodd, K., Oakley, A. and Storey, P. (1994). *Young People, Health and Family Life.* Buckingham, Open University Press.

Brustad, R.J., Wiggins, M.S. and Wyatt, F. (1995). Attraction to Physical Activity in Urban Children: Parental Socialization Influences. *Research Quarterly for Exercise and Sport Supplement,* 66 (1), A–78.

Buckle, D. (1995). The National Curriculum: The Teaching of Dance. *The British Journal of Physical Education,* 25 (3), 16–20.

Clay, G. (1996). Catching the Wave. *The Bulletin of Physical Education,* 32 (2), 6–7.

Evans, J., Penny, D. and Davies, B. (1996). Back to the Future: Education Policy and Physical Education. In N. Armstrong (Ed). *New Directions in Physical Education: Change and Innovation* (pp. 1–18). London, Cassell Education.

Green, K. (1995). Physical Education, Partnership and the Challenge of Lifelong Participation: A shared goal for the 21st Century. *The British Journal of Physical Education,* 26 (2), 26–30.

Goudas, M., and Biddle, S. (1993). Pupil Perceptions of Enjoyment in Physical Education. *Physical Education Review,* 16 (12), 145–150.

Harris, J. and Elbourn, J. (1997). Initiatives in Children's Physical Activity Promotion. *The British Journal of Physical Education,* 28 (1), 22–23.

Hendry, L.B., Shucksmith, J., Love, J.G. and Glendinning, A. (1993). *Young People's Leisure Lifestyles.* London, Routledge.

Jones, C. (1996). Physical Eduation at Key Stage 1. In N. Armstrong (Ed). *New Directions in Physical Education: Change and Innovation* (pp. 48–61). London, Cassell Education.

Kremer, J., Trew, K. and Ogle, S. (Eds.) (1997). *Young People's Involvement in Sport.* London, Routledge.

Manners, H.K. and Carroll, M.E. (1995). *A Framework for Physical Education in the Early Years.* London, Falmer Press.

Ogle, S. and Kelly, F. (1994). *Northern Ireland Health and Activity Survey: Main Findings.* Belfast, Sports Council for Northern Ireland.

Reid, B. (1995). National Curriculum: The Teaching of Games. *The British Journal of Physical Education,* 25 (3), 6–11.

Sallis, J. F. (1994). Determinants of Physcial Activity Behaviour in Children. In R.R. Pate and R.C. Hohn (Eds.), *Health and Fitness Through Physical Education,* (pp. 31–43). Champaign, IL, Human Kinetics.

Shultz, R.W., Smoll, F.L., Carre, F.A. and Mosher, R.E. (1985). Inventories and norms for children's attitudes towards physcial activity. *Research Quarterly in Exercise and Sport,* 56 (3), 256–265.

Siedentop, D. (Ed.) (1994). *Sport Education: Quality PE Through Positive Sport Experiences.* Champaign, IL, Human Kinetics.

Smith, M., Carlisle, C. and Cole, S. (1991). Teaching Fundamental Motor Skills in the Primary School: An Examination of the Effectiveness of a Developmental Physical Education Curriculum. *Physical Education Review,* 14 (2), 169–175.

Telema, R., Kannas, L. and Tynjala, J. (1995). Comparative and International Studies in Physical Activity and Sports: A Scandinavian Perspective. The Proceedings of 9th Biennial Conference of International Society for Comparative Physical Education and Sport. Charles University, Prague, Czech Republic, 2–7 July, 1994.

Weiss, M.R. (1993). Children's participation in Physical Activity: Are We Having Fun Yet? *Pediatric Exercise Science,* 5 (3), 205–209.

Wetton, P. (1997). *Physical Education in the Early Years.* London, Routledge.

Williams, A. (1995). National Curriculum Gymnastics. *The British Journal of Physical Education,* 25 (3), 12–15.

Williams, A. (1996). Physical Education at Key Stage 2. In N. Armstrong (Ed). *New Directions in Physical Education: Change and Innovation* (pp. 62–72). London, Cassell Education.

Wright, J. (1991). Gymnastics – Ideals for the 1990s? *The British Journal of Physical Education* 22 (4), 8–14.

6

Information technology: issues of control

Peter Dorman

During recent years a growing emphasis has been placed upon the role of Information Technology at all stages of the education process. In this chapter I am concerned first with definitions of Information Technology and then with an examination of its possible role in the early childhood curriculum. I will begin by widening the definition, paying special attention both to the role of the computer and the design of the software used. In particular I will raise the issue of control, asking who has control of the learning process, the teacher, the child or the computer system. Using examples from practice, I place the role of such systems firmly within a practical, investigatory and holistic view of early childhood education: a view in which teachers and children are co-learners using the systems as a focus for joint discovery and as a means to sustain children's place in the learning community.

First, what is meant by the term Information Technology? To paraphrase the National Council for Educational Technology definition (NCET 1995) Information Technology is to do with the handling and processing of information through the use of electronic devices. The information worked with can be in many forms, it could be words or pictures, equally it could be numbers or sounds. A response to this might be to question how such technology fits into an early years education, perhaps by questioning the validity of using computers with younger learners. Surely they deny a fundamental principle of early childhood education by replacing real life experiences?

A first answer lies in a wider definition of Information Technology for the term electronic devices is not limited solely to computers. Appreciating this allows us to see that Information Technology pervades our lives, we are surrounded by it in many forms. Think for a moment about your everyday, 'real world' experiences of IT: the microwave used to heat fast food; the washing machine with its pre-programmed settings; the telephone with its built in memory; the swipe card used for direct payments, bar-code readers in super-markets. The list is almost endless and the impact of the micro-processor on our lives immense. If we extend this through the use of tape and video recorders, television sets, cameras and camcorders, the growing use of fax and electronic communications we see that the influence of IT is all pervading. To acknowledge such develop-ments the use of tape recorders, play telephones, musical keyboards and programmable toys should form an integral part of the early years environment. Such 'natural' resources can be extended to include more specific hardware such as the various types of floor robots: Roamers, Pips or Pixies.

Computers form one part of these general developments in Information Technology; though by their sheer power and versatil-ity they have a very special part to play. It is also important to realise that the technologies of television, distance communication devices and computers, are not only developing rapidly in them-selves, but are becoming rapidly integrated. Systems are readily available now which simultaneously allow us to watch television, play audio CDs, type a letter, send and receive information across the world. Graphics displays have become enhanced, moving from two to thousands of colours in a generation. Three dimensional graphics will soon become commonplace, miniaturisation of systems will allow ready access to affordable portables. Coupled with the introduction of sound technologies which enable speech to be recorded, text to be read and spoken instructions responded to, we can see that change continues apace. It is perfectly feasible on a home computer system now to copy a video clip into a word processed letter, add a spoken message and then send the complete document to a friend in another country all within a few minutes and accomplished on the same system.

A utilitarian view of education would argue that an objective of any educational system ought to be to prepare children for the world that they are to enter and that children should therefore develop familiarity with Information Technology in all its guises. A more positive view is that education is not independent from the world, it is part of it and such a versatile resource should figure in the enterprise. It is not only adults who live in a technological world – so do children, children who come to school with expectations and assumptions about what they will find and use. For many their world now includes home computer systems, and for them it would be surprising to come into an educational system devoid of IT. We are beginning to experience Papert's (1980) predicted impact of the home computer on education.

We need, however, to step carefully between the two extreme positions. On the one hand is the techno-luddite who holds that all forms of IT are bad; but perhaps as limited a view is that of the techno-romantic (techno-naive may be a better description) who feels that IT will somehow, by its nature and uncritical use, solve all problems. As teachers our function should be to enable children to develop a critical understanding, a familiarity with and awareness of both the uses and the limitations of all forms of IT. The role of teachers is crucial here and should be to ensure that children develop appropriate Information Technology skills and that Information Technology is used effectively to both support and extend children's learning across curriculum areas. IT does not allow us to abrogate our responsibilities for making informed critical judgements.

At a fundamental level this requires us to consider how to apply and manage the technology for there are many ways of organising the use of computer systems. In many instances teachers will have little control over a school's general policy. For example, there is a tendency that as the more powerful machines described earlier are introduced into schools the older systems are moved down to the younger children. This is understandable (perhaps) but short-sighted (probably). Powerful machines are by their nature more flexible. They allow things to happen more quickly. They are more robust and less temperamental. By allowing more colour and better sound they enable access to a wide range of interactive programs through, for example, CDROM technology. Their power allows more intuitive methods of working when, for example, children trigger the animated sequences in 'Talking-books'. Whilst resources are always in short supply, careful consideration should be given to the use of powerful up-to-date systems with younger children.

Some older and, interestingly, some of the very new computer systems allow connection to be made directly to a standard television monitor. This is useful when you may want a large group of children to work collaboratively, for example, by representing children's information as a graph or to see an electronic book. In most cases, however, computers will be organised in a cafeteria style arrangement where one or more systems are located somewhere in a room and children come to them to complete tasks. Traditional QWERTY keyboards, which were designed both for adult hands and at a time when some method of slowing down fast typists was necessary, can cause problems. It is possible to purchase more child-friendly keyboards though they tend to be a little expensive; lower-case stickers can be placed on letter keys if required. Alternative methods of putting information into the computers or interacting with a program through a mouse, overlay board, stylus pen, track ball or touch screen are both valuable and, within National Curriculum terms at least, essential.

Siting computers is problematic in rooms which were often not designed for such equipment. They should be placed away from sand and water areas, not facing windows because of the difficulties which reflections may cause and in a place which can easily be overseen by an adult. Additionally, they also need to be placed securely on child-sized tables or trolleys which children themselves are not allowed to move. If possible the system should have a hard disk on which all programs are installed; this overcomes one management problem at least. To complete the set-up the system needs a printer, ink-jet colour for preference, so that text or pictures produced by the children can be displayed.

Despite the potential which computer systems have, by themselves they are lifeless and poor things. What gives them significance is the software they use and the purposes to which they are put. Computer programs do not just come into being, they are designed and constructed by people. Importantly, whoever designs the program has a view partly about what programs should look like but also about how children learn and the contexts in which this happens. Recognising the importance of software as the underestimated variable (Scrimshaw 1996) is a crucial first step in effective IT use.

Let us think about possible software designs first and the implications they have for learning. There are a number of possible models of software design to help us clarify our ideas. A useful one has been provided by Kemmis *et al.* (1977). Their analysis describes four models of software design.

They first describe **Instructional** software. Programs in this group are designed to teach a specific skill or piece of knowledge. Modern versions of this kind of program have lots of colour and sound effects with many things happening, but underlying all of them is a notion that knowledge can be broken down into parts, that the parts can be taught individually and that these parts can then be reassembled by the learner to form the original knowledge. So-called skill and drill programs or Computer Aided Instruction packages fit into this category.

Next we have **Revelatory** software. This is made up of programs which encourage learning through a series of simulations or adventures. It might be that children play the part, for example, of an animal trying to survive against all kinds of dangers. Children are able to try different strategies to see what happens. Learning happens as a consequence of what they do and their involvement with the program rather than simply by the presentation of facts. They can try things out in a safe environment.

A step beyond this is **Conjectural** or **Modelling** software. The earlier stages could involve children exploring ready made models of the outside world where, for example, they search through a computer-model of a house looking for a hidden mouse. At each choice point feedback from program instructions gives extra clues. During later stages children may use a program such as LOGO in which they can model worlds and ask 'what if' type questions; 'if I put in this number, what happens to the shape?' A great deal of research has shown that the use of this type of program allows children to develop a range of mathematical (Finlayson 1984) and cognitive skills (Clements and Gullo 1984) and exhibit behaviours typical of children at later stages of development (Lawler 1985).

The final type of software described by the model is termed **Emancipatory** software. This group includes labour-saving programs for the manipulation of text, pictures, sound or information. The use of this type of program allows the user to concentrate on the learning experience.

The descriptors above indicate a change in the content type of each program style. At the Instructional level, content is key. The body of knowledge held in the program, whether this is the sounds of letters in the alphabet, number sequences, spelling patterns or whatever, is the important element. The very reason for the program's existence is to pass this discrete body of knowledge to the user. The computer is used in this context as a teaching machine.

As we move towards the Emancipatory type of software the content of the program is reduced until with a word-processing package, for example, there is little discrete content. The program exists in order to simplify a particular task, in this case manipulating text.

Interestingly, however, as we move from instructional to Emancipatory software, computer specific content increases. To use a program designed to teach spelling we may only have to tap the computer space bar or move a pointer; a simple task which allows the computer to be largely ignored and program content concentrated upon. To use a word processor effectively, however, we have to learn a series of actions and commands which are only needed when using the program.

Using programs from this end of the spectrum requires program and computer familiarity, both on the part of teachers and of pupils. This is why such programs are often called a Software Toolkit. This is a phrase used to describe the use of a small number of generic programs of which different parts are introduced systematically to solve increasingly complex tasks. Such a methodical approach is the key to their effectiveness.

The implications for teacher confidence and computer familiarity are clear for we know that the potential word processing is constrained by teacher attitudes (Johnston *et al.* 1989).

Whatever software we select, however, we should always ask the crucial question, 'Who is in control, the computer or the learner?' For, as Alan Ellis commented as long ago as 1974, 'thinking about computers in education does not mean thinking about computers, it means thinking about education'. The question of control is fundamental, the use of content-specific software hands much control to the program designer, the use of content-free software enables the teacher to retain maximum content control. This is not to argue that there is simply one correct form of software which should be used at all times with children. A range of program types can, and should, be used but their use must be planned and integrated into an overall learning programme. The teacher must have clearly defined purposes when using any computer software. The selection of software should therefore be based upon:

- our own critical understanding of software types, styles and uses;

- overall learning objectives and, at an appropriate stage,

- the statutory learning opportunities which have to be provided for children in order to develop their Information Technology capability

Such issues and concerns are implicit in National Curriculum orders which recognise the wider definition of Information Technology by, for example, requiring the use of a variety of IT equipment which is to include but is not solely seen as that of computers (National Curriculum Programmes of Study 1a). The use of differing types of software for different purposes is also envisaged, content-specific software may be used to support subject areas but more generally a toolkit approach is assumed.

Let me outline how such concerns impact on practice with children by relating two possible incidents. A large group of three and four year olds were introduced to a Roamer, a large dome-shaped robot device, on the top of which is a pressure-sensitive keypad. By pressing on this instructions can be given which the Roamer follows. They were shown how to make the Roamer move forward by pressing the forward arrow, then a number, then the key marked 'Go' on the keypad. Sitting in a small circle, the device was sent across to children on the opposite side. Slowly the circle was made bigger and the numbers entered rapidly increased from single to double digit entries. One of the children then leaned over the pad and hiding her hand from her neighbours with the other, entered her instructions then sent the robot forward, a knowing smile on her face. The robot duly trundled across the space but, just as her friend reached out to pick up the Roamer it made a beeping noise then started off backwards across the room. The children of course laughed at the joke which she had played on her friend. What had happened was that, without being instructed, she had worked out that if one arrow made it move forward the other made it move backwards. Soon the Roamer was moving backwards, forwards, turning right and left, performing all manner of electronic dances.

On a second occasion two children were shown how to use a simple paint program: first the drawing tools and then how to change colours. After this they were left to experiment. Within a week not only had their friends learned these actions, they had also learned that with a few clicks they could open a different menu, switch on an axis of symmetry, go back to their pictures and draw symmetrical shapes. Within a few days all manner of faces, butterfly designs and kaleidoscopic patterns emerged. Much of the learning had been accomplished with little direct adult intervention. Rather the children themselves had made discoveries individually and in groups, sharing each piece of new knowledge as it was found, cascading it through the group. The paint package here provided a non-stressful and enjoyable setting in which children were able to try out ideas and modify first attempts.

Such occurrences highlight the manner in which the computer can be used in an experimental and exploratory manner allowing children a safe and supportive context in which to work. Learning by iteration, that is by doing, changing and repeating, is a powerful feature of some computer programs. In both incidents, discoveries took place through a process of self-initiated activities in which trial and error were used in a collaborative manner. They were not afraid to try out new ideas and different approaches. The role of talk was clearly central to the whole process, being used to support, extend, clarify and communicate understanding. Additionally too, it provided a flexible context for developing key social skills of sharing and turn taking as children learned to value each other's contributions.

A further important function of Information Technology illustrated by these incidents is the possibility for providing a framework for spontaneous activity. Both the software and the device are governed by inherent rule systems. In order to draw a symmetrical shape, for example, the rules of the program (move the mouse here, click on this icon and so on) had to be discovered. Only by completing a correct sequence of actions could the shape be drawn. In order to play a joke on her friend the girl had first to learn the rules used by the Roamer then work within these to meet her ends. In both incidents children were learning to work in a precise, disciplined and thoughtful manner with systems which allowed children to control parts of their environment.

Control is therefore not about the choice of software or hardware, such decisions simply make the process more or less efficient. It is really about choices in the way in which these are implemented and the contexts in which they are embedded. In these cases children were able, in a quite matter of fact manner, to teach adults. It was clear that learning was a joint enterprise and a shared experience. For some adults witnessing the confident manner in which even the youngest child may use a computer can be a daunting prospect. In this context adults may not always be the expert, for with computer systems we are all in a continual process of learning. In these cases the adult role had been to set up an environment in which learning could occur, to allow the time for investigation and consolidation, to delicately intervene when necessary but above all to value not just the product of the learning but the act of learning itself. In both cases the computer had been used as a tool for investigation. It had moved far from a simple model of Computer Aided Instruction and much closer to Computer Extended Thinking in which computers became objects to think with (Papert 1980). Rather than simply using computers to pass on a fixed body of knowledge they centred a problem solving approach to learning. Such an approach recognises that the unexpected and unplanned are worthwhile in themselves and can act as building blocks for future learning. Whilst computers have a function as powerful alternative modes of presenting tasks and reacting in an uncritical non-judgemental manner, their real impact is to change the whole locus of control.

Be clear, developments in Information Technology will not slow. Computer functions available by the time this generation of children are adults are almost unimaginable. The use of Information Technology within education should therefore not be grounded in some simplistic utilitarian preparation for adulthood, at the most pragmatic level we could never keep abreast of all developments. Rather it is about the creative implementation of systems as flexible tools to develop thinking and problem solving skills. It is about opening up possibilities, not closing them down. Through such an approach children are supported as flexible, enthusiastic thinkers engaged in an on-going process of change. We can decide to be a part of this – we do a disservice to children if we try to ignore it.

Issues

1. To what extent does the introduction of Information Technology question the traditional model of education and the traditional role of educator?
2. How should the previous experiences which children have of Information Technology be related to those which they have inside school settings?
3. What implications do the constant developments in Information Technology hardware and software capability pose for professional development?

References

Clements, D.H. and Gullo, D.F. (1984) Learning with new information technologies in schools: perspectives from the psychology of learning and instruction. *Journal of Computer Assisted Learning*, no. 6, pp. 69–87.

Ellis A. B. (1974) *The use and misuse of computers in Education*. New York: McGraw-Hill.

Finlayson, H.M. (1984) *The transfer of mathematical problem solving skills from LOGO experience*. Research paper no. 238, Edinburgh: Department of Artificial Intelligence, University of Edinburgh.

Johnston, D., Cox, M. and Rhodes, V. (1989) *The use of word processing in a primary classroom: teacher perception and classroom observations*. Paper presented to the Symposium on Computer Assisted Learning, the University of Surrey.

Kemmis, S., Atkin, R. and Wright, E. (1977) *How do students learn?* Working papers on CAL. Norwich: Centre for Applied Research in Education, University of Norwich School of Education.

Lawler, R.W. (1985) *Computer experience and cognitive development*. Chichester: Ellis Horwood.

NCET (1995) *Approaches to Information Technology, Key Stages 1 and 2*. Coventry: NCET Warwick University.

Papert, S. (1980) *Mindstorms: Children, computers and powerful ideas.* Hemel Hempstead: Harvester Press.
Scrimshaw, P. (ed.) (1996) *Language, classrooms and computers.* London: Routledge.

7

Design and technology: the subject integrator

Eric Parkinson and Caroline Thomas

Introduction

> it is evident that children enter formal schooling with a wealth of
> knowledge and experience relating to design particularly imaging and
> modelling, . . . which should be utilized and built upon.
>
> (Outterside 1993, p. 49)

Learning from and through the context of the home is a vital stage
in the education of the very young. These informal experiences will
provide encounters for a range of materials to chew, suck, tear, rattle,
bang and clank. Everyday objects, such as interesting kitchen utensils, mechanical toys and appliances, enable children to explore their
environment. Some encourage twisting and turning actions that produce interesting outcomes. Perhaps most important of all, above the
pleasure of enquiry and the early associations between cause and
effect, is the promotion of a positive spirit of inquiry itself. Homes
where young fingers are always excluded from 'messy' situations
will be deprived in mind as well as body. Moreover, the home provides an unstructured, unfettered environment that, unlike primary
education, has no pre-conceptions about the 'right' way to do anything. Within the limitations of the home situation, what is 'right' is
what suits the child. At school of course, increasingly a formal, structured environment takes over and children can build upon these
early home-based experiences. Children need to learn, for example,
more about how products are made in particular ways for different
purposes.

A useful working definition of Design and Technology is that it is
the application of skills and knowledge to create procedures and
products that assist human purposes, shape the environment and

perform practical functions. Elements now known as 'Design and Technology' formed part of early years education long before its inclusion in the formal structure of the National Curriculum for England and Wales (DES/WO 1990). Teachers encouraged children to represent ideas for products in a variety of media such as paper, card, fabrics and plastics. Cards, for example, became popular products to celebrate various festivals. Junk modelling, using recycled materials such as cardboard tubes, egg boxes and yoghurt pots, formed the essential building blocks of an unfettered style of craft work in many infant classrooms. Plasticene and other mouldable materials have a long history of use, as the medium lends itself to raw handling by eager young fingers and encourages the use of simple shaping and cutting tools. Cooking enabled children to mix, arrange and heat all manner of foodstuffs, and to explore the changes in materials.

Teachers used construction kits to enable children to represent the world as they perceive it, and model ideas for the future. They were also a means for enhancing children's social and physical development. Meccano, an all-metal kit, appeared in the early part of this century and set the tone for later developments. There has been an ever increasing range of construction kits in early years classrooms over the past ten years, but no one kit can fulfil all the aims of technological· endeavour. For example, some kits promote the copying and creation of structures, such as buildings, towers and bridges. Others, such as the LEGO product 'Early Simple Machines' assist with the construction of mechanisms used to work cranes, cars and roundabouts. Giant kits, such as 'Quadro', give children the satisfaction of building full-size products that can be used in games and role play experiences.

Adequate delivery of all subjects of the National Curriculum in the short early years day has led some teachers to implement the curriculum on a subject-based framework. However, this desire for simplicity, for a day defined by episodes of separate subject teaching, has some disadvantages. One of the greatest problems is that the curriculum can become disintegrated into fragments of subject teaching. This results in the loss of the capacity to combine skills, knowledge and attitudes though all-embracing contexts to empower effective learning. Life is cross-curricular, so why should learning in schools be different?

In addition, emphasis has been given to reservation of large parts of the school day for the development of literacy and numeracy skills (DfEE 1997). This means that large areas of learning are now 'fenced off' – they are unattached to learning in the core subjects. Schools are under pressure to constrain the teaching of Design and Technology.

Design and Technology provides for the integration of subject matter. The skills and methods employed are transferable to all subjects of the curriculum. There are opportunities to relate learning in other subjects to everyday life, as the problems encountered are authentic and relevant to the learner. Design may be a process that entails using a wide range of experience, knowledge and skills to solve problems. Plans are produced and put into action. Children need to examine the needs of others when designing their products, and in so doing develop their social skills through collaboration, discussion and negotiation.

The application of skills and knowledge from Mathematics, Science and English is essential to problem-solving in Design and Technology. A plan requires a clear statement of intention. The production of plans will develop pupils' ability to express themselves clearly and concisely in a written, graphical or verbal format. Evaluations of products and explanations about how they work can develop a wider range of vocabulary, although this will primarily be technical in nature. In solving problems in real life, information needs to be obtained from a variety of sources to solve them. This often requires an application of the reading and research skills taught in English.

Design and Technology tasks highlight the use of areas of Mathematics, such as the concepts of length, area, capacity and volume in real life contexts. When producing models, such as a chair for a doll, children use mathematical skills when measuring out materials and can appreciate the need for precision to obtain successful results. Food technology entails measuring out raw materials to produce a range of food dishes. When making simple masks, for example, children would need to plan the shape and size of their masks before making them. Children can think about what measurements they may need to make and how they can obtain these.

When examining furniture and buildings, children need to be aware of the shapes and patterns used to create stable and rigid structures and could apply these when engaging in bridge or tower building projects. When exploring packaging, they would gain an understanding of the applications of shapes and nets in their everyday environment. They can construct and create models using a range of regular and irregular three-dimensional shapes and explore the stacking of objects to make the optimum use of space. Johnson (1984) identifies a sequence of progression regarding block play activity. Within this sequence, she notes that children move on from simple repetition of blocks to make simple towers and rows to bridging activities and then to the recognition and use of pattern. She notes 'Children speak with blocks. They say in their own way what they have to say' (Johnson 1984, p. 42).

An analysis of some of the processes, skills and knowledge that underpin Science and Design Technology reveals similarities between the two subjects. Children explore and gain knowledge about materials, energy and force in both subjects. In Science, children examine the properties of materials through undertaking scientific investigations whilst in Design and Technology they may consider how these properties relate to 'fitness for purpose' in the design of products. For example, children can explore the structure and insulation properties of fabrics in Science. This might enable them to utilise this knowledge to evaluate the effectiveness of egg or tea cosies or 'dolls' made out of empty plastic bottles filled with warm water and even design and make their own products to keep things warm.

Energy is an abstract concept at the heart of the process of change. When changes occur, there is a transference of energy. Forces are associated with energy transfers. A child pushing a buggy made from reclaimed materials along the floor can find out about forces and energy. For instance, to make the vehicle move, energy is transferred from the child to the buggy. This energy is transferred through pushing, or by the child lifting the vehicle onto a ramp and letting it run downhill. When the vehicle moves across the floor it slows and stops.

Both Science and Design and Technology require a questioning of the natural and made world. In Science, typical questions arise from observations about the movement of the vehicle and instigate investigation: What makes the vehicle move? What makes it stop? How far will it go if it has bigger wheels? Will it go further if there is a cargo? Observation and question-raising are core scientific *skills* that lead to qualification, and then later to quantification. Measuring the distance the vehicle travels, and then recording and explaining the results, are also key scientific skills.

When encouraging the child to push the vehicle along, or roll it down a slope, the teacher can emphasise a technological dimension. The teacher can encourage the child to raise questions about the vehicle, taking account of the well-being of a teddy bear sitting in the vehicle. How will Teddy stay on the buggy? What can you use to keep Teddy in place? Is the seat appropriate? Teddy has a number of problems to overcome and these present the basis for technological challenge.

In emphasising the technological process, the teacher encourages children to frame their observations and questions as problems. If the teacher establishes simple objectives for a task, it is possible to measure a child's achievement. The child would need to specify the problem and then propose a suitable solution, after evaluating a range of alternatives. A child may model ideas by trying out possibilities with a range of media and evaluate the findings. Evaluation is not just a terminal activity in which the child asks, 'Have I solved my particular problem?' Evaluation is more overarching than this as it occurs at every stage of the design and make process.

Problem solving

Learning is most vibrant and effective when the tasks are interactive and when the learners are fully engaged in the process (Beswick 1987; Dobson 1987; Baldwin and Williams 1988; Bentley and Watts 1989). Design and Technology entails solving problems and this is 'active' learning. The learner takes responsibility for the problem by making decisions about how to proceed, before seeking a solution. Teachers can help children to formulate a problem by asking questions such as: 'What would happen if . . .?' 'Can you show me how . . .?' 'How does this work?' Children need help in learning how to formulate a clear definition of a problem or a clear and realistic goal.

Problems may have more than one solution. Teachers can help children identify a range of possibilities, by initiating discussion with individuals or groups either before or during an activity. These discussions can be either teacher-led or child-led.

In rich problem-solving contexts, new problems emerge throughout the design and make process. Learning occurs when the learner seeks to resolve these dilemmas (Lave *et al.* 1988). Hennessy and McCormick (1994) give the example of an 'emergent problem' as the production of a stable structure for a kite during construction. Design and Technology require the definition of new problems *during* the varying stages of the problem-solving process. If the child, in the construction phase, has difficulty gluing together a plastic straw framework, it may be necessary to use sellotape. This is an example of the solving of a problem during the design process. In the evaluation phase the kite may not fly well because the string is too heavy. This may need replacing with strong nylon thread to solve the problem.

Children, Piaget (1967) claimed, have problems 'decentring' and being able to consider a situation from a number of different viewpoints. Hughes (1975) and Donaldson (1978), however, claim that the provision of 'human sense' contexts – or familiar contexts – facilitate the decentring process. The essential nature of the design process provides an opportunity for perspective-shifting. In the teddy bear problem, the children are considering the teddy as the user of the product and are designing the vehicle for the teddy's needs. The teacher should encourage the children to think about the needs of the user by establishing a human sense context and by asking challenging questions. There are opportunities for role-play when children can act out their fears and fantasies and gain an insight into the lives and needs of other people in different situations.

Imagination and target-setting

Unstructured play is a core activity in the early years classroom. A rich play environment contains a number of raw materials for children to use. Children can use these in flexible ways to achieve the results they want. In this way lateral thinking can be enhanced as they will be using familiar objects in new ways. In free-play activities, children will devise tasks and model their own worlds. Within these worlds, role play is significant. The child controls the boundaries of this domain and each extension in language, social skills and manipulative skills is a new learning experience.

Design and Technology can provide the means of turning unstructured play into more structured play situations through setting children challenges and outcomes to achieve. For example, when children make sandcastles the teacher can encourage them to consider ways in which they could keep water in the moat. When children make tunnels they can be invited to explore ways of preventing a tunnel from caving in on top of a vehicle being driven through the sand.

Many early years children exposed to construction kits in free-play situations enjoy making cars. Besides free-play, some level of guidance or challenge can be introduced. For example, the teacher could encourage the children to discuss the types of movement produced by the mechanism and draw it to show which parts have been used to make it.

Work with construction kits can develop from stories. In the story of Goldilocks and the Three Bears, for example, the bears live in a house furnished with chairs and tables of appropriate sizes. Children could construct different sizes of furniture to go in the Bears' house. They would learn about the nature of sturdy structures, explore a variety of joining techniques and the effect on the strength of a structure of the type and arrangement of the pieces.

In classroom management terms, the teacher needs to decide the positioning on the structured to free-play continuum, and how to vary the teaching approach as circumstances dictate. Free play may also need to supersede structured play to build up confidence in using materials and equipment. In this example, it would enable the children to become familiar with the range of pieces in the construction kit and ways in which they fit together.

Inherent self-assessment

In a simplistic model of design activity, there is a tendency to see the overall process as a linear one of problem identification, solution formulation and evaluation. This simple model provides a structure from which we can plan and promote classroom activity. Welch (1997) suggests that evaluation informs **all** stages of technological endeavour. Evaluation assists in clarifying ideas in design and in making. The teacher should ask challenging questions to encourage children to think about their intentions, what they will do next, how well they have solved various emergent problems and the success of their product. This is a means of encouraging children to monitor and assess their own progress and performance as a matter of course. It is important to recognise and reward a child's evaluative behaviour. Teachers need to facilitate the application of a child's design and technology knowledge. When they appear to be 'stuck', teachers need to help pupils access and apply their knowledge to solve the problem.

Equal opportunities

Equality of educational provision and equal opportunities for all children to engage within that provision is an issue that all class teachers must take on board. One area that may present a particular problem to the class-teacher concerns the use of construction kits.

Several studies on construction activity, such as Claire (1992), Parkinson (1997) and Ross and Browne (1993) have brought gender issues into focus. Typically, these studies suggest that boys, in free-choice situations, tend to monopolise resources and engage in a different range of constructional activity to girls. For instance, Claire (1992) observed that girls' models were less well made and less sophisticated than those of boys. The walls of houses made by boys had proper joints and articulation whereas those made by girls consisted of bricks arranged in horizontal patterns or in piles. The bricks were not interlocked. Similarly, Ross and Browne (1993) found, with particular reference to construction sets, that boys preferred to engage with constructional activity. They reported that girls tended to construct 'passive' structures such as houses whereas boys made 'active' structures often emphasising motion. These studies indicate the disadvantage girls may have in working in mixed gender circumstances and the need to develop practical strategies to promote equal opportunities. It is vital to have high expectations of all children and by setting up structured tasks with children making products to fulfil a particular need, they may be encouraged to move away from stereotypical behaviour. In addition, exploration of materials and instruction in joining techniques by adults may enhance performance.

Design and Technology in the National Curriculum

The National Curriculum specifies the skills and knowledge to be taught. Children should

develop their Design and Technology capability through combining their designing and making skills with knowledge and understanding in order to design and make products.

(DfE 1995, p. 58)

In the early years, this can be achieved by children understanding a purpose for creating an environment or product, formulating clear ideas for their design in the form of a design proposal, producing the outcome and evaluating it throughout the production process. Children can communicate their ideas though discussing their model making and providing design sketches. These can vary from rough sketches of the overall product to drawings of part of a product. However, many young children find it difficult to visualise the end product. If they are asked to draw a car many draw any car rather than a vision of their model using the materials available to them. Children can be encouraged to interact with, and look at, the materials and place them together to see how they would fit. They can then try to draw a picture of the way in which they plan to use the raw materials.

To provide a structure for planning learning experiences to extend pupils' capability, the DfE (1995) specify three types of activity in which pupils should engage:,

– investigation, disassembly and evaluation tasks:
– focused practical tasks;
– design and make assignments.

Activities in which pupils can investigate, disassemble and evaluate simple products enable them to gain an understanding of the purpose of the product, the customer, the materials and components used to make it, the way in which it works and its effectiveness. For example, children can draw and discuss the design of a range of shoes. They can analyse the materials used to make shoes designed for different purposes. Their distinctive features, and the joining techniques employed, can be discussed. Children can evaluate the ways in which their shoe has been made to fit their feet. An understanding of shoe design would enable them to make their own simple classroom slippers from textiles and a cardboard framework. Alternatively this activity can take place in the context of establishing a class shoe shop or the Elves and the Shoemaker story.

Focused practical tasks enable pupils to develop and practise particular skills and develop their understanding of technological concepts. They can develop a wider knowledge about the properties of materials, of control and acquire practical strategies and techniques. It is during focused practical tasks that children need to be instructed in the safe use of tools and hygienic practices. For example, when constructing a picture frame out of wood for a classroom painting, children would practise measurement of raw materials, use the appropriate tool to saw wood and learn about personal safety. They could also gain a knowledge of the use of cardboard triangles to create rigid structures, appropriate glue to use and the need to use sand-paper to smooth rough edges to create a good finish. Children can also choose to cover the frame from a range of transparent materials and experiment to find out which material enables them to see their picture clearly. The skills and knowledge gained can be transferred to the design and making of wooden pictures on a cardboard backing or construction projects such as making wooden chairs for Goldilocks and the Three Bears.

'Design and make' assignments enable children to draw on the knowledge and skills gained from focused practical tasks and evaluation activities to create their own products. They should be encouraged to think for themselves, and make decisions about what materials, tools and joining techniques to use to make their products so that their creativity and organisational skills are enhanced. For example, having investigated how simple musical instruments, such as drums or shakers, are made to create different sounds, children can make drums using different containers and different materials as drumskins. During the focused practical tasks, they would experiment with joining techniques such as tape and elastic bands. The children would then design a set of drums or shakers and select the materials to make it. They can even make their own drumsticks to create different sounds and use their instruments to accompany class songs.

It is imperative that young children have the opportunity to work with a range of materials, for example recycled materials, textiles, mouldable materials, wood, food and construction kits. This is so that they are able to investigate and build up a knowledge about the characteristics of materials. This will enable them to make more informed choices about which materials to use for their design projects in the junior classroom.

Starting points

In early years education, starting points set up both a context for learning and an atmosphere for productive work. Some examples of starting points for Design and Technology reflecting current early years classroom practice have been selected to illustrate the approach to Design and Technology outlined.

Technology from stories and rhymes

Stories and rhymes form an attractive context for initiating Design and Technology, since they often invite problem solving from the perspective of the characters. They also provide powerful shared experiences for the class at the same time as promoting important literacy skills.

The story of The Three Little Pigs raises the question of where the pigs will live and provides a clear purpose for technological activity. Children could be inspired to think about the kind of house they would like to make for a pig to live in. The modelling of plasticene pigs helps children to identify with the characters of the story and build a house of an appropriate scale. In this way children will be encouraged to decentre and look at the situation from the pigs' points of view. The story introduces the idea of the *appropriateness* of materials for building houses. Mathematically, children will be exploring the use of shape and recurrent patterns to construct structures. Building bricks and construction kits provide a useful 'fast track' to constructing houses of brick, whilst re-used materials may give an alternative experience with adhesive tape, straws, card, paper and lolly sticks. From a scientific perspective children could make decisions about which joining techniques to use and experiment with joining straws together using tape and pipe cleaners.

To make a wolf-proof house, advanced thinking would be needed to select appropriate materials for construction and to consider methods of joining them in ways which wolves would find hard to disentangle. Young children often find it difficult to exhibit a 'design-before-you-do' phenomenon. Instead they design *by* doing. They select what they perceive to be wolf-resistant materials and join them in a range of ways, frequently changing their minds and expressing their opinions to their peers. The evaluation of the experience may be focused by key questions such as: Can the pig get though the door? Will the wolf be able to jump through the window? Can the house withstand the puff of the big bad wolf? This could lead to a discussion about the need for houses to have stable foundations.

Stories can also provide opportunities for role play and practising oracy skills. The children could alternatively design and make the props and the scenery and retell or act out the story of the Three Little Pigs. The children could empathise with the characters and explore how the wolf and the pigs felt in different situations.

Opportunities arise for varying the ending of the stories. In this example, the children could design and make a getaway vehicle for the three pigs or a machine to capture the big bad wolf.

Children can also construct books based either on a favourite story by retelling the story or by creating their own version of a story. In addition, another story can be used as a starting point and the children can predict a different ending or information books could be made of the class project with each child contributing one page. An investigation of the construction and layout of story or information books would provide a wealth of design ideas. Furthermore, evaluation of pop-up books and books with flaps and, in particular, analysis of ways in which the movement is achieved, could provide the stimulus for making books with simple moving mechanisms. Children could decide what kind of movement they want to create using forces, such as up and down or side to side, and design pages with movement. Instruction on ways of making flaps and pop-up characters would be the essential focused practical tasks for arming children with the techniques needed for their book making.

Design and technology from the 'home corner'

Role play and the rehearsal of domestic experiences are at the heart of home corner activities. However, the home corner as a focal point need not be restricted to situations from the home; children could be asked to design and make a shop, a garden centre or even a pizza parlour. Children can model pizzas in salt dough and plasticene and investigate the characteristics of compliant materials in Science. If plasticene is used they can add different toppings in a variety of colours of modelling clay and then go on to serve their creations to their companions. If they make salt dough the children can discover that moist dough can be moulded into a range of shapes but once it has dried out its shape cannot be altered except by breaking it. Salt dough can be painted and decorated in interesting ways. From examination of real life examples, children can design menus and give their pizzas special names. The children can role-play customers, waiters and cooks. Taking this even further, in the nursery, a child might even offer a delivery service on classroom large-play equipment such as a tricycle!

Environments can be created as a result of visits. Through identifying and investigating the layout of a local shop, important features such as the cash desk, the aisles and storage of food for ease of access can be explored. The children can re-create the environment using empty containers and products made out of salt dough, label and price them. Display systems could be investigated by children devising different ways of organising products in shops. Follow-up work in Mathematics could include writing shopping lists and handling money during role play. The children could even evaluate simple systems, for example the sequence of activities involved in shopping or those from ordering food to its arrival on the table, and mime these.

Celebrations and special events

Celebrations, such as Christmas, Birthdays and the Harvest Festival, as well as events such as Pancake Day provide a range of experiences with food. From a discussion base, children need to explore where foods come from and how they may be prepared and presented. From this basis, children may model food, as in the pizza parlour example, or they may participate in the preparation of foods in small groups under adult supervision. They will begin to learn that raw materials and a variety of utensils are needed to create simple products. They will learn how to use and take care of equipment and a wealth of practical skills, including an ability to measure out and combine ingredients. They will also gain an awareness of the need to follow instructions from recipes and safe and hygienic food preparation practices.

From the school's perspective safety is a key issue. Food should always be provided from known sources. Children may wish bring in foodstuffs but as nothing is known about their origin or storage history, it would be risky to accept them. Meat and fish products should not be used because of the dangers of food poisoning. Special care needs to be made of any product that is made from raw eggs. Vigilant supervision is needed during the mixing process to avoid any tasting of the mixture. It is also necessary to adhere to a regime of cleanliness which is underpinned by the use of a recognised germicide.

Observation and discussion of the components of a sandwich can provide the starting point for children to design their own dream sandwich for a Birthday or Christmas party. Children could choose from a range of breads and fillings that are safe to use. Children would practise how to cut bread and spread butter safely. A discussion of hygiene issues such as the need to wash-up utensils in warm water with a cleaning fluid would enhance personal safety. Design sketches of the proposed product could be made indicating the raw ingredients required. The butter for the sandwiches could be made from cream or milk by a churning process. From a science perspective, children would learn that the cream or milk has to be shaken until it splits into a liquid buttermilk and a solid butter. For celebrations Design and Technology activities could be extended to encompass the making of table decorations, woven place mats out of paper or textiles, napkin holders and decorations for fresh fruit cocktails.

Pitta bread or soda bread could be baked for the Harvest Festival in different size and shaped loaves. More experienced and ambitious children could try plaiting dough. A few additional ingredients could be added such as spices, seeds or dried fruit to appeal to different tastes. Evaluation can centre on describing how the product was made, its presentation, taste and appeal. If recipes are followed children can evaluate these and consider what else could have been included in the instructions to make them easier to follow. Children could make their own recipe cards in a written or picture strip format for others to copy when making simple products like chocolate cornflake cakes.

A range of materials with different properties may be combined. Sometimes this has the excitement of mechanical devices such as whisks when making Angel Delight to blend in air or to achieve a consistent mixture. If heat is applied, then a transformation may occur and changes in the state of the material can be explored in Science. When butter and chocolate are heated these change into liquids. However, when they cool they change into solids. Colours may change. New textures are there to be discovered – and so is the taste.

Children should be encouraged to articulate their preferences as part of the process of evaluation. How was the food presented? Was it easy to swallow? Did it look attractive? Did they *want* to eat it? What were the feelings for the whole class? They would soon gain an understanding that people like different tastes and textures and that this is perfectly normal.

Sand and water play

Sand and water facilities are standard items in most early years' classrooms. The justification for sand and water play has been rooted in Science. It involves finding out, firsthand, about the properties of materials through observation and the raising of questions. Water provides the excitement of finding out about the properties of fluids and fluid behaviour. Children can explore how liquids flow and fill the shape of containers into which they are poured and that they have a 'skin' at the interface with the air. Sand also has some of these properties and acts as a pseudo-fluid in that the individual grains of solid matter can be poured and take up the shape of a container. Children can investigate the size of the hole in a container and the effect this has on the flow of the sand. This is significant when thinking about the function of a sand timer. Sand offers different properties depending upon whether it is used wet or dry. Further justification for sand and water play comes from a social standpoint, where co-operation and communication assist effective learning.

From a Design and Technology perspective, wet sand can be moulded into various shapes to represent 'traditional' castle towers or a host of other designs from jelly moulds. Sand play can become the setting for adventures into imaginary worlds in which children can re-contextualise their lives in model landscapes, or empathise through play people and other creatures. An exploratory activity would consist of talking about all the different shapes they could make with the containers or with their hands.

Water play provides opportunities for floating and sinking. A 'classic' structured play activity for young children concerns changing a piece of plasticene from a sinking into a floating object. This is a design problem, in which the changing of the shape of a material with plastic properties changes its buoyancy characteristics. Through discussion children are able to predict that 'lumps' of plasticene will sink and will *generalise* from this basis that *all* plasticene sinks. Typically they say that it sinks because it is 'heavy'. When the plasticene has been rolled out thinly with the sides bent upwards it has boat-like characteristics. This apparent contradiction is a splendid platform for discussion. Children can put forward their tentative explanations. Although there is a strong link with science, the design ideas and the experiences with mouldable materials are essentially technological.

A range of sand and water play equipment is available on the market to encourage Design and Technology. For example, sand and water wheels encourage observation and experimentation. The association of cause and effect is made when evaluating the way in which the equipment works. Water pumps, usually made with a transparent barrel, enable children to see the 'workings' of mechanical devices and begin to understand ideas relating to the transfer of force and motion.

Washing and drying activities enable children to evaluate the effectiveness of materials such as paper towels used to dry their hands as they soak up water. They can observe the changes in different materials during washing day activities as the materials dry on the line. Consideration can be given to the most effective materials used to make waterproof clothing. Other starting points would be children thinking about what additional toys they would like to make for water play. These could include boats, planes, sieves and balls. The children would need to consider the materials that are suitable for making water toys and ways in which they can put them together. New joining techniques could be introduced. Having made the toy they could think about the process they went through, the toy's effectiveness and what they like and dislike about their toy.

Construction kits

Construction kits have a specialised set of pieces that can interlock to create structures and make things work. They also enable children to model design proposals before working in another material. The varying properties of kits suggest different approaches to construction. Some kits have wheels, and some kits even offer early experiences with levers, cams and cranks. Some offer building plans, worksheets, and even simple guide pictures. They can be used to support work arising from a variety of contexts and are objects of interest and sources of motivation in their own right. As they are often brightly coloured and have a variety of shapes, they are so interesting that children naturally engage with them. The mathematical element of the activities could involve children discussing the shapes and patterns created.

It is possible to incorporate the use of construction kits into a variety of classroom topics such as ourselves. Depending on an appropriate choice of construction kit, children could represent themselves in the tubular-based 'Reo Clic' or the interesting plastic framework units of 'Mobilo'. They could make their own personal items such as jewellery, glasses and interesting watches.

Differentiation can be achieved by the size and type of kits used as well as by the specifications placed on the design brief. When constructing a plan of a house, the simplest level would be requiring children to use their imagination to make a house. At a more advanced level they could make a plan of a house with a required number of rooms. Dimensions for the house or rooms could be attached to the design brief.

From a teacher's perspective, when choosing a kit to use with children some valuable pointers are safety, people, appearance and purpose. From a safety point of view, the component parts should be of appropriate size so that they cannot to be swallowed or jabbed in somebody's eye. In relation to people, it is worth considering the value of using kits that have play figures so that the children can externalise their feelings. The scale of the pieces needs to be appropriate for small fingers being employed and the kit needs to have interesting coloured pieces to capture attention. As kits have a range of functions choosing the right kit for the right sort of job is essential.

Construction projects

Construction tasks, such as the making of playground equipment or toy cars, enable children to join materials together in different ways. Through observing a collection of vehicles, children can gain ideas about the components and shapes of wheels that are used to create movement. Sticking wheels to a cardboard box illustrates the need for axles and wheels. Children can make a vehicle out of a cardboard box using cotton reel wheels and cane for axles. The initial problem entails fitting wheels to the cardboard box. Often children pierce the sides of the box, push through the cane and add the cotton reel wheels. Making a hole in cardboard requires consideration of the safe use of appropriate tools. On placing the vehicle on the ground, the wheels may not touch the ground. The need to resolve this problem depends on a child's perception of 'vehicle', their skill development and the important notion of 'fitness for purpose'. For many young children ideas of motion and wheels are not as significant as the function of a vehicle body that contains people.

Summary

This chapter has outlined the nature of Design and Technology in the early years curriculum. Design and Technology is both a practical activity and a way of working. Unfortunately, some teachers have perceived it as one subject too many in a timetable stretched by National Curriculum demands. This may be the case if a 'separate subject' curriculum model is followed. However, it can also be perceived as something that helps to *unite* the primary curriculum. The notion of engaging with problems, making decisions and working in an organised manner, in a context having a human dimension, is a powerful force in linking subjects together and making learning relevant. Although Design and Technology is related to Science, this is not exclusive. Children will use their scientific skills to find out about materials and in Design and Technology apply this knowledge to make something and evaluate its effectiveness. The cross-curricular potential of Design and Technology has yet to be fully exploited as a means of enhancing basic skills, especially early literacy, where communication through doing and making is a vital component. Some starting points have been provided to illustrate the value of this subject. Children need autonomy to develop their capability. They also require planned support tasks to expand their skills and knowledge, instruction in techniques and opportunities to work with different materials. These may vary according to the needs of individual children.

Issues

1. With an increasing emphasis on the 'core subjects' and the devotion of curriculum time to specialised periods of study, to what extent may foundation subjects such as Design and Technology be marginalised?
2. If they increasingly become players standing on the sidelines, watching the core subjects dominate the curriculum game, then will the *contexts for learning* offered by foundation subjects – especially design and technology – be diminished? Will children come away from their classrooms well-versed in obvious core skills, but impoverished in terms of stimulation through creative activity?
3. Will there be an economic effect? Will it be discovered, perhaps too late, that it is the creative side of the curriculum that underpins innovation and economic success in the advanced technological societies of the twenty-first century?

References

Baldwin, J. and Williams, H. (1988) *Active Learning: A Trainer's Guide*, Oxford, Basil Blackwell.

Bentley, D. and Watts, D. M. (1989) *Learning and Teaching in School Science: Practical Alternatives*, Milton Keynes, Open University Press.

Beswick, N. (1987) *Re-thinking Active Learning 8–16*, London, Falmer Press.

Claire, H. (1992) 'Interaction between girls and boys: working with construction apparatus in first school classrooms' *Design and Technology Teaching*, Vol. 24, No. 2.

DES/WO (1990) *Technology in the National Curriculum*, London, HMSO.

DfE (1995) *Key Stages 1 and 2 of the National Curriculum*, London, HMSO.

DfEE (1997) *Excellence in Education*, London, The Stationery Office.

Dobson, K. (1987) *Teaching for Active Learning: Coordinated Science Teachers' Guide*, London: Collins Educational.

Donaldson, M. (1978) *Children's Minds*, Glasgow, Fontana Press.

Hennessy, S. and McCormick, R. (1994) The general problem-solving process in technology education. Myth or reality?, in F. Banks (Ed) *Teaching Technology*, London, Routledge, pp. 94–108.

Hughes, M. (1975) *Egocentrism in pre-school children*, Edinburgh University, unpublished doctoral dissertation.

Johnson, H. M., (1984) 'The art of block building', in *The Block Book*, (Ed. Hirch, E.S.), Washington DC, National Association for Young Children, pp. 15–49.

Lave, J., Smith, S. and Butler, M. (1988) 'Problem solving as an everyday practice', in Lave, J., Greeno, J.G., Schoenfeld, A., Smith, S. and Butler, M. (Eds), *Learning Mathematical Problem Solving*, Institute for Research on Learning Report no. IRL88-0006, Palo Alto, CA.

Outterside, Y., (1993) 'The emergence of design activity ability: The early years', in Smith, J.S. (Ed.) IDATER93: International Conference on Design and Technology Education Research and Curriculum Development (pp. 43–49) Loughborough, Loughborough University of Technology.

Parkinson, E. (1997) Some Aspects of Construction Activity in Design and Technology Education in Jamaica and the UK – A primary Perspective, in R. Ager and C. Benson (Eds.), *International Primary Design and Technology Conference – A Celebration of Good Practice*, Volume 2, Birmingham, CRIPT at UCE, pp. 34–38.

Piaget, J. (1967) *Play, Dreams and Imitation in Childhood*, London, Routledge and Kegan Paul Ltd.

Ross, C. and Browne, N. (1993) *Girls as Constructors in the Early Years*, Stoke on Trent, Trentham Books Ltd.

Welch, M. (1997) *Year 7 students use of three-dimensional modelling while designing and making*, in Smith, J.S. (Ed.) IDATER97: International Conference on Design and Technology Education Research and Curriculum Development (pp. 61–67) Loughborough, Loughborough University.

8

Young children investigating: adopting a constructivist framework

Gill Nicholls

Introduction

Increasingly, questions are being asked about young children's abilities to investigate science concepts and the nature of the investigative skills they need. Yet there appears to be a lack of knowledge and understanding of how these skills are developed and acquired. There is no richer ground to be explored than that of the very young child trying to make sense of the science in their everyday environment. Touch, sight and hearing all play a crucial role, but how can these shape the young child's mind for future investigations in science? What role can teachers play in developing scientific skills? What approaches to the curriculum will nurture young pupils' interests? These questions are of significance and ones that we need to consider in the face of increasing demands on pupils to have baseline knowledge. It also requires educators to reconsider the place of science within the early years curriculum.

This chapter will explore the need to allow very young children to investigate science concepts from an early age as a way of enhancing their cognitive abilities in science and the development of their investigative skills. Observation and communication will be discussed and shown to be significant factors within a constructivist approach to investigations.

Investigative science

Investigation in science at every level is the process of finding out as much as possible about a particular situation, often science being the tool used to explore that instance, problem or situation. The statutory requirements of the National Curriculum at Key Stage 1 (KS1) requires pupils to be given the opportunity to ask questions: How, Why, What will happen if? To use focused exploration and investigation to acquire scientific knowledge, understanding and skills, as well as relate simple scientific ideas to the evidence for them.

(DFE 1995, p. 2)

And the Desirable Outcomes for children's learning (SCAA) relating to children under five, requires children at the start of compulsory schooling to have a knowledge and understanding of the world, which includes the scientific (SCAA 1996). How does this structure affect what young children do naturally, i.e. to ask questions and explore?

Brass and Budd (1995) suggest that investigation work in primary science can be a challenge, and that pupils can derive considerable enjoyment in thinking out scientific concepts for themselves (p. 121). The argument emphasises the child's ability to think scientifically and construct meaning for themselves. The constructivist paradigm is not new in science education and one that is often put forward as an acceptable approach. Constructivism is a 'less clerical and more human approach' (Fensham 1986, p. 37). If this is the case, what has it to offer the young child and investigative science?

Constructivism highlights the crucial role that activity plays in science learning and development. It gives priority to individual pupils' sensory-motor and conceptual activity. In this way constructivism allows for the analysis of thought to be considered as a conceptual process: a process that is located within the individual, and is typically concerned with the quality of individual activity that allows for the development of ways of knowing at a more micro-level. This development includes the pupils' interactive construction of classroom social norms and scientific practices. The usefulness here of the constructivist approach to young pupils investigating science is that it allows the metaphor of accommodation and mutual adaptation to be used as a means of explaining pupil behaviour, and hence allowing pupils to be involved in investigations in a natural way, not through false enforced situations.

'Constructivism emphasises that science is a creative human endeavour which is historically and culturally conditioned and that its knowledge claims are not absolute' (Mathews, 1996, p.) This definition is ideally situated as a description of very young children exploring new and exciting situations. The constructive approach starts from the premise that learning science is the personal construct of new knowledge. Our meaning for the world is constructed from our attempts to make sense of it. This is a very appealing framework for shaping our thoughts on a curriculum that focuses on young pupils investigating the science around them – one that encourages a sense of freedom to question, reason and make deductions based on pupils' own inquiries, investigations and understanding. Frensham argues that:

> Young learners are very likely to ask questions which do not fit tidily into the constructs of science, even though they seem simple.
>
> (Frensham 1986, p. 34)

Young children require an approach that allows questioning and concept construction but also takes account of the child's development, and realises that children need sufficient maturity in order to make sense of the scientific concepts being taught in the classroom. Where do scientific investigations fit into the discussion? It is generally assumed that during investigations pupils will use scientific process skills and develop scientific concepts and attitudes, but is this the case?

Harlen (1985) suggests that learning science helps children to develop ways of understanding the world around them and can bring a double benefit because science is both a method and a set of ideas; both a process and a product (p. 2).

The process of science provides ways of finding out information, testing ideas and seeking explanations, not only through the senses, but through the active participation and communication of ideas through a social context. The product of science is the ideas which can be applied to facilitate understanding of new experiences. Understanding depends on children working things out for themselves, but they need the process skills to be able to carry out investigations and communicate their findings or results.

Children investigate and explore naturally, observing very young children playing on a beach highlights this idea. Digging holes in the sand and watching them fill with water, pointing a finger and questioning why or looking quizzically when not being able to speak. The questions are there already: what is happening? where has the water gone? why does it do that? A perfectly natural enquiry, such interactions happen all the time for very young pupils, so why is there such a great desire to formalise investigations through the curriculum, and can a constructivist approach assist and make the process more personal and human? What is it that we want young pupils to achieve through investigations and how can opportunities be made so that the young child can develop their powers of reasoning without losing that natural curiosity of childhood?

The imposed framework

The National Curriculum at KS1 imposes a framework on teachers and pupils for the teaching of science. Investigative science falls under Attainment Target 1: Experimental and Investigative Science. Three broad aims are identified at this Key Stage:

1. Planning experimental work.
2. Obtaining evidence.
3. Considering evidence.

The context in which the above are to be derived are from the other three Attainment Targets within the curriculum – that of Life Processes and Living Things, Materials and their Properties, and Physical Processes – and should be used to teach pupils about experimental and investigative methods. On some occasions, the whole process of investigating an idea should be carried out by the pupil themselves (DFE 1995, p. 3). Specific to Science Investigations (SC1) are those skills concerned with the process of science investigations, sometimes called procedural understanding. The prominent place of SC1 in the curriculum has challenged many teachers in coming to terms with and understanding the principles of investigations. The National Curriculum stresses the importance of setting SC1 in the context of the other attainment targets and drawing upon the knowledge and understanding of science. SC1 is designed to help pupils to refine and clarify ideas and concepts. The attainment target structure is aimed at identifying progression in investigative skills. This has not proven to be an easy task.

What are the skills and processes teachers are required to identify and assess? They can be summarised in three broad strands:

1. ask questions, predict and hypothesise;
2. observe, measure and manipulate variables;
3. interpret results and evaluate scientific evidence.

These are seen as complementary not separate skills. Development of these skills will vary with individuals, but all three need to be nurtured together. Coates and Vause (1996) suggest that the aim of science education is to allow children to develop their own skills to plan fair tests, obtain evidence and analyse their findings, and that we cannot expect young pupils to do this without preliminary work. They imply that young pupils need time to enhance early skills of observation, descriptive language and measurement. The programs of study in the science curriculum state that 'focused exploration and investigations' are needed, while Attainment Target 1 (AT1) states that teachers teach pupils about experimental and investigative methods. On some occasions, the whole process of investigating an idea should be carried out by pupils themselves.

(National Curriculm Science 1996, p. 8)

What are the implication of such statements and how do they affect young pupils?

The implications of science investigations

Within the National Curriculum the various Key Stages have different weightings with respect to science investigations. The Key Stage of interest here is Key Stage 1. This carries the greatest weighting of all Key Stages. Fifty per cent of science should be devoted to 'investigations'. Understanding the implications of such a large weighting requires clear thinking surrounding the nature, purpose and range of activities that may serve the needs of very young pupils.

Aubrey (1992) suggests that by bringing the differences of nature and purpose into focus, a clearer understanding of the complexities of investigations within the early years may be constructed.

The quote from the National Curriculum above suggests that teachers need to expand their teaching strategies and methods for delivering the science curriculum to very young pupils. Teachers need to look carefully and examine the implications of what may be called the basic scientific skills of practicals, observation work, demonstrations and illustrative investigations. The implication for the present discussion is what are the skills or processes that young children need to fulfil the imposed framework, and what elements of these are naturally there to be nurtured, not moulded?

The Curriculum states observation as a key element. I would argue that young children are naturally observant, hence what is it that they do not have within that natural observational element that science investigations requires of them? Gott and Duggan (1992) suggest that observation tasks enable pupils 'to look at objects or events in a scientific way' (p. 138). The implication of this is that observation is a process not a skill and that it is concept driven. In this situation, children make sense of what they observe in terms of existing knowledge and understanding. The teacher's role is to develop children's observations in a more systematic way. Can the adoption of systematic observation help the continuity of the learning process?

Vygotsky (1978) and Mead (1934) have independently suggested that social experiences can shape the kinds of interpretative processes available to individuals. The constructivist approach may well be a way forward here, as constructivism makes cognition integral to social process. Very young people enjoy the social process of observation. Observation triggers questions in children's minds which can and often do lead to conversations and investigations of a self-motivating nature as they arise from children's own experiences. The role of the students' pre-instructional conceptions has been shown to be an important factor in learning. Conceptions are viewed as the individual's idiosyncratic mental representations, whereas concepts are something firmly defined or widely accepted in the case of science. However, the constructivist view is that there is no objective observation and that every observation is theory-laden, that is observations are determined by the conceptions held (Hanson 1965). This suggests that pupils will 'observe' different features of the same events or even observe the same features differently. Thus the role of social interaction becomes imperative as a forum for young children to talk about what they have seen, thus allowing them to internalise their own conceptions or theories. After all science is not only a way of knowing; it is also a way of doing. Any scientific theory is, to put it simply, the best explanation which scientists have produced up to the present. Theories are not final and certainly not true, hence is it not vital that children learn this from a very young age? Young pupils often will question and challenge 'truths' far more openly than later in life, so why do we try to mould them in their thinking of science so young? Surely science at this age should be about encouraging pupils to develop the ability to investigate and question things for themselves: to perceive problems, think of possible solutions and test their ideas.

Knowledge and investigations

Many of the activities of KS1 science involve tasks that regard pupils as small adults, and are mainly concerned in the effort to transmit science knowledge, connect new experiences with the children's old experiences, and demonstrate experiments or investigations (Chauvel and Michel 1990). As a consequence, observation of 'experimental' activities is often considered sufficient induction into the nature of scientific concepts. This is problematic but is in essence encouraged throughout the structure of the National Curriculum. It is a problem that needs to be addressed if learning is to be progressional and coherent. A possible answer lies in the nature of the knowledge we are trying to impart or at the very least involve very young children with. Science education can be thought of as developing three kinds of knowledge. The knowledge of 'that', 'why' and 'how to'. Knowledge 'that' is factual knowledge and evolves from and enables pupils to answer factual questions beginning with what, where, when and how. Knowledge 'that' is important in learning as it gives a description of how the world is thought to be and helps develop a framework for what pupils see happen or may happen in the future. This allows for surprises to happen when pupils ask the question 'why'.

'Why' knowledge helps to identify possible causes for what has been observed and give possible explanations to those observations. 'Why' knowledge is not factual, but allows pupils to develop questions which grow out of, and enable them to answer, questions beginning with 'why' and can be answered with 'because'. Frequently this type of knowledge is more complex than 'that' knowledge because it starts with facts and tries to explain them. This element of knowledge is very important when considering teaching and learning science with very young pupils and particularly investigative science. But science is more than just facts and asking questions it is about doing and inquiring.

Scientific knowledge is made up from both 'why' and 'that' knowledge. An equally important component of science is the knowledge of 'how to' . This is a more practical type of knowledge dealing with how things work in controlled and predictable ways. The testing of scientific ideas requires the 'how to' type of knowledge. Without this kind of knowledge and practical ability, the more innovative ideas in science and particularly children's science could never be tested or evaluated.

Knowledge and the kinds of knowledge within science are of specific relevance here, in that an understanding and realisation of the three forms can help put investigations into perspective when considering very young pupils. Investigations are not about major scientific discoveries, but about children developing their own investigative skills and becoming aware of the type and nature of the questions they ask. Young children naturally ask questions; as teachers we should be nurturing the types of questions they ask so that they become more systematic in their approach and ultimately solve problems. This does not mean we have to mould young pupils into certain scientific cultures, but guide them in their understanding of the world and specific scientific concepts. Such understanding will not happen in a vacuum. Communication is a key and essential element in investigative science.

The role of communication

The need to communicate clearly and effectively is neither new or inspirational, yet it is or can appear to be a stumbling block in science. The Curriculum specifies the need to use scientific terms at a very young age but is this necessary and how can young pupils be encouraged to develop such a language? Communication is at the heart of the KS1 curriculum and needs to be firmly established in any science work. The ability to talk about, record and communicate findings needs careful consideration prior to teaching. I would suggest that a constructivist approach which places the teacher's role quite clearly as a facilitator of knowledge construction (that is, as a guide in students' individual construction processes) is an appropriate approach to communication in investigative science. Here, 'teachers and pupils are seen as partners in the teaching learning situation. Consequently, pupils are given more command of their own learning and more responsibility for it' (Duit and Treagust 1995, p. 117). The nature and structure of communication within this context would consolidate Vygotsky's (1985) notion of learning within the 'zone of proximal development'. This can be considered as 'assisted performance' (Tharp and Gallimore 1988). This defines what a child can do with help, with the support of the environment, of others and of the self. Such a context allows for the introduction of scientific vocabulary as stated in the programs of study at KS1. Recent research by Ravanis (1994) has shown how free activity of children exploring magnets and magnetic material, in conjunction with appropriate support by teachers, can help pupils to construct the desired 'scientific' knowledge and vocabulary.

Communication is a key element to successful teaching and learning at any age. Investigation and exploration can be an ideal forum for young children to develop and progress their scientific ideas and scientific knowledge. Communication is a very important skill to develop in young pupils (Barnes 1976). More recently Harlen (1985, p. 39) has interpreted communication as 'an outward extension of thought'. What are the implications of this within the present discussion? If communication is essential to assisting young pupils' science conceptions, the time to think about investigations and talk about ideas is fundamental to development. I would suggest that a constructivist approach not only allows this to happen, but that it positively encourages communication and hence gives the pupils the opportunity to clarify their thinking with the support of the teacher. In this way pupils will reach a better understanding of the scientific concepts and be able to communicate them to their peers and teachers. Children need the opportunity to clarify their ideas as a way of evaluating what they have learnt. This is particularly true of very young pupils who continually ask the question why?

The role of the teacher is crucial to such an approach of learning science. Harlen (1992, p. 105) suggests that if communication is 'mainly a social event, with the emphasis on the opportunity to speak and little feedback in relation to content, then it may become something of a ritual'.

Facilitating constructive discussion without it becoming ritual or the enforcement of ideas due to lack of time or curriculum pressures, is fundamental to good long term learning of science concepts. Pupils need to hear other children's ideas as well as the teacher's in order to clarify their own thinking. However, this should be within the context of the learning situation. Curriculum constraints should not deter such a learning process. Very young pupils naturally ask questions and want to explore, communication is their principal mechanism, and investigations can be a powerful tool in the development of both their communication skills and their scientific knowledge.

Some points for discussion

Considering the use of investigations within the science curriculum for very young pupils draws attention to aspects of teaching and learning that may be informed by a constructivist view of learning. Teaching effectively is crucial to the development of any child, but in science it is essential that teachers understand how science differs from other subjects. This difference requires teachers to provide opportunities for the development of activities that nurture both scientific content and the progression of science skills and concepts. Young pupils frequently try to explain their physical world, science aims to explain the existing physical world by creating generalisations that fit all situations. This requires the use of hypothesis, an area that has not always been recognised in the early years teaching of science. It is very important that children are provided with opportunities to raise their own questions that will help them identify and ultimately understand fundamental science concepts (Cavendish *et al.* 1990).

From a constructivist perspective a central focus for planning investigations for very young pupils should allow for a comparison of the children's view of science and the accepted scientific view. This would then provide a means for establishing the intellectual demands of the areas under consideration for the learner. Thus with the teacher's help pupils can develop a more accurate scientific perspective of the concepts under investigation. Clement *et al.* (1989) suggest that a good teaching strategy is to expose the pupils' initial thinking and using this as a starting point to teaching. Such an approach would seem well suited to the naturally inquisitive child. Many approaches can be used in investigations but at the heart of the constructivist approach is the fundamental aim of supporting pupils in making links between their existing conceptions and the science view. Children are more likely to learn how to set up experiments and raise their own questions if they are fully involved in their learning and the decision processes that are required in investigative work.

Science learning from a constructivist perspective, involves epistemological as well as conceptual development (Carr *et al.* 1995). This would suggest that learning science requires the understanding of new conceptual structures, as well as developing a new rationality for knowledge. Science investigation for young pupils can and does fit well into this framework. It allows pupils not only to discuss empirical findings however simplistic they are, but to construct 'ways of seeing' such evidence. Learning through investigations involves socialisation. Teaching viewed in this way encourages practical activities and communication, but relies on feedback, checking conceptual development and providing appropriate learning activities.

It may be that pupils respond to things in terms of meaning they have for them rather than to constructs projected into their worlds by teachers. This would suggest that pupils be given the opportunity to investigate naturally and to question openly, rather than be moulded into the type of investigation needed and the nature of questions to be asked. Solomon (1995) suggests that at the core of a constructivist framework lies the child's thinking and learning about phenomena of the natural world which are likely to be central to good quality science teaching. Rogoff (1990) reinforces this argument by noting that in research children are considered to learn by observing or participating with others: the underlying assumption is that the external lesson (to be learned) is brought across a barrier into the mind of the child. Rogoff raises the issue that the process by which the barriers are crossed are not specified, and remains a deep problem (p. 195). However, if children are already engaged in social activity when they actively observe or participate with others then children may be viewed in the following way:

With the interpersonal aspects of *their* functioning integral to the individual aspects, then what is practised in social interaction is never on the outside of a barrier, and there is no need for separate process of internalisation.

(Rogoff 1990, p. 195)

This suggests that we consider the child from a different perspective, by focusing on what children's interpersonal activity might mean. This means that children need to be considered from the standpoint of focusing on scientific meanings and practices that the child considers and shares with others. This is an important aspect of observation and communication in investigative work. As Rogoff identifies, children are already active participants in social practice, implying that pupils engage in and contribute to the development of classroom science and scientific practices from the outset. A constructivist perspective therefore allows us to focus on the ways in which pupils can reorganise their activity as they participate in a learning science environment, and on the processes by which the curriculum is interactively constructed in the local situation of development.

Conclusion

In this chapter I have argued that science investigation for very young pupils should not be constrained by rigid curriculum frameworks, but prompted from natural curiosity and the need to know. It has not been suggested that science be trivialised. It has been argued that investigative skills will develop if young children are encouraged to test their own observations, questions, and hypotheses through constructing and reconstructing their scientific knowledge. Com-munication has been highlighted as a significant context for such development. Science investigations is a natural setting for pupils to test their conceptions of science. It is the teacher's responsibility to provide contexts that allow for such development to take place. The curriculum is only a framework to guide not to impose constraining structures on pupil learning. Investigations can and should be a method by which young pupils can explore science concepts and enhance their cognitive abilities through the development of fundamental skills such as observation, hypothesis making, and communication. New ways of seeing are important, and children are keen to learn. As educators we should encourage and nurture new ways of seeing and doing. Children need environments that enhance creativity and allow ideas to be freely expressed and promote active learning. Teachers and pupils need to be part of the learning process, such a process cannot and should not be passive. It should provide an environment that allows failure to be turned into success through challenging, constructing and deconstructing scientific concepts. Investigations should not be moulded and contrived so that pupils come away with certain terms and possible concepts. Investigations should be a medium for challenging present conception, developing future conceptions and progressing their scientific understandings. In planning for scientific development through investigations teachers and teacher educators need to consider ways of enhancing and widening learning environments as a way of facilitating young pupils conceptual development in science.

Investigations and exploration are important in the early development of scientific skills, knowledge and attitudes. A constructivist approach for developing skills, knowledge, attitudes and conceptual development can provide a useful framework in :

i. developing the skills of observation, hypothesising and communicating;
ii matching the conceptual needs and abilities of children;
iii. developing the natural curiosity of young pupils in the classroom.

Constricting such activities at an early age nips children's scientific capability 'in the bud'. A prudent way forward would be the incorporation of activities which capitalise on children's natural curiosity, providing a variety of media and situations to help them 'make sense' of their world.

Issues

1. During some thematic work on 'Growing', children at a nursery were encouraged to observe the differences and similarities between a baby and an elderly grandmother. They took photos with an 'instamatic' camera and used them to develop a display which was part of their work. What other types of recording of their activities could have been encouraged? What other areas of learning would have been involved?
2. Some children were making ice lollies as part of a theme on 'Hot and Cold'. Although the teacher had arranged for a small fridge (with a freezer section) to be placed in the room, some of the children selected to try to freeze their lollies outside. The weather had been cold but the temperature was certainly above freezing point.

What did the teacher learn from the children's decision and how could she have moved the children on? How would the approach you suggest fit with a constructivist perspective?

3. If the National Curriculum is 'slimmed down', or revised, by distilling each area to include only the most important aspects or topics, in order to ensure a balanced and broad curriculum with all the subjects/areas as an entitlement, what should the statutory science curriculum for children in the Early Years and KS1 comprise?

References

Aubrey, C. (Eds) (1992) *The Role of Subject Knowledge in the Primary Curriculum*. London, Falmer Press.

Barnes, D. (1976) *From communication to Curriculum*. Milton Keynes, Open University Press.

Carr, M. *et al.* (1995) The constructivist Paradigm and some implications for science content and pedagogy. In Fensham, P. Gunstone, R. and White, R. (Eds) *The Content of Science*. London, Falmer Press London pp. 147–160.

Cavendish, S., Galton, M., Hargreaves, L. and Harlen, W. (1990) *Assessing Science in the Primary Classroom: Objective Activities*. London, Paul Chapman.

Chauvel, C. and Michel, V. (1990) *Les science des la maternelle*. Paris, RETZ

Clement, J., Brown, D. and Zietsman, A. (1989) Not all preconceptions are misconceptions. Finding anchoring conceptions for grounding instructions on students' intutions. *International Journal of Science Education*, Vol. 11, No. 5, pp. 554–565.

Coates, D. and Vause, J. (1996) Experimental and investigative science at Key Stage 1. *School Science Review*, Vol. 78. No. 282. pp. 17–22.

DFE (1995) *Science in the National Curriculum*. London, HSMO.

Duggan, S. and Gott, R. (1995) The place of investigations in practical work in the National Curriculum for Science. *International Journal of Science Education*. Vol. 17, No. 2, pp. 137–147.

Duit, R. and Treagust, D.F. (1995) Students conceptions and constructivist teaching approaches. In Fraser, B. and Walberg, H. J. (Eds) *Improving Science Education*. Illinois, Chicago University Press.

Fensham, P .J. (1986) Science for all. *Educational Leadership*, Vol. 44, pp. 18–23.

Gott, R. and Duggan, S. (1992) *Investigative work in the Science Curriculum*. Open University Press.

Hanson, Norwood, R. (1965) *Patterns of Discovery*. Cambridge. England Cambridge University Press.

Harlen, W. (1985) *Teaching and Learning Science*, London, David Fulton.

Harlen, W. (1992) *Teaching and Learning Primary Science*. London, Paul Chapman

Johnstone, J. (1996) *Early Explorations in Science*. Buckingham, Open

University Press.

Matthews, M. (1994) *Science Teaching: The Role of the History and Philosophy of Science.* London, Routledge.

Mead. G.H. (1934) *Mind, Self and Society,* Chicago, University of Chicago Press.

Piaget, J. (1978) *The Development of thought equilibration of cognitive structures.* London, Blackwell.

Ravanis, K. (1994) The discovery of elementary magnetic properties in preschool age. Qualitative and Quantitative research within a Piagetian framework. *European Early Childhood Education Research Journal.* Vol. 2, No. 2, pp. 79–91.

Rogoff, B. (1990) *Apprenticship in Thinking: cognitive development in social context.* New York and Oxford, Oxford University Press.

SCAA (1966) *Desirable Outcomes for Children's Learning on entering compulsory education,* London: SCAA.

Solomon, J. (1995) Constructivism and quality, in Murphy, P. (Ed), *Subject Learning in the Primary Curriculum.* London, Routledge.

Tharp, R.G. and Gallimore, R. (1976) The use and limits of social reinforcement and industriousness for learning to read. *Technical report No. 60.* Honolulu, Kamehameha Schools. Early Education Program.

Vygotsky, L.S. (1978) *Mind in Society.* Harvard University Press.

9

Young children's perceptions of the world

Stephen Scoffham

By the time they come to school most children have already acquired a range of ideas about their geographical surroundings and the wider world. These notions tend to be rather confused and reflect a general fear of the unknown. This chapter considers how a positive teaching programme can help to promote more balanced images.

In his treatise on education the seventeenth century philospher John Locke (1693) described young children 'as travellers newly arrived in a strange country of which they know nothing' (p. 137). If we accept Locke's premise that the newborn baby is devoid of ideas, one of the challenges for educational research is to account for the way children acquire their subsequent knowledge and understanding. This question concerns geographers on a number of different levels. Much of the information which children obtain about their environment comes from first hand experience. However, children also acquire ideas about distant places which they have never seen or visited. How can we help to ensure that the perceptions which they develop are not coloured by bias and prejudice?

Knowledge of the wider world

One of the simplest ways of exploring what children know about the wider world is to ask them to list the countries they can name. A study of 222 children by Wiegand (1991) revealed that seven-year old children could on average recall five or six different countries. However, their ideas were generally confused and real and imaginary places were mixed up in their minds. For example, some of the children mentioned Legoland and Narnia along with cities like Paris and New York. The eleven-year olds, by contrast, were much less likely to mix fiction and reality and could typically name about fifteen countries.

An undergraduate study of 60 children by Palmer (1993) produced similar results. Only half the four year olds tested were able to name any country at all. The six year olds did better but still confused places with countries. The eight year olds showed increasing knowledge particularly of Europe, while the ten year olds were beginning to piece together the world map. Significantly both Wiegand and Palmer found that few children were able to name individual African countries. Indeed South America, southern Asia and the Third World hardly appear to feature on their mental maps (Figure 9.1).

One of the most interesting aspects of these studies is the difficulties young children encountered in distinguishing between countries and places. Palmer commented that many six year olds named places believing them to be countries. Examples include Chessington Zoo which one child thought was 'Great fun, in England, but might be a country'. Others suggested a farm ('pigs, donkeys and horses live there'), the sea ('fishes think that is a country') and Christmas, maybe meaning the North Pole or the place where Father Christmas lives.

Piaget investigated this confusion as part of his early research in the 1920s. He was struck by the way young children, when questioned if they were they were Swiss, would frequently answer 'No, I am Genevan' i.e. from Geneva. This led him to study how children make sense of their physical location. He postulated three stages. Initially children view a country simply as a unit along with towns and districts which they regard as roughly equal in size and importance. In due course they accept their nationality but still deny they can live both in a town (Geneva) and a country (Switzerland). Finally they recognise the way that small units can be located in larger units in the country-town-district hierachy. The crucial moment comes when children abandon the idea that places are separate and appreciate instead that they fit into each other in a nesting relationship rather like the different parts of a Russian doll. Subsequent research by Jahoda (1963) and Harwood and McShane (1996) supports Piaget's original hypothesis, although children nowadays seem to adopt the hierarchical model at an earlier age than they did in the past.

Ideas about places

If children are able to name a place, the next step is to see what else they know about it. In one study (Jahoda 1963) children were asked to identify various national symbols such as the national anthem, songs and flags. The results showed that at six years old children tended to have extremely vague or mistaken ideas but that their understanding progressed steadily so that by age eleven most were able to offer cor-

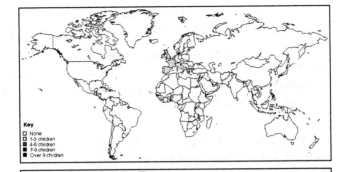

Countries named
by four year olds

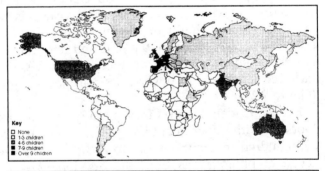

Countries named
by six year olds

Countries named
by eight year olds

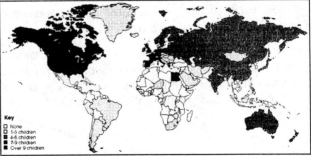

Countries named
by ten year olds

Fig. 9.1 Countries named by children of different ages. Although children name more countries as they grow older, South America, Africa and southern Asia hardly feature in their mental maps.
Source: Palmer 1993

rect answers. Jahoda commented on the great intellectual distance which children traverse within the span of a few years.

> At the outset their responses reveal an almost complete ignorance of the wider geographical and social world surrounding them: some five years later the outlook of most of them is no longer fundamentally different from that of an adult.
>
> (Jahoda 1963, p. 150)

Another approach is to use word association exercises. A survey of eight and nine year olds' ideas of Africa by Storm (reported by Fyson 1984, p. 65) revealed a great diversity of notions with a strong emphasis on the physical and natural environment, especially wildlife. Similar results have been obtained in small scale student studies conducted at Canterbury (Elliott 1992; Friend 1995; Harrington 1995; Gambrill 1996).

The study by Gambrill (1996) is particularly revealing. Using word association, sorting exercises and stimulus photographs she investigated children's images of Africa across the primary school years. Not only did the range of images increase as the children grew older, but their notions seemed to change from chance associations to more generalised stereotypes. The six and seven year olds (years 2 and 3), for example, focused chiefly on the wild animals and the heat. The same things were mentioned by the nine and ten year olds (years 5 and 6) but the children also had an increasingly negative perception and included references to poverty, lack of food and general lawlessness (Figure 9.2).

Further evidence comes from a study by Graham and Lynn (1989). Working with upper infant and upper junior classes they interviewed 320 children in groups of six to eight. The children were shown a range of photographs from the developing world and invited to discuss each picture using an open-ended schedule of questions. Graham and Lynn were surprised to find that

> a large proportion of infants and many less mature upper juniors associated the scenes in Bengal and Bangladesh with a hunter-gatherer life style. One infant group, in no way an exception, thought there would be no roads and people would rub sticks to make fire, 'cos there's no matches'.
>
> (Graham and Lynn 1989, pp. 29–30)

Another junior group discussing daily life in Bangladesh declared 'They sleep on skins from bears they've killed with spears'. However, there were also some more encouraging responses. One girl said, 'I'd love to see the village and hear the legends there'.

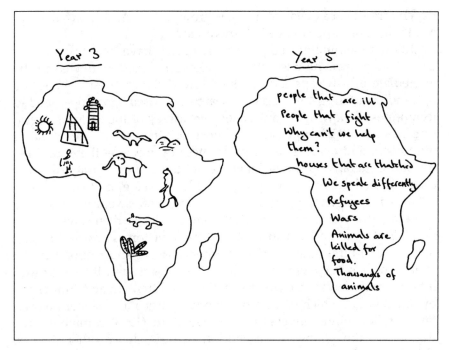

Fig. 9.2 Children's images of Africa
Source: After Gambrill 1996

Graham and Lynn (ibid.) speculate on the underlying reasons for these perceptions. They suggest that stereotyping of Third World countries may be related to the child's stage of development. Young children appear to relish stories about the simple hunting life and books about prehistoric times are popular library choices. The idea of 'primitive savages' reflects and amplifies their notions.

Working in a very different context (suburban United States) Hart (1979) makes a similar observation. He notes how scary places such as woods and abandoned buildings hold a particular fascination for children of a particular age and are frequently associated with fearsome animals such as snakes and bears. Hart argues that this fear, which is echoed in many fairy tales, may well reach back thousands of years into the roots of our culture and our psychological history.

Children's attitude to ethnic diversity

If young children hold biased images about the developing world, it raises a number of important questions. How do these ideas develop?

Do children's ideas change as they grow older? And in what ways can their images be changed or modified?

Children's ethnic attitudes and prejudices have been extensively investigated over the past 50 years. However, tests conducted in the immediate post-war period involved forced choice questions and are open to criticism. More recent research has used more open-ended techniques. Following a comprehensive survey of the research literature Aboud (1988) suggests that most children are aware of racial differences and express racial preferences by the time they are three or four. Generally speaking infants seem to have an affinity for their own national group. They appear unable to take more than one factor into account and, when pressed to support their opinions, simply express a preference for people who are similar to themselves.

While it may be hard to quantify different forces and influences, there can be little doubt young children observe and respond to the racial tensions in contemporary society. In this respect their views do little more than mirror current thinking. Children are also influenced by role models, which in Britain and other parts of the western world, fail to reflect ethnic diversity. Siraj-Blatchford (1996) comments that this leaves the young white child with little choice other than to absorb negative views about black people.

Not only does Aboud draw attention to the very early age at which attitudes develop, she also highlights the way children's ideas alter as they grow older. Although the research evidence is not conclusive it appears children become less biased from about the age of seven. For example, when Vaughan (cited in Aboud, 1988) asked white children if they would choose a Maori for a playmate, none of the eight-year olds, 30 per cent of the ten year olds and 40 per cent of the twelve year olds responded positively.

Elliott (1992) decided to probe further and investigated in a small scale student study how children's ideas change with age. Working in a predominantly all white school, she asked the children to list the words they associated with India. The seven year olds (year 3) gave an average response of eight words most of which were to do with animals and food. By contrast the ten year olds (year 6) children showed a much wider understanding giving an average of seventeen responses covering different aspects of the culture, environment and people of India.

Specific questions about food and diet revealed more about the children's perceptions. The seven year olds exhibited some very confused and distorted images. For example, along with fruit and vegetables they listed muck, brains, snakes, bugs and dirty water in their answers. Several of them appeared to believe Indians eat eyeballs. One child commented: 'I've seen it on Indiana Jones and they eat them for afters'. By contrast the older children gave a more balanced response. One girl speculated 'I don't suppose they have kettles'. Bats and flies were still mentioned as part of the diet but the children also included many more foods they would eat themselves.

These findings are supported by a major UNESCO study into children's ideas of nation cited by Carnie (1972). This indicated that between the ages of seven and eleven children become increasingly knowledgable and favourably disposed towards people of other lands. Friendliness to foreigners appears to peak around the end of the junior years followed by a downward curve in international and interracial goodwill during adolescence.

Aboud (1988) attributes the shift in attitude of seven and eight year olds to fundamental changes in the way children think. She argues that between the ages of four and seven children are naturally egocentric and make superficial judgements based on emotional preferences. As they grow older they begin to think cognitively. Consequently they are no longer so concerned with superficial appearances and better able to make balanced judgements.

Stereotypes and preconceptions

The research suggests that children often develop attitudes to other people and other countries *before* they have any appreciable knowledge of them. Lowenthal (1961) and Marsden (1976) both point out how stereotypes influence and distort our perceptions. What we see and the information we receive appears to be filtered by the categories we have already established in our mind. When we are confronted with evidence which fails to conform to our previous beliefs we tend to ignore it. In other words we only see and hear what we want to.

The influence of stereotypes was noted by Graham and Lynn (1989), who lamented the way children quickly jumped to conclusions when scanning photographs. Even Bengali children, who might be expected to be aware of conditions in the developing world, appeared reluctant to accept modern images of Africa. For example, one of the photographs showed an airport with two African women, one dressed in a rather dowdy European suit and the other in an expensive-looking traditional dress. The children's comments revealed strong prejudices. They decided the lady in European dress might be a teacher or air hostess, while the other 'collects sticks and hay to make brooms'.

The same point was noted by Elliott (1992), who presented children with 25 pictures of India. To test their preconceptions she asked them to decide which ones they thought were of India and which ones they thought showed other places. She comments:

> The children quickly disregarded fifteen of the pictures that didn't match their pre-conceived images and were very reluctant to accept that they were all of India once this had been explained. One boy's reaction to this was: 'No way are they all of India, Miss. You've gone brain dead!'
>
> (Elliott 1992, p. 27)

Furthermore, it seems that the preferences which young children exhibit often precede even the simplest factual knowledge. Wiegand (1992) describes a number of studies in which infants expressed a clear liking for particular countries, although they could say almost nothing about them. One explanation is that young children may absorb attitudes just as they acquire any other facts, and accept them without question or criticism.

Developing more balanced images

A key question for educationalists is how best to modify the rather confused and unbalanced images which children appear to hold from an early age. Are they best challenged while children are still young or should this be left till they are older and more mature? Also, what techniques and approaches are likely to yield results?

As in so many areas of geography, fieldwork and first hand experience would seem to provide an ideal solution. Wiegand (1991) investigated how travel affects children's knowledge and understanding. He found that at the most basic level children who had travelled were able to name the countries and places they had visited and describe the route they had taken. Much more importantly he also discovered that the children had gained an almost universally positive impression from their travels. This meant they were ready to view stereotypes more cautiously and to match them against their own experiences and observations. Speculating on whether travel broadens the mind Wiegand concluded:

> At the very least they have powerful impressions that can be shared with other children. At best, some children begin to see the world from the point of view of other people – the essence of international understanding.
>
> (Wiegand 1991, p. 58)

Classroom teachers, being mostly unable to organise overseas visits, need to adopt other strategies. Stratta (1989) describes a small scale study in which he explored the geography and culture of Bangladesh with children aged seven and eight. Using maps, photographs, stories and reference books he gradually introduced and expanded the topic. Practical activities such as cooking and eating Asian food proved particularly successful. The highlight was a visit from a local Bengali woman, Mrs Rashid. As well as bringing a number of every-day items such as bamboo, cooking utensils and money for the children to handle, she brought some clothes for them to try on. Stratta concludes that while he was unable to achieve a radical shift in atttitudes and beliefs in a period of just a few weeks he did succeed in raising the children's level of awareness.

A student study by Friend (1995) amplifies these findings. Working with a group of six and ten year olds Friend assessed what the children thought of Africa before and after a short teaching programme. The results were generally encouraging but she found a significant difference between the groups. The young children were willing to abandon their previous ideas and adopt new, more positive, images. By contrast the older children tended to hold onto negative attitudes which they retained alongside their new ideas. While it would be unwise to generalise from such a small sample, Friend argues that it seems easier to alter images while children are still infants. By the time they reach the upper juniors stereotypes have already started to become entrenched.

It appears that longer teaching programmes can achieve more substantial results. Harrington (1995) taught a class of eight and nine year olds (year 4 and 5) about Nairobi over a nine week period. The work was based an ActionAid photopack *Nairobi, Kenyan City Life* and involved a large stimulus display. At the beginning and end of the project Harrington investigated the children's attitudes and ideas about Africa using drawings, word associations, labelling and sorting exercises. What emerged was that the children had acquired a much more balanced and mature image of Africa as a result of the project. Also, although some of the class still expressed negative images, they were much less likely to jump to conclusions. (See Figure 9.3.)

Studies such as these are particularly important because they suggest that teaching programmes at junior level can and do change children's attitudes. By the time pupils reach secondary school stereotypes become much harder to shift. Milner (1983) describes a longitudinal study of children's attitudes by Zeligs. The pupils, who were twelve years old at the beginning of the study, were re-interviewed at ages fifteen and eighteen. The opinions they expressed and the reasons

Results before teaching programme	Results after teaching programme
Hot and sunny 68%	Elephants 82%
Desert/sand 39%	Rich and poor 43%
Elephants 36%	Hot/sunny 43%
Black and Asian people 32%	Deserts 29%
Camels 29%	Trees 29%
Mud/straw houses 21%	Kenya 25%
Palm trees 18%	Black and Asian people 21%
Little food 11%	Nairobi 18%
Little water 11%	Safari 14%
Different language 11%	White people 14%
Beaches 11%	Poaching 11%
Sea 11%	Cities 11%

The children were given a word association test before and after a teaching programme. Both tests show that the children see Africa as a hot, sunny place with sand and elephants. However, after the teaching programme the children also mentioned cities, white people and real places.

Fig. 9.3 Changing images of Africa
Source: Harrington 1996

that they gave for their beliefs changed remarkably little over the period.

In a brief review of the literature Marsden (1976) discusses the difficulty of breaking down 'attitudinal rigidity' . He argues that because stereotypes become lodged in our emotional life they are not easily dislodged by logical argument or factual evidence. A survey of 3,000 American students reported by Hibberd (1983) lends weight to this view. Despite a course on the Third World their impressions of Africa hardly changed between the ages of 12 and 17. 'Teachers need to work very hard indeed,' Hibberd declares, 'to counteract false or unbalanced images already formed' (p. 68.).

Classroom implications

The reasons for teaching children about distant places and cultures from an early age appear compelling. Without intervention infants are liable to accept uncritically the bias and discrimination they see around them. Stereotypes promoted in advertisements and stories of war, famine and disasters in the media further distort their perceptions. At the same time the influence of parents and peer group pressure may also serve to confirm negative views. From here racism and all its attendant evils are only a short step away. By contrast if children are exposed to a balanced teaching programme and given access to appropriate information and ideas they will be more likely to judge people as equals whatever their race or nationality. (Figure 9.4.)

Exploring this theme further, Aboud (1988) adds a note for educators in her study on racial attitudes. Children aged seven and over, she argues, are cognitively capable of making their own judgements. They can in some measure decide whether to be influenced by the prejudice but in order to make a reasonable choice they need access to appro-

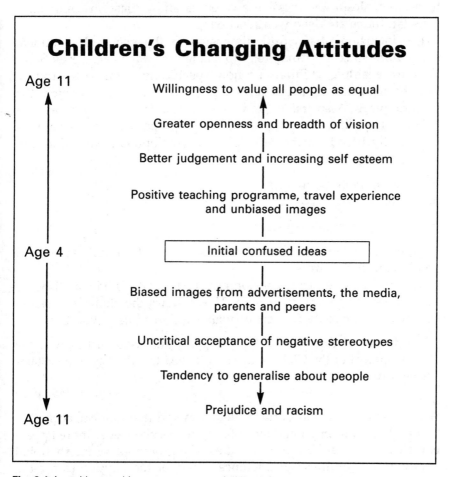

Fig. 9.4 A positive teaching programme can help to influence children's attitudes and perceptions

priate information. If this is not forthcoming they are unable to make a sensible choice and a 'golden opportunity' is lost. Hicks (1981) makes the same point in a different way. He contends that if we do nothing about fostering tolerant multi-ethnic attitudes we tacitly assent to the current norms of British society including racism.

If Hicks seems to be overstating the case it is salutory to consider a survey of attitudes among sixteen to twenty four year olds (*Guardian* 1996). Almost 30 per cent of youngsters interviewed denied that all races are equal. A subsequent investigation of 16,000 people of all ages across the European Union produced similar results. Eight per cent of Britons considered themselves 'very racist' and a further 24 per cent believed they were 'quite racist' (*Guardian* 1997). The conclusion seems to be that, despite successive awareness and education campaigns, racist attitudes are deeply entrenched.

The inclusion of a world dimension in the geography national curriculum since 1991 may help to change the balance. At Key Stage Two, for example, children are now specifically required to study a locality in a developing country. In turn this has prompted the Geographical Association and other organisations such as aid agencies to produce teaching and photograph packs. These are almost universally based on the principles of development education and stress the importance of:

(a) creating positive images

(b) challenging stereotypes and

(c) celebrating ethnic diversity.

As a result teachers now have access to a range of carefully structured and balanced resources.

In a further significant development Oxfam (1997) has published a curriculum for global citizenship. This reviews the challenges facing schools in the twenty first century and declares unequivocally:

> an education based on principles of equity and social justice, with the development of the Global Citizen at its heart, is the key to a sustainable future.
>
> (Oxfam 1997, p. 2)

As we come to the end of the millennium and the political, economic and ecological interdependence of nations becomes ever more apparent, we need to reaffirm our priorities. The promotion of international goodwill and multi-racial tolerance is one of the key issues for the future. It surely makes sense to see that young children are introduced to other peoples and cultures before prejudices and stereotypes become established. Any school curriculum which fails to do this is seriously flawed.

Issues

1. What is the difference between a stereotype and an image? Do they both contribute to the process of learning?
2. Why is it important to teach children about distant places from an early age?
3. Does global education need to be approached in different ways in different parts of Britain? Contrast inner city urban areas with all white rural communities.

References

Aboud, F. (1988) *Children and Prejudice* Oxford, Blackwell.

Carnie, J. (1972) 'Children's Attitudes to other Nationalities' in Graves, N. (Ed) *New Movements in the Study and Teaching of Geography* London, Temple Smith.

Elliott, J. (1992) *Children's Knowledge About and Perceptions of a Distant Land* (Unpublished undergraduate dissertation) Canterbury Christ Church College.

Friend, C. (1995) *Can Postive Attitudes be Developed Towards Economically Developing Countries in the Primary Phase?* (Unpublished undergraduate dissertation) Canterbury Christ Church College

Fyson, N. (1984) *The Development Puzzle* London, Hodder & Stoughton.

Gambrill, A. (1996) *Children's Images of Distant Places* (unpublished dissertation) Canterbury Christ Church College.

Graham, L. and Lynn, S. (1989) 'Mud Huts and Flints: Children's Images of the Third World' *Education 3–13* Vol. 17 pp. 29–32.

Guardian (1996) 'Britain's Youth the most Intolerant in Europe' *Guardian* 6.2.96.

Guardian (1997) 'Third of Britons Admit Racism' *Guardian* 21.12.97 p 7.

Harrington, V. (1995) 'Children's Attitudes to Developing Countries' *Primary Geographer*, Vol. 23, pp. 24–25.

Hart, R. (1979) *Children's Experience of Place* New York, Irvington.

Harwood, D. and McShane, J. (1996) 'Young Children's Understanding of Nested Hierarchies of Place Relationships' *International Research in Geographical and Environmental Education* Vol. 5 pp. 3–29.

Hibberd, D. (1983) *Children's Images of the Third World*, Teaching Geography, Vol. 9, No. 2, pp. 68–71.

Hicks, D. (1981) 'Teaching About Other People – How Biased are School Books?' *Education 3–13* Vol. 9 pp. 14–19.

Knight, P. (1993) *Primary Geography Primary History* London, Fulton.

Jahoda, G. (1963) 'The Development of Children's Ideas About Country and

Nationality' *British Journal of Educational Psychology*, Vol. 3.3, pp. 143–153.

Locke, J. (1693) *Some Thoughts on Education* Aldershot, Scholar Press, (1970).

Lowenthal, D. (1961) 'Geography, Experience and Imagination' *Annals of the Association of American Geographers*, Vol. 51, pp. 249–53.

Marsden, W. (1976) 'Stereotyping and Third World Geography' *Teaching Geography*, Vol. 1, No. 1, pp. 228–231.

Milner, D. (1983) *Children and Race* London, Ward Lock Educational.

Oxfam (1997) *A Curriculum for Global Citizenship*, London, Oxfam.

Palmer, L. (1993) *What Countries Do Children Know and Why?* (unpublished dissertation) Canterbury Christ Church College.

Piaget, J. (1929) *The Child's Conception of the World*, London, Kegan Paul.

Siraj-Blatchford, I. (1996) 'Why Understanding Cultural Differences is Not Enough' in Pugh, G. (ed) *Contemporary Issues in the Early Years*, London, Chapman.

Stratta, E. (1989) 'First Year Juniors and Cultural Diversity' *Education 3–13* Vol. 17 pp. 21–27.

Wiegand, P. (1991) 'Does Travel Broaden the Mind?' *Education 3–13* Vol. 19 pp. 54-58.

Wiegand, P. (1992) *Places in the Primary School* London, Falmer.

Acknowlegement

The author is grateful to Mary Young for her comments on earlier drafts of this chapter.

10

Assessment and learning

Beryl Webber

Assessment is an integral part of the learning process. For very young children this process is informal and even unnoticed. The relationship the child has with the adults around him or herself dictates the extent to which the child uses self assessment as a mode of developing a further and deeper understanding of the world. The adults respond to the child by informing, sharing, explaining, questioning or modelling in response to the immediate learning needs.

The child revises and extends the judgements made. The understanding developing from these experiences are stored away until required in another context at another time and place. An assessment judgement has been made by the adult, planning for the next stage of learning. The child has used the experience to build up an understanding or clarification of the world around.

Mary Jane Drummond in *Assessing Children's Learning* says that teachers making assessments:

> must be subject to this one, central, inescapable principle: that children's interests are paramount. Assessment is a process that must enrich their lives, their learning and development. Assessment must work for children.
>
> (Drummond 1993, p. 53)

The story of Jessica illustrates 'this one, central, inescapable principle' espoused by Mary Jane Drummond.

Jessica is a regular visitor who likes to look across the field behind the house to the paddock where three or four horses have a stable, spending time entertaining themselves by gambolling and exploring their territory.

Jessica first indicated that she had noticed the horses when she was about a year old. She communicated by waving her arms, grunting and smiling in delight. During the year following, Jessica continued to enjoy watching the horses. She did not speak clearly but communicated in her own style which she perfected. She must have been focusing closely on spoken language because, by the time she was two years old she enlarged her repertoire by suddenly speaking in complete sentences. No longer did she grunt but one day she said quite clearly,

'A horse and, and, and more horse.'

She was pleased with her response and sought affirmation. The adult responded with the usual congratulatory smile and encouragement but added that they could see two horses.

Thereafter, the two horses were noted and counted as her understanding of one to one correspondence developed and when she could conserve two. She was able to see two without counting.

By the age of three, Jessica was able to seek out three horses and count them accurately. She was later able to identify two horses and say,

'I can see two horses. The other one is in the stable. He's eating his dinner?'

This led to

'What do horses eat?'

There had been observable learning in her language development. Mathematical number concepts had been acquired as Jessica grew older. The scope and range of language and mathematical concepts did not develop without the enriched discussions and debate which are the norm for many children in a supportive family environment. At times, specific learning points were noted and thus assessments were made. For example, recognising that Jessica could understand more than one object, it became part of a game to encourage her to conserve two and know that the name given to identify one more than one is two. The interrelationship between learning and assessment can be seen quite clearly.

A young child makes sense of the world by communicating and the adults support this learning by making judgements and deciding how best to enable the child to think and understand more about a rich and varied world. Thus, mathematical concepts are developed and language is enriched. The child asks the questions as further understanding is known by the child to be necessary. Thus Jessica wanted to know what horses ate and asked her question. She had assessed her own knowledge base and found that it required to be extended.

At no point during this development was anything written or were any formal assessment tasks undertaken. It is usual and possible to make on the spot assessments of one child in a familiar setting. There would have been no purpose in recording any of this particular development. Had Jessica still been communicating by grunting by the time she was three or four years old then some formal assessment tasks and certainly professional observations would have been necessary and the findings analysed.

Moving from an enquiring and self assessed environment of informal assessment, and entering into the formal education system can be difficult for many children. These children are demanding and have assessment skills and learning expectations that need to be recognised and integrated into a formal structure of curriculum and assessment requirements.

The assessment of young children has become an industry for a variety of reasons, mainly because the Education Reform Act of 1988 set in train a system which required a national monitoring network of specialist personnel and funding arrangements that enabled LEAs through the country to appoint or retrain staff to become assessment teams who were to support schools in the implementation of the new requirements.

The Education Act 1988 stated 'The curriculum for every maintained school shall comprise a basic curriculum' (Education Reform Act 1998). For the first time in the history of education a curriculum was to be defined and taught with assessment procedures to support and ensure delivery of this prescribed curriculum.

Children aged seven, eleven and fourteen were to be assessed. These were to be the named Key Stages and the results of the assessments of all these age groups were to be published.

Teachers were to make assessment judgements at the end of each Key Stage based on a criterion referenced model of assessment rather than the norm referenced model which was seen to be required in any rank ordering of pupils. It also included a battery of nationally administered tasks and tests.

When the statutory testing was introduced for seven year olds, there was an overwhelming response from teachers through the Local Education Authorities and School Evaluation and Assessment Committee that if these children were to be assessed and schools to be made accountable for the performance of their pupils, then it was necessary to take account of the starting points and age of children on entry to school. Education of young children became the focus of national attention. Teachers felt that they should not be held responsible for poor performance when so many other factors had not been taken into account. It was still the intention of the government to publish league tables for seven year olds. Teachers cited a range of variables that needed to be taken into account:

- How long a child had been in the primary school. This could vary by up to a year depending on month of birth.

- The demographic make up of the intake of pupil. There were many children for whom English was an additional language.

- The varying LEA policies of the integration of pupils with a range of special educational needs.

- The money allocated to schools via the LEA. Some school have a far lower ratio of teachers to children, with some having the support of ancillary staff whilst others had larger classes and no classroom support.

- The range of interpretation of the administration of tasks and tests by teachers across the country.

Many of these concerns have been eliminated by the development and refinement of the test items and training of teachers. The range of educational starting points has been addressed by the introduction of the economic term 'value added'. This was applied for the first time to the performance and subsequent progress of such young children. A nationally administered baseline assessment was the inevitable outcome of the debate.

Prior to this time there had been an informal system of assessing what had been taught. Teachers of young children expressed concern about how little knowledge was retained by many children during a long summer holiday. They made judgements on reading progress, mathematical development and to a lesser extent, the wider curriculum that was taught. There was a support network of educational psychologists who undertook diagnostic testing for children with special educational needs. It is interesting to note that Gipps (1994) in her book *Beyond Testing* raises the issue of diagnostic testing and how the role of the classroom teacher is changing with training now available for the teacher to undertake some of the detailed testing and assessment formally completed by psychologists.

Can assessment be divorced from learning?

'Assessment is at the heart of learning' is the often quoted statement from the Task Group on Assessment and Testing (1988) which was set up to report on the assessment requirements of the National Curriculum. It has taken six years and a revision of the National Curriculum for this powerful statement to even begin to be understood.

The first National Curriculum legislation required teachers to collect evidence of learning based on clear criteria *'read write and order numbers to ten'* was one such criterion for which teachers needed to produce evidence.

What could be considered as evidence exercised the minds of those involved in the implementation and monitoring of the assessment arrangements. Was it possible for the teacher to store information gathered from large numbers of children based on a new and far more detailed curriculum? Teachers felt they were no longer engaging in the professional and challenging task of teaching, rather they were the collectors of evidence and deliverers of a prescribed curriculum.

In a study of KS1 teaching undertaken by a small team from Canterbury Christ Church College, it was found that:

> There was a strong feeling that the changing nature of the assessment requirement added extra burden. Two comments from different teachers serve to demonstrate this view.

> It [managing assessment] takes over the whole school life.

> The amount of evidence meant that I was working from October to Easter all night and one day each weekend to collate, plan, just keeping up with the mountain.

> (Hall *et al.* 1997)

In the early days of the implementation of the National Curriculum and its accompanying assessment arrangements, there was wide ranging discussion regarding the nature of evidence. Much was written at the time but gradually teachers became more compliant and the Key Stage 1 assessment procedures were gradually accepted by teachers.

In 1996 a review of the National Curriculum was undertaken and fundamental changes were made to both the structure of Programmes of Study and also to the criteria for assessment. No longer were teachers required to deliver a curriculum and gather evidence of achievement of success by meeting given criteria. They were now required to design a Key Stage scheme of work appropriate to the needs of the pupils in their schools and to assess the performance of each child against a level or performance description. But Teacher Assessment was seen as different and of equal status to the National Curriculum tests.

These changes were not greeted with the enthusiasm that might have been expected. A measure of autonomy was being returned to the teacher and professional judgements were required for the end of Key Stage Teacher Assessment in the core subjects English, mathematics and science. Many teachers were not sure this was what they wanted. It had become comfortable to follow a rigid statement led curriculum for which there were clear criteria. Had a dependency culture of teaching been established?

It has taken two years from the implementation of this revised model for schools to feel comfortable and able to move forward in translating it into a workable model for the benefit of the children in their schools. At staff development sessions during which schools endeavour to put policy into practice concerns are often expressed regarding the next change following the five year moratorium on curriculum change promised by Sir Ron Dearing in the review of 1996. There is a deep suspicion that those involved with the next review will wish to make change for change's sake in order to justify the time and money that will be spent on the next exercise. The need to make one's mark is a common and understandable human condition.

Meanwhile, the informal assessment of the younger children continues and children start their formal schooling bringing with them an accumulation of conceptual, intuitive and factual understanding and knowledge which is unique to each child.

The child on a train

The following transcript is an approximation of a discussion between an adult and child of about 3 or 4 years old overheard on a train journey.

A. *How do you like being on a train?*

C. *It's noisy.*
   Why is it noisy?

A. *It's moving fast and it's on tracks – like those over there.*

C *Are we on tracks?*

A. *Yes.*

C. *How does it stay on the tracks?*

A. *The wheels are smooth and they fit over the tracks.*
C. *The tracks are noisy.*

A.   *The noise is the wheels on the tracks.*

C.   *The wheels are noisy. The wheels on my cars make a noise in my car park.*

(Maybe this was a reference to a toy.)

The child and the adult were engaged in a type of conversation that is fairly common in public places. The enthusiastic child wanting to learn and understand and the slightly embarrassed adult trying to respond whilst not wanting to draw attention to her or himself.

However, the child was learning, building on previous experiences and self assessing by questioning. This mode of interaction and observation has been formalised by teachers of very young children. Many assessment schemes have been developed so that the strengths and range of experiences of the children can be extended. This should continue whilst embracing the new Baseline Assessment models introduced to all schools in September 1998.

A new dimension to assessment could and should be added to assessment knowledge through Baseline Assessment. A national picture of children's attainment on entry to school, whether at four or five, will reveal, a perspective – albeit narrow – to cover aspects of literacy and language, mathematics and personal and social development.

However, this bring about a downward pressure on young children and bring a change in their relationships with their parents?

David (1996) expresses concern that parents often do not communicate with their very young children, as was illustrated by the adult on the train.

> Even if it were suggested that the dominant construction of babies is 'person in the making', the permeation of our culture with attitudes negating personhood is evident in the lack of interaction in public places. Only a minority of British adults seem to direct conversation, gaze or touch to children in this age group when in public places, except when the child demands attention, by crying for example.
>
> (David 1996, p. 2)

In an article by Parkin in the *TES* 11 (1997), Margaret Lochrie of the Pre-school Learning Alliance is quoted as saying:

> Assessments could be used to capitalise on parents' fears. You don't have to be very tied into current affairs to know that lots of children are failing, or being failed. So parents are vulnerable to clever marketing . . . Pre-schools involve parents a lot, so there's more information

and a more rounded view among them. They see the point isn't cramming their children for tests but ensuring they have opportunities. If they concentrate on that the baseline assessments will take care of themselves.

(Parkin 1997, p. 7)

This new initiative could raise awareness and give a higher profile to the learning experiences of young children or it could have the reverse effect of narrowing the wide range of experiences to what is required by the 'test'. In attempting to raise the standards in school of individual performance and offer a model for 'value added' analysis, will the informal assessments and credit for diverse pre-school experiences be replaced by a formal and narrow assessment procedure at the start of formal education? It will be essential that this system is monitored closely by those responsible for the education of young children into the twenty-first century.

Involvement of parents in the assessment of their children is a requirement of the baseline national framework. It will be up to schools to consider how this is implemented in their own establishment and outline programmes. Somewhere in the middle of these concerns there needs to be a debate regarding the development, learning experiences and analysis of the assessments that are made by parents, other involved adults and children themselves during these vital early years of a child's development. Managed well, explained clearly and by directly involving parents, Baseline Assessment could be the way into this debate.

Schools and representative bodies for young children need to lead the way and not leave the reporting in the hands of journalists seeking to undermine the process in the interests of raising the sales of their newspapers rather than giving a balanced and careful consideration to the issues.

Parents are too often intimidated by the school environment and teachers are often sceptical about prior achievement. Where there is a good relationship between home and school, teachers will initiate home/school links to break down barriers and will welcome visits and involvement of parents with the ongoing education of these young children. Baseline Assessment will bring together all parents and early years teachers.

All Baseline Assessment models include, at the very least, an opportunity for parents to discuss the outcomes of Baseline Assessments with the teacher within a term of the assessments taking place. This will be the forum for teachers to expand upon the minimal requirements and share with parents the range of interests, talents and strengths in all aspects of the curriculum. Teachers must continue to stress the importance of art, music, understanding of the world, dance, drama, PE and access to the technological world, as well as recognising the importance of the basic tools of literacy and mathematics. All this within a framework of personal and social development which it is essential to establish before any formalised learning can take place.

The keen mathematician

The following extract is taken from notes from an observation of a four year old in school who brought with him a tremendous knowledge and understanding of mathematics.

Rob enters the classroom alone is greeted by his teacher. He does not respond. He is attracted by a working model of a water mill and operates the mechanism – concentrating, unaware that another child has joined him. Rob says nothing and drifts towards blackboard, picks up chalk and writes 60 x 18 and writes 480 beneath the sum.

Speaking for first time (ten minutes in class) he asks the teacher to look at his work. Teacher asks how he worked out the sum. He responds by shrugging and saying 'I just know'.

Teacher suggests that he join some children in the outside play area. He joins 2 girls and 2 boys playing in a boat. The girls are the 'drivers' sitting together on a seat behind a steering wheel. Rob joins them. Not enough room. He starts pushing the girls. A brief argument ensues and girls leave to tell a member of staff. They move away to another play area. Rob joins the boys and for a few minutes they play alongside each other. The boys drift away and Rob plays an articulate game of lifeboats. Language noted.

'captain', 'drown', 'catch', 'life raft', 'sea is rough', 'waves', 'engine'.

A later observation on the same day. This was a teacher-led logical reasoning sorting game. Each child in turn turned over a card and laid it on a grid according to the criteria of colour and shape.

Four children take turns. Rob places his card with no difficulty. He attempts to dictate to the other children as they are seeking the correct position on the grid. He is held back by the teacher who asks him to keep ever so quiet and not help the other children.

Rob in the reading area. Rob is looking at a book alongside another child. They do not communicate, except to exchange books at the request of the other child. Rob is examining a picture book and starts to tell himself a story. He is called by the teacher to bring his book and share it with her. He re-tells the story of the Enormous Turnip which is the book he has chosen. He responds well to the one to one situation and for the first time during the observation period of about seventy five minutes, he is interacting and smiling.

Rob is a very articulate child who would score highly in the core subjects but he requires a programme of interaction and communication with his peer group to enable him to work and play collaboratively. It is interesting to observe that the inclusion of assessment of personal and social development in the National Framework for Baseline Assess-ment was included as a direct result of consultation with early years specialists and practitioners. It was not included in the draft proposals.

Somewhere between the informal and ongoing assessment undertaken by parents, teachers and children themselves and the structured narrowly focused assessments required for national and local accountability, there must be a balance. The introduction of national assessment for seven, eleven and fourteen year olds has given rise to discussion on the range of purposes of the assessment judgements made by teachers and by the national testing programme as well as those more detailed diagnostic assessments required to pinpoint particular learning needs. There is a difference and teachers of young children need to be very clear when sharing the results of baseline assessment

As Clemson and Clemson write in their section on assessment in *Mathematics in the Early Years*:

> Without assessment of children's progress in their learning, purposeful teaching is replaced by serendipity. We have to know what children have learned, where they are finding difficulties in learning, and by implication, what new learning opportunities should be offered in order to structure teaching and the content of lessons.
>
> (Clemson and Clemson 1994, p. 97)

Schools, and in particular teachers of young children, need to be clear in their own minds about the purposes and the difference between the ongoing day to day assessment and 'snap shot' assessment required for national purposes and be able to communicate this message to the parents of young children who will be concerned to know how their child is measuring up to the next child or considering how best to 'coach for the test'.

The comparative results in aspects of language, literacy and mathematics will be available to schools. It is not intended at the time of publication that these results are to be made widely available. Comparisons between schools in the locality could be used to ensure parity of opportunity across schools with similar intakes. They should not be used as a guide to the 'best school'.

The school and national assessment procedures are at a watershed and the schools and their teachers need to take the initiative and make the best use of the required assessments and use the information wisely alongside the whole range of assessments, formal and informal, that are made on and by us all from the moment we are born.

All educators of young children need to all play their part in providing the best learning environment for 'people in the making'. The Baseline national initiative with the ongoing training, moderation and analysis of results that are required, is a good continuing forum for this debate. These are changing times and early years education now holds centre stage, teachers need to take this opportunity to explore and articulate their beliefs and make them known to parents.

Issues

1. Profiling and Baseline Assessment are combined in some Baseline Assessment models. How clear are we on the differing purposes for the two strands?
2. Sir Ron Dearing's revisions for the National Curriculum required a change to the model of assessment at the end of the Key Stages. Teacher assessment's ongoing use of planning etc., and the National Curriculum end of Key Stage tests were supposed to summarise the achievement and the end of the Key Stages. How does this differ from the Baseline model?
3. How can teachers ensure they use teacher assessment to inform their planning?
4. Look at some video material of an adult interacting with a preschool child in a learning environment. Identify the assessment opportunities which have been seized by the adult or child in their questioning/discussion of what they have been doing.

References

Clemson, D. and Clemson, W. (1994) *Mathematics in the Early Years* London: Routledge.
David, T. (1996) British Babies: People or Possessions? in Hayes, D. (Ed) *Debating Education* Canterbury: Canterbury Christ Church College.
DES (1988) *Education Reform Act 1988* London: HMSO.
DES(1988) *National Curriculum: Task Group on Assessment and Testing: A report,*

London: DES/Welsh Office

Drummond, M. J. (1993) *Assessing Children's Learning* London: David Fulton

Gipps, C. (1994) *Beyond Testing* London: Falmer Press

Gipps C. and Murphy, P. (1994) *A Fair Test* Buckingham: Open University Press

Hall, K., Webber, B., Varley, S., Young, V. and Dorman, P. (1997) A Study of Teacher Assessment at Key Stage 1. *Cambridge Journal of Education*, Vol. 27 (1) pp. .

Parkin, J. (1997) A Sales Pitch too Far? *Times Education Supplement* 11 April.

SCAA (1997) *The National Framework for Baseline Assessment* London: SCAA publications

11

Continuing professional development

Vanessa Young

'If we're going to come in after school particularly for the NC we want to be told what we've got to do . . . I want to know what I'm supposed to be doing and I want it to be delivered by the adviser who's supposed to know. I want it to be useful and I want it to be useful in the shortest possible time.'

(cited in Morrison 1992, p. 158)

This comment from a Key Stage 1 Curriculum Co-ordinator serves two functions. Firstly, it seems to reflect the attitudes encountered by many of us involved in what is now called 'continuing professional development' (CPD). Secondly, it encapsulates a number of significant current trends in relation to CPD. In this chapter, I would like to examine more specifically these trends and their implications for the profession.

Let us examine more closely the comment from our KS1 Co-ordinator. What she seems to be saying on behalf of her colleagues is:

– we feel coerced into being involved in INSET;
– we are having to attend at unsociable hours;
– we have no ownership over the content;
– our only interest in the content is in so far as it helps us to fulfil statutory requirements;
– the provider is the expert, we are simply passive receivers;
– we do not want to have to think too much, or make decisions;
– we do not want anything that is not immediately useful;
– we only want tried and tested solutions;
– we want the solutions instantly.

This stance is symptomatic of a number of trends in CPD which have been evolving as a result of the wealth of legislative initiatives in education over the last 10 or 15 years. Three of the most significant are: **prescription, pragmatism** and, in evaluation terms, an emphasis on **outcomes**.

Prescription

Prescription has manifested itself in a number of different ways. Most obviously, perhaps, the National Curriculum has laid down by law the subject areas that are to be taught in schools and within those subject areas, content and assessment criteria. Certain subjects have been accorded high status (and, by definition, others marginalised). Furthermore, within the most prestigious subjects of English and Maths, a small section of their content, i.e. reading and arithmetic, has been elevated beyond the realms of any 'broad and balanced' curriculum so that we're in danger of returning to what Richards (1997) refers to as a 'neo-elementary school curriculum' in which more and more time is devoted to the so-called 'basics' of numeracy and literacy and only rudimentary, superficial coverage of other curriculum areas is provided.

In terms of CPD, this prescription has had an impact in a number of related ways. Firstly, the redirection of funds from LEAs to schools provided a strong financial lever, thrusting not only power but responsibility onto the school. With the minds of head teachers firmly set on having to deliver an unfamiliar and often challenging new curriculum (not to mention meeting Ofsted criteria, and satisfying newly empowered parents), LEA and Higher Education providers had, as a consequence, little choice but to fall into line and give the 'customers' what they wanted. Secondly, the setting up of national priority areas and the abandonment of local priorities under GEST in 1991 ensured that the agenda for CPD was firmly in government hands. Now, the last bastion – Higher Education (HE) – has fallen into the clutches of the government through the transfer of HE funds for CPD from the Higher Education Council for England (HEFCE) to TTA control (HEFCE circular 27/95). This allows the TTA to dictate not only course content, but also process and outcomes and, as a government quango, it is reasonable to assume that this powerful body will be more intent on carrying out the wishes of its masters than its subjects. By these means, the retraining of the primary profession to deliver the National Curriculum has been assured.

Pragmatism

Linked with this trend for prescription is the move towards a much more pragmatic, means-end approach both to initial teacher training and continuing professional development. This has involved, fundamentally, the denigration of theory evidenced by the continuing attacks over the past decade on 'educationists' i.e. the researchers and theorists of education (Goodson 1997). This denigration would seem to apply both to abstract, critical thinking in relation to bodies of knowledge *per se*, and more specifically, to the kind of educational theory that reflects unfashionable 'progressive' ideology such as that embodied in the Plowden Report. This last was clearly the inevitable stance of a government whose policies were firmly rooted in alternative ideologies; the attack on abstract, critical thinking, however, could be construed more cynically as a means of distracting teachers from asking 'why?' by concentrating their minds on simply 'how?' to deliver this new curriculum.

There are a number of clear indications of this trend. The first is what appears to have been a deliberate sidelining of educational scholarship in the setting up of the National Curriculum. Goodson (ibid.) observes that the government chose to spend £750 million on what he describes as 'a series of curriculum definition exercises' rather than fund educational research to ensure a sound philosophical basis for this huge national initiative. The second indicator is the introduction of school-based training for trainee teachers which places a specific and significant emphasis on the practical rather than the theoretical. This is 'on the job' *training* as opposed to *education* in its broadest sense (as described by Stenhouse 1975). The third indication is the erosion of long term Masters level courses (Golby 1994). He observes a proliferation of part time courses and modularised degrees which he describes as 'too often like strings of beads – without the beads!' (Golby ibid.). The nature of these courses (or their survival) could be further affected by the TTA's emphasis on the assessment of the impact of CPD in terms of outcomes in the classroom (TTA 1996; Golby 1994).

These indications point to a parallel trend, namely the shift from 'knowledge acquisition to performance enhancement' (School Management Task Force 1990 in Golby 1994); in other words away from theoretical, educational knowledge towards professional skills and competences. These are manifest not only in the 14/93 directive (DfE 1993) on primary initial teacher training, but also in the TTA's new framework of national standards for the profession which specifies the target standards which teachers must achieve to move from one rung of the career ladder to the next (TTA 1996 and 1998).

Outcomes

One of the main items on the TTA's agenda is to make teachers and INSET providers more accountable for funding provided for CPD. At a recent conference, Anthea Millet of the TTA quoted some of the findings from the Mori survey carried out for her organisation (at the government's behest) into the effectiveness of INSET. In this survey, although 89 per cent of teachers who responded thought their CPD experiences were useful or very useful, only 26 per cent thought they had had any impact on their classroom practice. This raised questions about the cost-effectiveness of GEST funding. The TTA propose therefore that evaluation of CPD should, in future, focus much more specifically on outcomes in the classroom (TTA 1996). This merely echoes what was noted by the DES almost a decade before:

> At the heart of evaluation is the effect on pupils. Given that the ultimate purpose of most INSET is directly or indirectly to improve the quality of learning, the evaluation process must seek ways of showing this to be happening
>
> (DES 1987, in Morrison 1992, p. 158)

On the face of it, this seems a very reasonable expectation. Surely there must be some perceptible return for public funds, and if CPD is not about improvement in the classroom, what is it about? However, the key phrase here is 'directly or indirectly'. English (1995) highlights the enormous difficulty of attributing outcomes in the classroom to in-service training activities asking questions such as:

- How long might it take for any changes to manifest themselves?
- Can it be guaranteed that any observed changes are a direct result of the in-service training?
- Is it likely that a single factor has brought about the change or might there be several contributory factors and if so, in what proportions? (English 1995, p. 296)

Additional questions might be asked concerning the nature and desirability of that change and who defines the criteria.

This emphasis on outcomes in the evaluation of CPD is paralleled in school evaluation where calls for accountability have demanded the setting of targets and the measurement of outcomes. As Gillian Shepherd, then Secretary of State for Education, stated in the *Times Educational Supplement*:

> We have to make sure that schools are fully accountable and that results are transparent.
>
> (Shepherd, *TES* 9 February 1997)

Discussion

Having described these trends discretely, it is important to realise that of course all three are inextricably linked, indicating a set of values which are of themselves coherent and complementary. If we look at the paradigms in Table 11.1 (Young in Hayes (ed.) 1996, p. 153), we can see that these values relate most closely to the 'institutional' model.

Table 11.1   Comparison of values

INSTITUTIONAL	PROFESSIONAL
collective	individual
'majority' needs	'minority' needs
instrumental	ideological
training	education
'how'?	'why?'
short term solutions	long term problem solving
reactive	proactive

This is especially the case with regard to the last five features: instrumental rather ideological (in the educational rather than political sense); focusing on training rather than education; requiring 'how?' rather than 'why?' questions; demanding short term solutions rather than long term, problem solving approaches; reacting to a prescribed 'top-down' agenda rather than setting ones own.

So what are the problems with this model of CPD for the teacher of children in the early years, or indeed any teacher? It seems to cater for the needs of our KS1 Co-ordinator very well in that it suggests short term, useful solutions to the delivery of the most important statutory requirements and it is provided by experts. In order to answer that question, we need to examine more critically the issues raised by the three trends of **prescription, pragmatism** and emphasis on **outcomes**.

The prescribed curriculum may at first seem comforting in an illusory way. It suggests that there is a consensus of opinion on what is essential knowledge taking away some of the burden of decision-making. At a time when teachers appear to be so over-worked (ironically, as a result of the National Curriculum and matters related to the 1987 Education Reform Act (Campbell *et al.* 1991 in Morrison 1992), this may well come as a relief for teachers. This perception of prescription as desirable was illustrated recently by a comment from a local head teacher during a consultancy visit. In seeking advice on writing a scheme of work for her school, she declared that she wanted something whereby her teachers would not have to think! Although, this perhaps says more about the stat. of exhaustion experienced by many in the profession at the moment, it does indicates a worrying capitulation when a work force of 'non-thinking' curriculum deliverers is seen as a panacea.

The prescribed curriculum, however tempting, presents a number of problems. Firstly the organisation of National Curriculum content into discrete subject areas smacks very much of a secondary school model. It ignores the traditional areas of experience and the primary teachers' concerns to deal with the child in a holistic way; and although reception and pre-school children are not legally required to follow the NC, emphasis on judging schools through the performance of children in the NC (i.e. on outcomes) and the use of these results in school league tables, will inevitably lead teachers to 'teach to the test'. Within these discrete subject areas, the further narrowing of the curriculum to focus on literacy and numeracy places even further constraints on teachers of children in the early years. What value is attributed to other experiences such as play, development of relationships and all those other important areas which are not to be 'pinned down' within a specific subject?

This issue of value, coupled with the pressures of bureaucratic accountability represented by Ofsted, league tables and the Parents Charter, is vital when it comes to CPD. In a culture which is 'customer orientated' and therefore obsessed with measurable outcomes that indicate 'value for money', what is dictated is a CPD provision as narrow and as limited as the curriculum it serves. Our KS1 Co-ordinator was not interested in any experiences that did not help her fulfil her statutory obligations, she was understandably only concerned with giving up her valuable time for that which she perceived as being immediately useful.

The issue of time in itself is a significant one, in as much as perceptions about its deployment are inherently bound up with those values. In 1991, Campbell *et al.* made a study of KS1 teachers' working hours and discovered that in just a year since a similar study was made, a KS1 teachers' working week had risen from 50 hours to 55 hours. A 1994 report for the National Education Commission on Time and Learning (in Woodilla *et al.* 1997) made the following observation about teachers' perception of time:

> the greatest resistance of all is found in the conviction that the only valid use of the teacher's time is in front of the class; the assumption is that reading, planning, collaboration with other teachers and

professional development are somehow a waste of time.

(cited in Woodilla et al. 1997, p. 297)

This attitude is understandable given the time pressures inflicted on teachers since the introduction of the NC with its constantly moving goal posts. The instrumental (as opposed to ideological), pragmatic approach demanded by our KS1 Co-ordinator, appears to be a direct consequence of curriculum prescription on the one hand and emphasis on outcomes on the other.

Most serious perhaps of all the attitudes underlying our KS1 Co-ordinator's statement is a passivity and lack of confidence about her and her colleagues' own knowledge and experience. This indicates a profession with low esteem, driven by extrinsic rather than intrinsic motivation. Helsby and McCulloch (in Goodson 1997, p. 17), in their conclusions from a wide survey of teachers, have no doubts as to the cause:

> The introduction of a centralized and prescriptive National Curriculum appears to have weakened the professional confidence, lowered morale and left them uncertain both of their ability to cope and of their right to take major curriculum decisions. These findings are consistent with the views of increased State control of the curriculum undermining teacher professionalism.

In Millett's 1995 TTA Annual Lecture *Securing Excellence in Teaching* she announced that:

> the cornerstone of our programme will be to establish national standards to help teachers and schools set targets for teachers' development and career progression and to help focus and improve training programmes at national, local and school levels. The national standards will seek to establish clear and explicit expectations of teachers in relation to different key roles. Establishing these agreed standards throughout the profession will provide a focus for setting targets, for planning training and development programmes and for reviewing performance
>
> (Millett 1995 in Graham 1996, p. 126)

This policy initiative, some might argue, should provide the profession with a long-needed career structure which could go some way towards raising teacher morale and confidence. Graham (1996), however, sees it as yet another 'nail in the coffin' for the profession with worrying implications which could be far-reaching.

Firstly, the emphasis is on competence and therefore skills, marginalising once again theoretical aspects of education. Secondly, standards, once defined by the TTA, will be fixed and non-negotiable.

Thirdly, these are not optional extras to enhance a teacher's CV – on the contrary, promotion or lateral transfer could be blocked until the prescribed standards have been demonstrably achieved. These are highly significant features and, as Graham (ibid.) observes, represents a major shift in conditions of service.

> As we have seen in ITT, the initial unexceptional and relatively common-sense parameters [have] rapidly become elaborated into a highly debatable framework of ideological control expressed as mandatory requirements policed by OFSTED.

This may appear to be an extreme, uncompromising response, but the insidious nature of these developments needs to be recognised. His diatribe highlights a further, even more profound issue that relates to the notion of 'professionalism'.

The emphasis on set standards places the TTA Framework firmly in the 'training' rather than the 'education' camp. The freedom to take an unfashionable stance, examine long-held assumptions, be critical of the status quo afforded by long term, academic work leading to higher degrees are not features of the Framework. The danger then is that the term 'professional' becomes redefined. Goodyear alerted us to this problem as long ago as 1992 before The Framework was even a 'twinkle in the TTA's eye':

> The meaning of 'professional' has slid away from the rich suggestiveness of say 'professional judgement' or 'professional integrity' towards the narrower end of its continuum, where it is synonymous with 'proficient' as in 'they made a proficient job of it . . . professional development covers management training from those teachers already heads or senior teachers, and refers primarily to the acquisition and extension of skills needed to implement and assess the NC for all others.
>
> (Goodyear 1992 in Golby 1994, p. 71)

This is worrying, especially as Goodson (1997) reminds us that teaching (as arguably any profession) is seen as a profession precisely for its basis on thorough research and theoretical bodies of knowledge.

What has been described is a rather depressing scenario. Is there nothing within the current developments which relates to professional development in its original, broadest, sense? One could be forgiven for seeing hope in the TTA's commitment to promoting the idea of teaching as a research-based profession, giving funding directly to the teachers to carry out their own classroom-based research. David Hargreaves, at the launch of the TTA's Corporate Plan in 1996, attacked educational research as an 'esoteric activity of little relevance to practitioners' (Hargreaves, 1996). The TTA's initiative of individual teacher researchers, would seem to go some way to answering him and other critics of traditional research. On the face of it, it seems a beguiling idea, implying a process that is:

- reflective
- teacher initiated
- intrinsically motivated
- sharply relevant to the classroom both in terms of defining research questions and making use of findings
- action orientated.

There are, however, a number of inherent problems with this proposal. Although the impetus for research may well come from classroom practitioners, the need and focus will almost certainly pertain to imposed agenda items related to the prescribed curriculum; indeed as the TTA holds the 'purse strings', relevance to the imposed agenda would presumably be a criterion for granting the necessary funds for carrying out the research. Regardless of the integrity and commitment of individual putative teacher-researchers, there are studies which suggest that, in the present climate, externally imposed factors are overwhelmingly influential on teachers. English (1995), in his research study, found that external factors such as the National Curriculum and its associated procedures had far more significance for teachers than any other factor. In contrast, teachers in the 1970s were influenced only a little by the government, valuing, above all, their autonomous decision-making (Taylor *et al.* 1974 in Kyriakides 1997) English worries that the dominance of these external factors raises doubts about the effectiveness of the changes initiated, arguing that when teachers lack control and ownership, it is unlikely that the effects of imposed change will be sustained for very long. As Golby (1994, p. 71) points out, meaningful change is intrinsically dependent on teachers' values which underpin all their actions:

> Practice can only be fully professional when informed by consideration of aims and values and the relationship of particular activities to overall purposes. The view of professionalism here is of practitioners who have reflective commitment to guiding values, seeing their daily work as an embodiment of those values and seeking through continuing review and deliberation on their work constantly to improve it

A further problem with this notion of the individual teacher researcher is the lack of external perspective that it implies. With a traditional MA course, teachers would be required to 'step outside' their own situation by reading the work and research of others in the field and coming together to discuss and debate ideas with colleagues and tutors outside their own institutions. This is particularly crucial when teachers base their dissertation on a case study of their own school or critical events from their own classrooms. That is not to say that individual teacher researchers would not seek these opportunities for detachment or alternative perspectives, but it would, in reality, be much more difficult to achieve. The researcher also needs to be sensitive to the ethics involved in school-based enquiry and be aware of appropriate data-gathering techniques and approaches. Process knowledge of this type in relation to research has to be learned in the same way as any other knowledge. This implies some kind of teaching and guidance from those who are themselves experienced in research. These people are not usually found within the school context.

Lastly, all those involved in research need to have an audience for their findings if the process is to carry any significance beyond the individual teacher in their individual classroom. This is challenging enough for those teachers involved in formal Masters programmes with tutors who can offer opportunities for dissemination and guidance on publication; one wonders how this will realistically be achieved by the lone individual.

Recommendations

The action research approach by its nature is practice orientated, which in reality is both its strength and its downfall. Although laudable in its intentions in helping teachers to improve their practice (Carr and Kemmis 1986 in Goodson 1997), experience with teachers working in this way has revealed a number of problems inherent in the process. While not insurmountable, these can only be exacerbated in the case of the classroom researcher working in isolation. The main areas of difficulty are:

– establishing enough detachment from their work to maintain a critical distance;
– seeing connections between their own work and the work of other (published) researchers and writers;
– generalising and speculating from the specific to contribute to the larger community of researchers in education, and therefore the development of professional (in its original sense) knowledge.

Research in the classroom with a view to evidence-based practice is undoubtedly 'a good thing', but in order to give it significance, it needs to have meaning and relate to ideas outside that particular classroom. If not, we are in danger of constantly reinventing the wheel. There are a number of implications arising from this point:

1. Teachers must read and be aware of the work and research of others, whether academics outside the classroom or other teachers. This will inform not only the conclusions drawn from the work but, perhaps more importantly the questions asked in the first place. This relates of course very closely to teachers' perceptions of the value of theory.

2. Teachers must have a forum for disseminating their work. In the first instance of course this should be to colleagues within their own school. It is my experience that most teachers stumble at this first hurdle as there is no infrastructure within many schools for the dissemination of knowledge. Secondly, if the work is to be truly influential, it needs to be shared with others in the field of education outside the immediate school – not just teachers from nearby institutions, but also all those in the wider education community. This could be achieved through publication in journals, professional association magazines or conference papers for example; indeed any opportunity to engage others in thinking about an educational issue that may result in long term change rather than a short term 'fix' would be important, not just for others, but for teacher researchers themselves.

3. The manner in which work is disseminated will have an effect not only on whether it is read by the appropriate audience, but also how it is used. Fisher and Selinger (1992) alert us to the dangers of a 'bolt on' adoption of recommendations without any understanding of the philosophy or aims underpinning the work, making it therefore difficult to make judgements about whether or not it is appropriate to their children or contexts. As Carr and Kemmis point out 'Practices are changed by changing the ways in which they are understood' (Carr and Kemmis 1989, p. 91 in Aelberry and Golby 1995, p. 11), not simply by employing new techniques. Attention must therefore be paid to the methods of dissemination in relation to audience.

4. Teachers should have opportunities for seeking accreditation for their work outside the TTA framework with its instrumental goals. These should include Masters level awards that value not only the practical, but also the intellectual – that challenge and address 'why?' questions, not just 'how?' and 'what?' questions. This would involve a shift in perception from both academics and teachers. Firstly, it calls for 'Masters degrees that take practice seriously' (Golby ibid.). Pring puts it thus:

Academic respectability must be found in professional relevance, but that requires not only space and time for teachers to be academic but also a re-examination of what it means to be academic.

(Pring 1991 in Golby 1994, p. 72)

This is an issue, of course, in that it could be interpreted as a call for 'downgrading' the standard of Masters level work. Goodson points out the dangers:

The advocacy of practice driven theory marks an attempt to drive theory onto a particular highway, possibly a narrow one with many cul-de-sacs on either side

(Goodson 1997, p. 7)

Rather than denying the importance of practice, he recommends that work should move between 'theoretical pre-occupation' and 'practical predilection' in ways that challenge both (Goodson ibid.).

What is also required is a shift in perception by teachers about the value of theory and its contribution to practice, not just in improving performance for specific teachers in specific classrooms, but in challenging and developing ideas and insights within the education profession as a whole. This seems particularly important for early years teachers, if we are to convincingly withstand such crass ideas as the 'mums' army' proposal and the devaluation of teachers of young children that that implied.

5. We need to reconceive our understanding of the purpose of CPD. Fullan in 1991 suggested that the ultimate aim of in-service training should be:

less to implement a specific innovation or policy and more to create individual and organisational habits and structures that make continuous learning a valued and endemic part of the culture of schools and teaching.

(in English 1995, p. 305)

This in turn has implications for the evaluation of CPD and the demand for tangible outcomes as evidence of effectiveness. Eraut in 1987 (in Havland, Kinder and Keys 1993) advised that there should be a distinction made between INSET evaluation which should focus on the link between INSET and teachers' attitudes and behaviour, and school-based evaluation which should focus on the link between school policy and practice and pupils' attitudes and achievements. This seems to be an important distinction which we ignore at our peril.

Finally, all these recommendations point to the importance of maintaining the crucial links between Higher Education and schools. For the good of the profession, all of us involved in education should foster the challenging dynamic between 'theoretical pre-occupation' and 'practical predilection' (Goodson ibid., p. 9). As Taylor observed:

> any profession whose essential theoretical and practical knowledge does not have a high place in universities and other institutions of higher education, must count itself deprived and, in the long run, be diminished in status.
>
> (Taylor 1987 in Goodson ibid.)

Issues

1. How prescriptive should a government be over

   a) curriculum content, and
   b) teaching methods or styles?

2. To what extent would you agree that theory has become degenerated in recent years? What are the indicators in your own professional context of this trend and what are the long-term implications?

3. How realistic or desirable is it to evaluate the success of CPD by measurement of outcomes in the classroom?

References

Aelberry, F. and Golby, M. (1995) Doing an Improper Dissertation: Academic and Professional Relationships. *Teacher Development*, May, pp. 5–12.

DES (1987) *LEA Training Grants Scheme: Monitoring and Evaluation DES Note* London: HMSO

DfE (1993) Circular 14/93 The Initial Training of Primary School Teachers: New criteria for courses.

English, R. (1995) INSET: initiating change or merely supporting it? *British Journal of In-service Education*, Vol. 21, No. 3, pp. 295–301.

Fisher, E. and Selinger, M. (1992) Teachers and researchers: Practical constraints and possible approaches towards an effective partnership. *Teacher Development*, October, pp. 175–81.

Golby, M. (1994) Doing a Proper Course: The present crisis in advanced courses. *Teacher Development*, May, pp. 69–73.

Goodson, I. (1997) 'Trendy Theory' and Teacher Professionalism. Cambridge Journal of Education, Vol. 27, No. 1, pp. 7–22.

Graham, J. (1996) The Teacher Training Agency, Continuing Professional Development Policy and the Definition of Com-petences for Serving Teachers. *British Journal of In-service Education*, Vol. 22, No. 2, pp. 121–132.

Hargreaves, D. H. (1996) Teaching as research-based profession: possibilities and prospects, TTA Annual lecture. London: TTA.

Harland, J., Kinder, K. and Keys, W. (1993) *Restructuring INSET: Privatisation and its alternatives*. Slough: NFER.

Hayes, D. (Ed) (1996) *Debating Education: issues for the new millenium?* Department of Education: Canterbury Christ Church College.

HEFCE (1995) Circular 27/95 *Redistribution of HEFCE Funding for teaching in the academic Year 1995–6*. Bristol: HEFCE.

Kyriakides, L. (1997) Influences on Primary Teachers' Practice: some problems for curriculum change theory. *British Educational Research Journal*, Vol. 23, No. 1.

Morrison, M. (1992) Time for INSET, Time to Teach: Evaluating school-based development in an infants school during a period of change. *Teacher Development*, October, pp. 157–169.

Richards, C. (1997) The Primary curriculum 1988–2008. *British Journal of Curriculum and Assessment*, Vol. 7 No. 3, pp. 6–8.

Stenhouse, L. (1975) *An Introduction to Curriculum Research and Development* London: Heinemann.

TTA (1996) *Corporate plan*. London: TTA.

Woodilla, J., Boscardin, M.L. and Dodds, P. (1997) Time for Elementary Educators' Professional Development. *Teaching and Teacher Education*, Vol. 13, No. 3, pp. 295–309.

12

Inspections of under fives' education and constructions of early childhood

Tricia David and Angela Nurse

Following the previous government's inception of a voucher scheme to enable the parents of four year olds to access free nursery provision for them, all settings which wished to become recognised for the redeeming of vouchers for cash were expected to undergo inspections of their educational provision. The mixed nature of UK preschool provision has been well described elsewhere (see, for example, David 1993; Pugh 1988). The types of settings which became eligible to redeem vouchers included maintained and private nurseries, preschools/playgroups and reception classes. Although childminders are now welcomed as part of the new Labour Government's local authority Nursery Partnerships, they were discounted under the previous regime, as not constituting 'group provision' unless two or three childminders banded together (to form a playgroup of sorts).

All the private and voluntary settings are inspected every year by local authority social services departments, under regulations according to the Children Act 1989. Schools do not normally come under this regulation. Further, the private and voluntary nurseries involved in the funded provision for four year olds outlined above are regulated by inspections arising as a result of the 1996 Nursery Education and Grant Maintained Schools Act; the inspectors who carry out this work have qualified under different conditions and training from those of the primary inspectors. Classes for children under five in maintained schools are inspected by Ofsted teams at the same time as the 5-11 classes and maintained nursery schools are also subject to inspections by Ofsted's primary inspectors.

When the nursery inspections were first mooted, they were subjected to a discourse of derision by some members of the press. The 'light touch' which was intended to typify their approach was interpreted as 'letting providers off lightly' – more lightly than those in the

165

maintained sector, who were subjected to the scrutiny of 'proper Ofsted inspectors' (Ensing 1996).

In this chapter we intend to 'read between the lines', to examine some of the evidence available concerning the two types of educational inspections of provision for children under five, in order to pose important questions about the expectations and demands our society currently places on small children, their parents and educators.

There are many aspects which could be considered, for example, in their reports Ofsted (1997c, 1998) point to: the need for staff in all types of settings to increase their knowledge and understanding of the six areas of learning, particularly that concerning *knowledge and understanding of the world;* and particularly technology and information technology; for curriculum planning to be more thorough and focused on the *Desirable Outcomes* (SCAA 1996); for a review of the policy of admitting four year olds to reception classes and the monitoring of such provision; for greater account to be taken of the Code of Practice for Special Educational Needs (SEN) (DfE 1994); For the planning and provision of outdoor activities to be improved. Further, Ofsted (ibid) suggests that the highest proportion of weaknesses in promoting the *Desirable Outcomes* in the areas of *language and literacy, mathematics* and *knowledge and understanding of the world* exists in the playgroups (although there are strengths and weaknesses in all types of settings). The 1998 Ofsted report, drawing on inspection evidence, states that while providers are aware of the Code of Practice for SEN, they are not universally confident in identifying the stages used by the Code, with the result that planning is of variable quality.

For their earlier report (Ofsted 1997a), the inspectors had actually carried out some inspections of reception classes using the nursery inspection framework (Ofsted 1997c is the second edition of this document), whereas for the second report (Ofsted 1998) evidence from the inspections carried out by Registered Nursery Inspectors was compared with that from inspection reports published following maintained sector inspections. The 1998 report also signals up the intention of Ofsted to further consider issues in reception classes.

Comparing the results

So what is the reality? Are the voluntary and private/independent nursery providers being let off more lightly than those in the maintained sectors? Or, looking at the issues from a slightly different perspective, are children in different sectors experiencing different childhoods? (Chapters related to this include David (in this volume), and David and Powell in *Young Children Learning*).

For the work reported in this chapter, we decided to subject two sets of inspection reports to scrutiny and relate their contents to other key publications concerning the education of children under five years. We gathered 24 inspection reports from maintained schools where children under five years old were being educated, which had been included in the Chief Inspectors list of 'excellent schools' for 1997. We ensured that our sample of inspection reports was drawn from the different regions but limited the research to England. We then gathered an equivalent number of nursery inspection reports from an equivalent geographical spread and included only those which had been designated in the 'top group' – that is, they were to be reinspected in two to four years. (Note: none of these is identified in the text in order to maintain the anonymity of the schools and nurseries involved in the sample.)

By analysing the two sets of reports, we began to see a picture emerging which contained a number of different messages. In this chapter we will limit ourselves to the messages concerning 1) play as a vehicle for young children's learning; and 2) the education of children under five years with special educational needs.

Play and learning in the early years

The early pioneers of nursery education, such as Owen, Froebel, Montessori, Steiner, McMillan and Isaacs, who have influenced practice in the West over two centuries, clearly concluded play to be an important vehicle for learning for young children. More recently research (see for example, Sylva 1994; 1998) has lent support to their conclusions. In her book *Just playing?* Moyles (1989) discusses the way in which learning through play involves a spiral of engaging with knowledgeable others (in a meaningful, Vygotskian, social and instructional interaction), interspersed with free play periods in which the new skills and knowledge are practised, experimented with and 'owned'.

In their 1990 publication about the education of children under five, HMI (DES 1990) demonstrated key principles underpinning such provision. These included:

- the important role of parents as primary educators;
- curricular breadth and balance;
- purposeful play;
- equality of opportunity;
- the knowledge, concepts, skills and attitudes in different areas of

learning. In other words, inspectors were in no doubt that play constitutes a key vehicle for learning.

Four years later, Ofsted (1993) used data from its inspections of schools to examine provision for four year olds in reception classes. In their conclusion to that report the inspectors claimed that in the best classes for such young children there was a balance between teaching and learning practices that were teacher-directed and play, which was child-directed:

> In the poorer classes teachers over-directed work and under-directed play. They used play as a reward for finishing work or as an occupational holding device. By contrast, in the effective classes play was used positively to develop children's abilities across a wide range of activities.
>
> (Ofsted 1993, para. 25)

Since that time it has been difficult to find the word *play* in any of the English documents published as guidelines or frameworks for providers or for inspectors. For example, in the English version of SCAA's (1996) *Desirable Outcomes* document, we find the opening page stating:

> INTRODUCTION
> This document is for people who work with children of pre-compulsory school age across the full range of provision in the private, voluntary and maintained sectors in England. Separate documentation applies to Wales. The desirable outcomes are goals for learning for children by the time they enter compulsory education. They emphasise early literacy, numeracy and the development of personal and social skills and contribute to children's knowledge, understanding and skills in other areas . . .
>
> (SCAA 1996, p. 1)

Meanwhile, colleagues in the same types of settings, in Wales, were being urged to consider:

> Pan feddwn dalent plentyn
> I weld llais a chlywed llun . . .
>
> (When I had a child's talent to see a voice and hear an image . . .)
> Introduction
> In the opening lines of his epic poem Afon (The River) Gerallt Lloyd Owen longs for the magic of early childhood. It is the time when the world is there to be explored and the adventure of discovery is all around.
>
> (Curriculum and Assessment Authority for Wales 1996, p. 1)

In addition to these contrasting introductory sections to guidelines about young children's learning, the Welsh paper includes explicit comment advocating play in a section devoted to 'the importance of play' (Curriculum and Assessment Authority for Wales 1996, p.2). Nothing of this nature is included in the English guidelines, play gaining simply a cursory mention (SCAA 1996).

What are we to make of the stark contrast in approach reflected in the two sets of documentation? Are young children in Wales so different from young children in England? Or is it that national expectations, in other words the constructions of childhood, implicit in this documentation are different and if so, why? What messages are being transmitted to educators and parents about governmental policy and thinking for and about children aged under five?

It would seem that for the under fives in England in the 1990s childhood is to be less playful, less celebrated, less creative, less romantic, more pressurised, more serious, more confined, more directed (especially in relation to literacy and numeracy) than early childhood in Wales or most of the other European countries and than the childhoods experienced by their own parents. Yet strangely, research evidence shows that early formalisation actually has a negative effect on children's later academic and emotional progress and play is also important if the country is to produce creative entrepreneurs (Sylva 1998).

In addition to this, while being told that the English version of the *Desirable Outcomes* (SCAA 1996) does not constitute a curriculum, it is difficult to see how one is to avoid such an interpretation, a point other writers have asserted (for example, Anning 1995). Private and voluntary providers of nursery educational settings for four year olds are taking as their learning objectives for planning the sets of statements identifiable in the six paragraphs referring to *Personal and Social Development; Language and Literacy; Mathematics; Knowledge and Understanding of the World; Physical Development;* and *Creative Development*. This is hardly surprising, since the Registered Nursery Inspectors must use these in their search for evidence that a setting is promoting the children's ability to meet the *Desirable Outcomes* listed (Ofsted 1997a).

While Registered Nursery Inspectors work in the voluntary and private sectors, Ofsted Section 9 (of the 1992 Education Act) inspectors cover classes for children under five in maintained nursery and primary schools. Could it be that different childhoods are being experienced in the different settings, differing constructions of childhood being applied, legitimising even further the narrowing of opportunities for young children because 'real school' is seen as best?

Add to this all the other narrowly directed initiatives, such as the Literacy and Numeracy hours in Year R, which (even though this may not have been the intention) seem bound to have a similar, worksheet mentality impact to those Sylva *et al.* (1992) found in certain nurseries at the time the National Curriculum was being implemented and one appreciates how difficult it will be to ensure that children under five in England enjoy a broad and balanced curriculum with the aims 'wellbeing; belonging; contribution; communication; and exploration', the aims of the *Te Whariki* (New Zealand) early years curriculum, or the philosophy, concerning curriculum planning, for the young children in the Italian region of Emilia-Romagna, of Loris Malaguzzi summed up as

> our schools have not had, nor do they have, a planned curriculum with units and sub-units (lesson plans) as the behaviourists would like. These would push our schools towards teaching without learning; we would humiliate the schools and the children by entrusting them to forms, dittos and handbooks . . . the school for young children has to respond to the child.
>
> (Edwards *et al.* 1993, p. 85)

In Reggio Emilia children are seen as curious, loving, creative, eager to express themselves through a plurality of symbolic languages. They hold an image of the child as 'rich, strong, and powerful' (Rinaldi in Edwards *et al.* 1993, p. 102).

Not only is the joyless, 'input-output' model of the current approach for English provision one which is a daunting prospect for our four year olds, it has very worrying consequences for children under four. As preschool staff become sensitive to how children they have provided for 'perform' in Baseline Assessment tests, we seem likely to see a growth in 'teaching to the tests' by both parents and early childhood educators.

So at the same time as we offer support and training to attempt to limit the damage, we might also fruitfully explore ideas from other countries, such as Hungary and Denmark, where the children's later reading attainment is higher than that in England but their early education emphasises first hand experience and play, **not** early writing, reading and mathematical notation. Mills (1998) compiled strong evidence that too early formalisation damages children's later educational achievements. She claims that expecting all children to be capable of writing their own names, some letters, etc., by the time they begin Year R is forcing something which children will acquire very quickly a couple of years later. Her case is highly persuasive, especially when one observes how much of a young child's day can be taken up with laboriously, perhaps for some even painfully, trying to satisfy an adult's requirement to record a bland statement of 'news' or its equivalent.

On the other hand, there is powerful evidence from other research in England and Australia (Hall 1987; Reynolds 1997) that, given the opportunity to use the necessary tools for recording and the incentives to engage through play in emergent, child-directed literacy most under fives will take over the process and request more materials, resources and information. Their drive to communicate in many different ways, to use 'a hundred languages', and their enthusiasm for the tasks they set themselves lead one to think this empowers children. In both the publications cited above, the children are portrayed as rich, strong, and powerful. Perhaps both Mill's (ibid.) carefully structured approaches to developing attending, listening and memory skills, combined with skills fostering appropriate group behaviour, spoken language and phonological awareness, and motor skills, together with opportunities for emergent literacy engagement in the widest sense are needed.

However, if we are to continue to promote a play-based approach to early years education, we must also pay heed to the evidence that even those regarded as highly skilled practitioners fail to capitalise fully on the educational potential of play (Bennett *et al.* 1997). What is fascinating about the conclusions reached by Bennett's team (ibid.) is that they suggest teacher inset should take the form of supported action research, with inputs providing new research knowledge – a model very similar to that reached not only in the Goldsmiths project (Blenkin *et al.* 1995) but also the model practised half a day a week in Reggio Emilia.

What then is happening in under fives' education? Is a play-based curriculum in evidence in English early years education, or is it being transformed as a result of the pressure from other sectors and the National Curriculum and concomitant initiatives, and because parents are anxious for their children's test results on entry to school and they assume early formalisation to be the answer? Or can we even tell whether self-directed play takes up a significant proportion of time in an under five's day, because the evidence of inspection reports uses language which rules out the word *play*? And if so, why? Should we be concerned about the ultimate effects of imposed terminology (Nutbrown 1998)? Certainly we would be wise to question overly formalised teaching sessions, which the 'new' terminology might encourage, for any significant proportion of the day for children under five – in fact, probably for children under eight. In their survey of the issue, Blenkin and Kelly proposed that the concept of infancy 'must be resurrected before it is too late' (Blenkin and Kelly 1994, p.9). Are educators feeling pressed into treating two, three and four year olds as if they were five, or seven year olds 'with their legs cut off'?[1]

Play in under fives' classrooms in the maintained sector schools and in the voluntary and private sector nurseries

A documentary analysis of 24 reports of inspections of classes for children under five years old in maintained primary, first or nursery schools, which were carried out according to Section 9 of the Education Act (Schools) 1992, revealed that *play* is rarely mentioned. In some instances it is clear that the inspection team has been led by, or included, an inspector with expertise in the early years and although *play* is still relatively infrequently used to describe children's learning activities, other phrases (for example, *learn by exploration, lively and interesting practical work*) and the ways in which young children's joy and enthusiasm are allowed to shine through the descriptions, convey the play-type, experiential nature of the pedagogy. In one case, an inspector criticises provision for the youngest children (despite the fact that all 24 reports were of schools listed by Ofsted as excellent in 1997):

> where teaching is unsatisfactory it does not fully take into account the characteristics and specific learning needs of very young children.

At another point in the report this team also criticised the use of some inappropriate worksheets they had observed in an under fives' classroom.

Meanwhile, in the 24 inspection reports for the voluntary and private sector provision for four year olds (inspected according to Section 5 of the 1996 Education and Grant Maintained Schools Act), there is almost twice the number of uses of the word *play* to describe children's learning activities. In all, the total frequency of use in the 24 maintained sector reports is only 49, in the voluntary and private sector the total frequency is 89, making the averages for comparison 2.0:3.7 maintained sector:voluntary and private sector. However, when

---

[1] This was a favourite phrase used by Gwen Stubbs when she was Early Years Inspector for Staffordshire. It was used to bring home to practitioners the special nature of very young children's learning and the cruelty and stupidity of using inappropriate teaching methods.

the number of pages presented as reports for each sector are taken into account the frequency rating is reversed. The loss of the word 'play' from discourse of nursery education may be heralded by these inspection reports. Further, this difference in terminology certainly raises questions about the possibility that children are now experiencing very different constructions of 'being four'.

Perhaps inspectors are pressed into using certain terms by the guidance for the two types of inspection (Ofsted 1995, 1997c, 1998)? It is, after all, difficult to find the word *play* in the guidance documents, though it must be said that in the two publications providing guidance for voluntary and private provision *play* is used – for example:

A well-planned programme of personal and social development helps children work, play and co-operate with others.
(Ofsted 1997c, p. 37; Ofsted 1998, p. 41)

A positive interpretation of this use of euphemisms would be the difficulty many parents have in understanding that their children can learn through play activities which are skilfully offered, encouraged, observed and sometimes extended by adults aware of the possibilities and of the rationale for them. However, there is a danger that the formalised language will lead to alternative interpretations of what young children should be doing for the majority of their time in nursery education.

Too early formalisation?

Although it is important to beware of importing too easily the practices and policies for young children adopted in other countries, the study by Mills (1998) has raised many important questions concerning over formalised early childhood education. Play, or playful approaches to learning have a number of advantages. These include:

- the children's intrinsic motivation and curiosity to engage;

- the self-posed 'questions' of play activity are meaningful and relevant to the child (or children) involved;

- there are usually many possibilities in play, rather than a 'right answer' to be sought, so play is non-threatening, although it is often challenging;

- 'ownership' and control of the situation by the learners strengthens both motivation and learning;

- the 'what if' quality of play encourages creativity; rules can be invented and broken (see Chapter 2 in this volume by Teresa Grainger and Kathy Goouch on children's playful subversion of adults' agendas);

- much play is social, encouraging interpersonal skills, although it can be solitary;
- different forms of play exercise the body and the mind – especially allowing for both sides of the brain to be developed. As Tina Bruce says, play is 'an integrating mechanism, which brings together all we learn, know, feel and understand' (Bruce 1991, p. 60);
- play is pleasurable!

Under fives with special educational needs

The Education Act 1981, strengthened by the Code of Practice (DfE 1994), specifically highlighted local authorities' duty to provide for children under five whose learning difficulty (or difficulties) call for special provision to be made. The Code of Practice (DfE 1994) suggests a child has a learning difficulty if he or she:

a) has a significantly greater difficulty in learning than the majority of children of the same age
b) has a disability which either prevents or hinders the child from making use of educational facilities of a kind provided for children of the same age in schools within the area of the local authority
c) is under five and falls within the definition at (a) or (b) above or would do if special educational provision was not made for the child . . .

Special educational provision means:
(a) for a child over two, educational provision which is additional to, or otherwise different from, the educational provision made generally for children of the child's age in maintained schools, other than special schools, in the area
(b) for a child under two, educational provision of any kind. (Section 156)

(DfEE 1994, par 2.1)

The Children Act 1989 broadened the definition to include 'children in need' and to impose duties on all local authorities, including education departments, to provide for these children. This has been interpreted variously across the UK, generally according to the provision already available, rather than reviewing and extending existing provision to meet the needs of such under fives specifically. In some areas this has increased the LEAs' reliance on voluntary, and sometimes private, provision substantially. These sectors have responded by including children with special needs alongside their local peer group or by creating specific sessions for children with developmental delays, disabilities or behaviour problems. They have frequently taken on children whose difficulties have been complex and challenging to understand and manage. Often these are the very children other providers have been wary of admitting, at least not without substantial support both in financial and 'people' terms. Additionally, the staff in such settings take on a family coming to terms with the child's difficulties and consequently, often distressed, frustrated and understandably angry (Herbert 1994).

Many professionals with long years of training and perhaps many years' experience find these situations problematic, even when there is appropriate personal and professional support.

Despite the importance of their role, many playgroups and nurseries have had to carry out their work in isolation. Many work calmly and efficiently, liaising with and taking on tasks suggested by advisory teachers, therapists, and psychologists. They make contact with local assessment centres and schools, attending review meetings, and providing progress reports – all for a fraction of the costs of placement somewhere more specialised. As Wolfendale writes (1997), 'The nursery/playgroup/day care practitioners play a significant "front line" in keeping close, detailed records on children which constitute the basis from which more "specialised" assessment can take place'.

So in spite of the lack of training, what are the benefits of the current situation, particularly if a truly holistic view of the child's (amd the family's) development is taken? Firstly, playgroups are local. They give parents, and often the extended family, a chance to become embedded within the local community and to develop friendships and links as children grow. These links may have been difficult to forge for families working away from their own communities, extended families and childhood homes. The staff who work in playgroups are usually members of the community. They are also, usually, very approachable. So there can be a sense of 'working through this together' which may not be so easy to achieve if a barrier is set up through an intervention perceived as 'professional knowledge and expertise' (Carpenter and Herbert 1997). Parents can have more control over the situation and so become confident in taking decisions and making choices. The most overwhelming reason for inclusion in some form of mainstream provision is that, for many children, this may be the only opportunity they have to learn and grow alongside their peers. Children learn as much from their interaction with other children as they do from adults. They learn not just formal skills but how to operate in the wider world with its own set of rules and expectations. They can learn to socialise and negotiate, to care more for themselves and make choices in a situation that can be structured to give them access to opportunities available to *all* children of the same age or stage. It can allow children choice to initiate and carry through their activities, rather than to be constantly adult-directed. As Herbert and Moir (1996, p. 56) affirm, 'it is the right of all children to be given the opportunity to grow, to play, to socialize and to learn alongside their friends within their local community'.

As the whole 'voucher' system and its requirements were being introduced, one of the most heated debates concerned those children with special needs who attended voluntary or private settings. These arguments were not only based upon supporting the children financially through the voucher funding but also on the nature of the curriculum they would follow and the expected outcomes for each individual. As Wolfendale (1997) argues, hardly any texts are currently available concerning this area.

The *Desirable Outcomes for children's learning* (SCAA 1996) contains little that is specific but does include a paragraph in its introduction concerning children with special educational needs which indicates that they may continue towards achieving these outcomes throughout their school years. The paragraph also highlights alternative means of communication. The six areas of learning do not contain any specific references to children with special needs but the common features of the 'good practice' section includes references to assessment, planning, and recording progress, working with parents, liaison with other agencies and carers, and training. Within this is the expectation that 'early identification of children's particular needs leads to appropriate intervention and support' (SCAA 1996, p. 6).

As a response to the criticism that this was not detailed enough to support and safeguard those with special needs, SCAA (now QCA – Qualifications and Curriculum Authority) responded by advising those settings choosing to join the voucher scheme to use the Code of Practice (DfE 1994) and Registered Nursery Inspectors were instructed to view what they were seeing in all settings in the light of these guidelines.

The complete Code of Practice (DfE 1994) is a complex, detailed document, which many education authorities and schools had recently implemented amid much torment and anxiety. A shortened version was circulated to the nursery settings – but this nevertheless exhorted providers to take account of the full Code, which was also supplied in nursery information packs. Although the voucher scheme ended with the installation of the new government in May 1997, the *Desirable Outcomes for Children's Learning* (SCAA 1996), the inspection system and the requirements concerning young children with special educational needs still stand.

The DfEE (1997a) guidance on using the Code of Practice in nurseries highlighted the need for planning to have regard for the principles set out in the Code, as well as recognising that staff in nursery settings would need training to enable them to do so. As always, the source of this training and who is to fund it is not made clear. Settings have had to arrange much of their training for themselves, using what is available locally, rather than being able to link with any nationally co-ordinated scheme. The commitment and quality which many have been able to achieve for themselves have formed part of the inspection evidence, particularly in those groups whose special needs provision and practice have been highlighted as good. Ofsted has recently reported on a survey of twenty-one institutions, statutory, private and voluntary, and concluded that 'curricular provision for, and the early identification of, children's special educational needs promotes the Desirable Learning Outcomes in over three-quarters of all institutions', although not all settings were confident yet in identifying children's specific needs, linking these to the stages set out in the Code of Practice and then planning how to meet these needs (Ofsted 1998). This is a complex process and one which experienced schools can find difficult, particularly for very young children who have developmental as well as curricular needs.

In contrast to the results concerning *play* from the two sets of inspection reports we analysed, those relating to provision for children with special educational needs seem to concur with the inspectors' own survey (Ofsted 1997a). There appears to be powerful evidence for training for voluntary and private providers, to develop their ability to offer better support to children with learning difficulties. However, the inspectors themselves, with a few exceptions, seem to lack the ability to write anything which is detailed enough to offer providers pointers from which they can learn. In almost every case the Registered Nursery Inspector's report on a group's provision for children with SEN is a single line. In contrast, the reports on the maintained sector usually contain several paragraphs concerning special educational needs in a school, with a variety of points in each, for example, one maintained sector report states:

There are five pupils with statements of special educational needs (SEN) for whom extra support is provided. A further 27 pupils are identified on the SEN register.

The school has shown its commitment to pupils with learning difficulties by allocating funds for additional specialist teaching support . . . Documentation is fully maintained and parents are involved . . . Pupils' progress is being monitored effectively through individual action plans . . . Well-trained specialist assistants are appropriately deployed. . .

There is a comprehensive policy for SEN with good management . . . good links with support agencies and services . . . good balance of support strategies helps to maintain pupils' confidence and sef-esteem. Early assessments are used as indicators of pupils likely to need additional support. All staff co-operate closely to provide a coherent and effective programme of support.

While these are longer than the RgNI reports, these paragraphs would still only give a minimal idea of what the setting in question (or another using the report as guidelines) might do to improve provision for children with special needs. So while the frequency of comment was the reverse of the earlier analysis on *play*, since the maintained provision received 81 paragraphs of comment (total in 24 reports) and the voluntary and private sector reports contained only 44 sentences (total in 24 reports), there is still much to be done to improve both the provision itself – across the board – and to improve the ways in which inspectors' comments can contribute to that improvement.

Our review of the 48 inspection reports' *special needs* sections reveals a lack of detail and depth to the analysis of good practice and provision. A number of fundamental difficulties occur in discussing children's needs at this stage. One of these has been the meaning of the phrase 'early identification'. This can be defined as either early in a child's life or early in a child's school career. The consequent interpretation obviously impacts upon the sort of assessment made, the resulting programme and the resources needed to support the child. Another has been the confusion between 'special needs' and 'special educational needs'. A child with special needs does not necessarily have, or go on to develop, educational needs if the need is appropriately and sensitively handled. Yet another difficulty is that much of the estimation of the number of children with special needs in early years settings, particularly for early inspections, depended upon the number of children with a statement rather than understanding and using the stage approach advocated by the Code of Practice. Using statements to establish under-fives' needs masks the number of children who may need specific support at this stage. It also obscures the difference between providing a developmentally appropriate curriculum and one based on the early stages of the National Curriculum where children may not have the underlying competencies and skills to ensure success. Inspection evidence from schools highlights this. Not all reports on schools which admit children under five include a section on the early years or under-fives. Even in those that do, special needs is rarely mentioned specifically or in any depth. Usually 'good practice' is highlighted or links with other agencies are mentioned. General sections on special educational needs provision rarely pinpoint the under-fives. Sometimes 'early identification' is mentioned, but without defining clearly the meaning of this. Nursery school inspections, by their very nature, include a section on special needs but again interpretation is coloured by the dependence of the system on statement figures to establish need. This is also apparent for nursery inspections in the voluntary and private sectors where 'not applicable' frequently appears. Little consistent detail is given of the procedures, systems and teaching methods used to prepare for and support these children and give them access to the curriculum. Partly this is a reflection of the often incomplete understanding that people involved with very young children, including those in a professional capacity, have of the complexity of needs in the very young, how to assess them and then how to support and monitor them. Wilson (1998) recognises this early in her book where she writes:

> Children with special needs vary tremendously. Not only do they have the same type of variances as the general population (e.g., different interests, likes, dislikes, temperaments, abilities, etc.), they also vary by type and extent of disability.
>
> (Wilson 1998, p. 7)

None of the inspection reports considered mentioned differentiation or considered how special educational needs were met in a curricular context, whatever form the curriculum took. Conversely no exceptional practice was described. Most used acceptance of the Code of Practice as a catchall rather than a starting point.

For the future, much more training needs to be done at *all* levels if Early Years Development Plans (DfEE 1998) are to meet fully the needs of all children within their area of concern and the inspection system is to ensure that provision is not only good but equitable and open to all children.

Conclusions

In this chapter we have attempted to 'read between the lines' of two sets of inspection reports – 24 concerning provision for children under five in maintained schools deemed excellent by Ofsted and 24 nurseries in the voluntary and private sectors which were graded in the 'top' category (to be reinspected in two to four years). In particular, we have discussed two areas where the entitlement of some of our children may be threatened. Firstly, we have explored the potential demise of play as the vehicle for learning, and secondly, we have discussed the need for more support for early childhood educators working with children with special educational needs.

The new Nursery Partnerships and the unprecedented focus on comprehensive early years services is such an optimistic development that we must ensure it is successful for the children themselves, as well as for other stakeholders. The inspection system can be a very positive aspect of that success and of the development of high quality edu-care provision for all. The main areas which need reform – and most are currently being evaluated in this respect – are:

- inspections of reception classes;
- extra training concerning special educational needs for all inspectors relating to early years settings;
- coordination of the Social Services Children Act inspections and the Registered Nursery Education inspections;
- a more supportive culture around early years inspections;
- the education and training of early years practitioners to work together in this field so that they can not only develop the quality the inspections are intended to seek, but they feel confident to articulate the problems raised by inappropriate aspects of the inspection framework and system.

An additional call for a review of Ofsted's powers has also come from the Better Regulation Task Force, who are challenging the agency's lead role in the inspection of 'childcare' settings (Ghouri 1998).

The Standards Fund, funding allocated to local authorities for inservice training, includes in 1998-99 a substantial tranche for under fives providers and since one area of priority is special educational needs it is to be hoped that specialists will work with educators to develop and professionalise their caring approaches, so helping them be even more effective – though in a way which does not mean their professionalisation begins to erode their approachable, 'working through the difficulties together' style!

Following their research with teachers about learning through play, Wood and Attfield (1996, p. 93) argue that:

> In early childhood education there is a tendency to regard all that children do in their play through rose-tinted glasses. The reality can be rather different.

and they suggest

> Educators can also create play/learning environments which reflect their own intentions but at the same time are responsive to children's intentions. Awareness of children's intentions can only come about through a curriculum model which encourages them to express those intentions and to fulfil them . . . where enabling structures are used, play can become more than just an occupational activity which is relegated to the margins of the school day. Educators can make valuable connections between children's ongoing cognitive concerns and the forms of knowledge which serve as an organising structure for curriculum content.
>
> (Ibid, p. 88)

The reduction of the use of the term *play*, because it is often misunderstood or denigrated, may have had honourable beginnings. The inspections of under fives' establishments were intended to raise the status of early childhood education (Ensing 1996) and they do have the capacity to raise the standards of provision, if all work together to make the process a constructive one. However, it is important to signal some anxiety at the apparent disappearance of *play* from the vocabulary of early childhood educators and inspectors, since it may be another marker that childhood is being changed in England. It could seem that to be taken seriously early learning must stop being fun (when in fact quite the reverse should be true!). Other developments (such as statutory homework for young children) draw attention to the growing similarity with the intense, future/work-oriented childhoods of Japanese children. Anthropological studies of Japanese childhood (James 1998) have argued that in Japan childhood is protected as a separate phase of life but it is a childhood full of study, homework and anxiety, its aim being the production of future workers.

Meanwhile, in her survey of research evidence, Sylva (1998) shows how over-formalisation in the early years has not only damaging effects on academic progress, it has long term emotional consequences and costs too. While the government's aim of a literate and numerate nation is laudable and to be supported, perhaps they should exercise some caution in how their strategies affect early childhood education, since presumably they do not want a literate, numerate nation whose emotional illnesses prevent them from working or contributing to the 'common good'.

Making meaning for young children, especially those with learning difficulties, must be based on the learner's own experience and on the sense they have made of earlier experiences with parents and carers in their home settings. To be suddenly plunged into a setting where someone tells you what to do, and the 'doing' that is expected is largely in terms of forms of communication using symbolic representation, may be a leap too far for many children in this age group. Young children are highly capable thinkers but to ask them to engage in tasks which are irrelevant and meaningless is just a waste of their precious time, because they need other activities as foundations (Willes 1983). Research shows overly adult-directed approaches to be counter productive in the long run (Sylva 1998).

As Wood and Attfield comment in their discussion of the ideas of Bruner and Vygotsky and justification for play:

> Newman and Holzman (1993) have argued that play can be seen as a revolutionary activity because it is concerned with learning leading to development and meaning-making, either in individual or in collective zones of proximal development. This has led us to question whether play is inadequately represented in the curriculum partly because its significance is not fully understood but partly because we are wary of its revolutionary nature.
>
> (Wood and Attfield 1996, p. 73)

Issues

1. How could the nursery inspection systems (by Social Services Officers/Inspectors, Registered Nursery Inspectors, and Ofsted Inspectors) be rationalised to be equitable to providers but to improve quality assurance for parents/carers and children?
2. Reflect on a play incident you have observed (or use the examples from earlier chapters in this volume, for example, Chapters 2, 3 or 4) and think of a variety of extensions which adults could have provided through intervention, to further the children's learning but maintain the playfulness of the incident.
3. What types of comment by inspectors would be constructive in relation to appropriate support for children with special educational needs?

References

Anning, A. (1995) *The Key Stage Zero Curriculum: a response to the SCAA Draft Proposals on pre-school education* London: ATL.

Bennett, N., Wood, L. and Rogers, S. (1997) *Teaching Through Play* Buckingham: Open University Press.

Blamires, M., Robertson, C. and Blamires, J. (1997) *Parent-Teacher Partnership*; London: David Fulton.

Blenkin, G. and Kelly, A. V. (1994) The death of infancy. *Education 3–13* Vol. 22, 2, pp. 3–9.

Blenkin, G., Hurst, V., Whitehead, M. and Yue, N.Y.L. (1995) *Principles into practice: improving the quality of children's early learning* London: Goldsmiths' College, University of London.

Bruce, T. (1991) *Time to play in early childhood* Sevenoaks: Hodder and Stoughton.

Campion J (1992) *Working with Vulnerable Young Children* London: Cassell.

Carpenter, B. and Herbert, E. (1997) Fathers: are we meeting their needs? in B. Carpenter (ed) *Families in context* London: David Fulton, pp. 50–61.

Curriculum and Assessment Authority for Wales (1996) *Desirable Outcomes for Children's Learning Before Compulsory School Age: A Consultation Document* Cardiff: ASESU Cymru.

David, T. (ed) (1993) *Educating our Youngest Children: European Perspectives* London: Paul Chapman Publishing.

Dept of Health and Social Security (1989) *The Children Act* London: HMSO.

DES (1990) *Starting with quality* (Rumbold Report) London: HMSO.

DfE (1994) *Code of Practice on the Identification and Assessment of Special Educational Needs* London: DfE.

DfEE (1997a) *Guidance on using the Code of Practice in Nurseries* London: DfEE.

DfEE (1997c) *Excellence for All Children* (Green Paper) London: DfEE.

DfEE (1998) *Guidance: 1998–99 Early Years Development Partnerships and Plans* London: DfEE.

Edwards, C., Gandini, L. and Forman, G. (1993) *The Hundred Languages of Children: the Reggio Emilia Approach to Early Childhood Education* Norwood, New Jersey: Ablex.

Ensing, J. (1996) Inspections of early years in schools in C. Nutbrown (ed) *Respectful Educators – Capable Learners. Children's Rights and Early Education.* London: Paul Chapman Publishing, pp. 11–22.

Ghouri, N. (1998) Advisers attack Ofsted early years role. *Times Educational Supplement* No. 4280 10 July, p. 8.

Hall, N. (1987) *The emergence of literacy* Sevenoaks: Hodder and Stoughton.

Herbert, E. (1994) Becoming a special family, in T. David (ed) *Working together for young children* London: Routledge, pp. 81–92.

Herbert, E. and Moir, J. (1996) Children with Special Educational Needs – a Collaborative and Inclusive Style of Working, in C. Nutbrown (ed) *Respectful Educators – Capable Learners. Children's Rights and Early Education* London: Paul Chapman Publishing, pp. 56–68

James, A. (1998) From the child's point of view, in C. Panter-Brick (ed) *Biosocial perspectives on children* Oxford: Oxford University Press

Mills, C. (1998) *Britain's Early Years Disaster* Survey of research evidence for Channel 4 Television Documentary 'Too Much. Too Young'.

Moyles, J. (1989) *Just playing?* Milton Keynes: Open University Press.

Nutbrown, C. (1998) *The lore and language of early education* Sheffield: University of Sheffield Division of Education.

Ofsted (1993) *First Class: the standards and quality of education in reception classes* London: HMSO.

Ofsted (1995) *Guidance on the inspection of nursery and primary schools* London: HMSO.

Ofsted (1997a) *Guidance on the Inspection of Nursery Education Provision in the Private, Voluntary and Independent Sectors* London: The Stationery Office.

Ofsted (1997b) *The quality of education in nursery voucher settings* London: Ofsted/DfEE.

Ofsted (1997c) *Guidance on the inspection of nursery education provision in the private, voluntary and independent sectors* London: The Stationery Office.

Ofsted (1998) *The quality of education in institutions inspected under the nursery education funding arrangements* London: Ofsted.

Pugh, G. (1988) *Services for the under fives: developing a coordinated approach* London: National Children's Bureau.

Reynolds, B. (1997) *Literacy in the Pre-school* Stoke-on-Trent: Trentham Books

SCAA (1996) *Desirable outcomes for children's learning on entering compulsory education* London: SCAA.

Sylva, K. (1994) The impact of early learning on children's later development. in C. Ball *Start right. The importance of early learning* London: RSA.

Sylva, K. (1998) Too formal too soon? Keynote address presented at the Islington Early Years Conference, Building on Best Practice in the Early Years, 9 July.

Sylva, K., Siraj-Blatchford, I. and Johnson, S. (1992) The impact of the National Curriculum on preschool practice. *International Journal of Early Childhood* Vol. 24 (2) pp. 41–51.

Willes, M. (1983) *Children into pupils* London: Routledge and Kegan Paul

Wilson, R. A. (1998) *Special Educational Needs in the Early Years* London: Routledge.

Wolfendale, S. (ed) (1997) *Meeting Special Needs in the Early Years* London: David Fulton.

Wood, E. and Attfield, J. (1996) *Play, learning and the early childhood curriculum* London: Paul Chapman Publishing.

13

Evaluating policy and practice

Carl Parsons and Carol Precious

Introduction

In the midst of league tables, standards and demands for effectiveness in education there remains a place for nurturing, facilitating growth, allowing exploration, as well as the more direct promotion of learning. This chapter seeks to lay out a comprehensive approach to evaluation in the early years of education but presents it as a set of options from which to draw. Teaching, and managing the learning of young children, has always got to be intensely about actually planning, doing, providing and interacting, matched, if necessary, by a modicum of reflection and analysis. It is therefore important that professionals who seek a degree of autonomy and self government in their vocation use that modicum of reflection in a targeted and useful way.

What is evaluation?

Evaluation can be defined as the purposeful gathering, analysis and discussion of evidence from relevant sources about the merit, quality of provision and the impact of courses and experiences on pupils. Put simply, evaluation is about a) getting useful information, b) collecting it in reliable and systematic ways, c) reporting into decision-making cycles and forums and d) supporting planning, development and accountability.

Some other items akin to evaluation are set out below

Monitoring   is routine collecting and organising factual data
                    – how money was spent, number of person
                    in-service days, courses complying with criteria
                    etc.

Assessment	is of pupils
Appraisal	is of teachers
Review	is the process of examining and discussing all available evidence on lessons, a subject or a strategy. Evaluation, along with information from monitoring and assessment, may feed into review.

Evaluation can be formative or summative. Formative evaluation is about an ongoing activity where the evaluation can feed in to alter the course of the activities. Summative valuation is usually retrospective.

Why do evaluation?

There are a number of reasons why valuable professional time should be devoted to evaluation. It can function to maximise information about the quality and impact of what we teach, how we teach and the way we organise teaching and learning and thereby help improve courses. It can also motivate staff and encourage team work. It can actually motivate pupils, and others asked to provide information who might feel valued by the special attention, and enhance relationships between learners and teachers. Where parents and others (visiting performance groups, health professionals, members of the community) are part of an evaluation, just doing evaluation can improve communication and commitment to the school. Evaluation can serve accountability demands from parents, the community, those who provide funding and those who inspect us. To that extent it is politically expedient at a time when colleagues are under scrutiny and under pressure to give evidence of being effective and adaptable.

What must be remembered is that one never evaluates comprehensively. Evaluation is always selective in focus and needs to be modest in scale to be feasible within the constraints of doing the job.

Evaluation techniques

There are eight main approaches to gathering data for evaluation purposes (see Table 13.1). It is important to choose approaches which suit your style, workload and audience. It is worth noting that a multi-method approach is best.

Table 13.1 Evaluation techniques and their main characteristics

	Characteristics
INTERVIEWS	– can control the setting in which data are gathered – can ensure questions are understood – can probe, penetrate and get at underlying feelings – can check more easily that answers are accurate
QUESTIONNAIRES	– can get at large numbers relatively quickly – can get representative samples from which to generalise – can be open 'almost essay style', or highly structured 'box ticking' variety
OBSERVATION	– advantage over the above self-report methods is that this involves actually seeing it happen – can involve written record, audio tapes, photographs or videos
STANDARDISED TESTS	– often valid and reliable measures of a situation at one time – allow comparisons between groups or for change in the same group over time
AUDIT SHEETS	– structure the collection of information – simple method to ensure coverage and avoid omissions
EXAMINATION OF OFFICIAL STATISTICS AND DOCUMENTS	– usually easily accessible background data – test scores, Pandas, examination results, attendance rates, free dinners etc. – stated objectives of a course, content, policy statements etc.
FIELD NOTES/ INFORMAL AND INCIDENTAL REPORTS OF EXPERIENCES, CASE STUDY, DIARIES	– can participate and record what happens as it happens, identifying issues only as they arise – exploratory technique – can record events over time – can record inferences, feelings and interpretations alongside a record of events
GROUP REFLECTION	– sharing meanings – pooling experiences and judgements – challenging assumptions – checking common practices – elicits personal feelings

This may seem rather scientific and 'researchy' but like a drama can be played out at the level of Shakespeare at the National Theatre or The Little Red Hen at the front of the class. Evaluation should be an activity designed for its context and purpose, but designed in the knowledge of its limitations.

The evaluation panorama

To put in perspective the focus of an evaluation and the techniques used the notion of an evaluation panorama is helpful. This separates out the different contents of professional work in education from national context through institutional context, and from process to the product or outcomes in terms of what the children have learned. In respect of this last, it is important that professionals develop a confidence to set their goals, in terms of pupil learning, as wide as they judge appropriate. Table 13.2 sets out this spectrum. The national, regional and local context refers both to requirements laid down in law as well as regulations which may apply locally. It is not all about restrictions, however. There are projects and funding opportunities available locally or regionally which may benefit the school. There may be supportive links established and school consortium arrangements which the school can join with.

The institutional context is the totality of provision in terms of school policies, visions, missions and commitments; the allocation of roles; the physical environment and resources available. The process refers to all that takes place in the encounters with children. It is all the interactions and experiences, it is all the contacts with staff and other children and the teaching and learning activities that take place. The product concerns outcomes. It is all the knowledge, attitudes,

Table 13.2 The evaluation panorama – from specification to product

National, Regional and local context	Institutional context	Process	Product
National curriculum and desirable learning outcomes; national policies; priorities; funding at national and local levels; local efforts and initiatives.	Policy and mission; roles; physical environment resources.	Interactions; experiences; school and community inputs.	Knowledge; attitudes; values; competences; dispositions; behaviours.

values, competences, dispositions and behaviours that the child acquires as a result of the processes (though it is never that simple) within the contexts provided. Figure 13.1 sets out the evaluation panorama to indicate the different aspects of the teaching and learning enterprise that are candidates for evaluation.

Spelling out the different areas which may be examined for evidence of quality, elements of the context can be scrutinised. What are the children's needs? How do they learn? How do they develop? What do they come with? (See Drummond and Nutbrown 1996.) It is in the uniqueness of what they are and what they bring (not what they are not or what they lack) that we find our starting point in the education of young children. We can judge ourselves by the depth and seriousness of our thinking in this area.

There are national and some local requirements to which the school must conform (SCAA 1996). Compliance with the National Curriculum is easily checked. The quality of the policy mission and

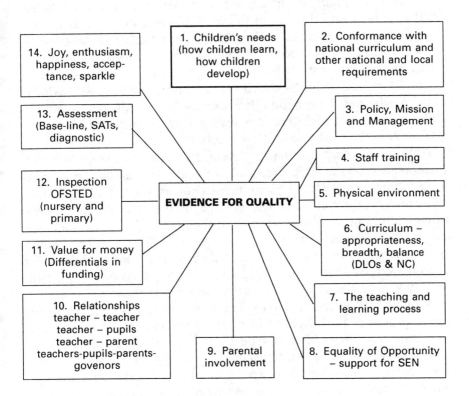

Fig. 13.1 Sources for evidence of quality

management is less obvious (Parsons *et al.* 1994). It is, however, fundamental that we have sorted out how as a staff we should do our work, how we are to act as a team in defining our goals and pursuing these. Staff training too should be optimised to make sure both that staff are developed and that the needs of the nursery or school are being fulfilled (DfEE 1998). The physical environment is a most important part of the context, immediately experienced by children, staff and parents. Some aspects of the physical structure of the building may not be amenable to significant change in the short term yet much can be done to create an environment which speaks eloquently of what the school is about. Less fancifully it is easy to set down what one sees as the feasible requirements of a good physical environment for young children and defined evidence of poor quality in this area.

Curriculum appropriateness is a matter of professional judgement and there is considerable scope for teacher and whole school choices about how to manage the content and learning opportunities for the children.

Evidence for quality of the process of teaching and learning (Ofsted 1995) is to be found directly in the work teachers do with their children. Parental involvement (SCAA 1996) is essential and relationships of all sorts need to be good if teachers are to be effective in guiding the learning of their pupils. Equality of opportunity (Long 1996; Smedley 1996), especially in the provision for children with special educational needs, and the general differentiation that needs to go with our outlook on young children, is a vital source of evidence about the quality of early years provision in a school.

While partnership with parents is central, the relationships between teachers, teachers and children and with support staff and governors are also important (Bartholomew 1996). Outcomes are of various sorts, some more in the control of teachers than others, some of more developmental importance to teachers and their work than others. Ofsted inspections mention value for money (Ofsted 1995) and will also cover the full curriculum range offering in their reports the Key Issues For Action (KIFAs). Assessment and recording is of course important, mainly so that we can target our work rather than show 'value added' or achieve well in league tables. The central objective is to foster the development of the whole child on the very broadest of fronts. This brings us to notions which have been ever present in the minds of early years teachers but in recent times not always confidently voiced. There are outcomes embedded in existence in a quality early years environment. These are the ever present excitement and joy of being there and doing things, the enthusiasm and happiness with which tasks are pursued, the acceptance of all and the 'zip' and 'sparkle' integral to the experience we would want children to have during these years and which we would want them to take away with them; to that extent this constitutes an outcome. Finally, returning to children's needs there is the assessment of the extent to which these have been demonstrably met. Have staff responded to how children learn and develop, met needs, and acted in ways which acknowledge differential needs?

Excellence in Schools (DfEE 1998a) states:

> Our children are our future as a civilised society and a prosperous nation. If they are to have an education that matches the best in the world, we must start now to lay the foundations, by getting integrated early years education and childcare, and primary education right.
>
> (DFEE 1998a, p. 15)

Early years education and the quality of children's early learning experiences from before statutory attendance in pre-school settings and Reception classes through to the end of Key Stage One are the focus of recent government legislation. Local Education Authorities were required to have in place from April 1998 Early Years' Development Plans (DfEE 1998). In these plans early years provision is co-ordinated and recognises the role of all those who work with young children. While most early years practitioners welcome the unprecedented focus on children under five, there is also a degree of scepticism because there are many motives involved, not least the wish to improve standards of literacy, to reduce crime (encouraged by the American High/Scope nursery programme's longitudinal research results indicating this benefit among many others, according to Schweinhart *et al*, 1993) and the need for improved levels of childcare provision. These are, of course, key reasons to support the development of provision but they do not begin with the premise that young children, as citizens – or at least future citizens – should be entitled to play and learn with friends in appropriate settings, that early childhood is an important stage in its own right.

Since the Rumbold Report (DES 1990) the search for a quality curriculum for our youngest children has resulted in the establishment of 'goals for learning by the time they enter compulsory education' (SCAA 1996) which are embodied in the Desirable Outcomes for nursery education and other preschool education, including four year olds in Reception classes. The Desirable Learning Outcomes do not constitute a curriculum for four year olds, rather setting out achievements, organised into six areas of learning:

- Personal and Social Development;
- Language and Literacy;
- Mathematics;
- Knowledge and Understanding of the World;
- Physical Development;
- Creative Development (SCAA 1996).

Following on from this is the Dearing revision of the National Curriculum (1995). These initiatives have sought to define a suitable curriculum for children from the ages of three to seven involving inspection criteria upon which standards for quality of provision and children's learning are measured through Ofsted Nursery and Section 10 Inspections.

Baseline Assessment, trialled from September 1997, and SATs testing at Key Stage One initiated in accordance with the National Curriculum, seek to measure children's achievements at both the point of entry into statutory education and at the end of the first Key Stage. However, these statistics offer measurement of the outcomes of children's learning rather than an in-depth analysis of the processes, the child's intentions and thinking which are hidden from our view by raw statistical data. Whilst such statistics may be an indicator of the outcomes of quality education, they belie the educational activities *per se* which underpin the children's achievements. It is the essential quality of young children's learning experiences that quantitative, summative assessment fails to identify.

Through observation and reflection upon children's activities we enrich our knowledge and understanding of children as individual learners and are enabled to integrate theories of learning with first hand evidence.

> Children's learning is so complex, rich, fascinating, varied and variable, surprising, enthusiastic and stimulating, that to see it taking place, every day of the week, before one's very eyes is one of the great rewards of the early year's educator.
>
> (Drummond and Nutbrown, 1996, p. 103)

It is the very complexity and diversity of children's learning that challenges our notion of quality and ways in which this might be defined. However, learning takes place within specific contexts, it is affected by the quality of the curriculum offered, the interaction between adult and child and what we value pedagogically. The product or outcome is the final stage.

The nature of early learning is essentially playful and purposeful having a particular importance for the child at one particular time and within a specific context. Children learn through exploratory play and first hand experience, hypothesising, taking risks and finding out how things work.

It is evident from the preceding chapters that the interface of preschool learning and learning within the constraints of a partially subject orientated, school-based experience presents problems that must be faced and surmounted if we are to bridge the gap and ensure quality of learning. Reflecting upon a common theme, all the chapters in this book, especially chapters such as Mike Radford's *Co-constructing reality* and Tricia David and Sacha Powell's *Changing childhoods* (in *Changing Minds I*), suggest that each child starts school with a unique set of learning experiences across a potentially wide range of activities.

One aspect of evidence of quality (as it might be defined in a caring, democratic society) is how successful we are as children's secondary educators in smoothing the passage between children's early experiences in the home and building upon these strengths towards the more formal school curriculum of early years experiences within the constraints of the legislated curriculum within the institutional context. Difficulties occur when we attempt to reconcile what we know of early learning in the home, the expectations of school and how we make links between preschool experiences and the need to build upon and translate children's knowledge and skills into an integrated approach towards learning.

Questions arise as to whether the two are compatible within the top down needs of the prescribed curriculum and the bottom up theories of early years education. However, as David and Nurse have commented in the preceding chapter, quoting from the work of Wood and Attfield (1996), a skilled early years teacher should be able to be flexible, to be sensitive to

> the meanings which children communicate in their play and how these then inform curriculum planning. They need a dual perspective here as well as a two way flow of information which is dependent on observation of children playing, supportive interactions in play where appropriate and a feedback system for children to relate and reflect on what they have been doing and learning.
>
> (Wood and Attfield 1996, p. 88)

The decision by the previous government to encourage the development of increased nursery provision funded by the Nursery Education

Voucher System has been augmented by the new government, although the Voucher Scheme was discontinued on their election in May 1997. Additionally, the legacy of goals for preschool learning – the Desirable Outcomes (SCAA 1996) – have been retained for the time being and it is these which form the basis for the inspections of voluntary and private provision. Section 10 Ofsted Inspectors also use these when looking at under fives in primary school classes. The Ofsted report on *The Quality of Education in Nursery Voucher Settings* (Ofsted 1997) identifies the quality of the teaching as the most significant factor determining the effectiveness of the curriculum received by the children. The Standards Fund budget for improving the quality of teaching in under fives' settings in 1998-99 includes in its priorities: the upgrading of early years teachers' knowledge and understanding of children's development and learning; wider access to training in provision for the specialised learning support for children with special educational needs. A survey of the research literature also indicates that teachers and educators seem to require training in science (in other words to prioritise training in relation to *Knowledge and Understanding of the World*), maths, and IT in particular (David 1996). Further evidence from Ofsted's (1998a) own survey of inspections shows that overall the private and voluntary sector needs training in: questioning techniques (to engage children in debating why and how things happen); practical problem solving and number operations in maths; communicating through the use of represention (for example using symbols); associating sounds with patterns and rhymes, with syllables, and with words and letters; and using the strengths of local communities to engage children in learning about cultural and religious events. Key points for action to improve the quality of provision clearly identified training needs for staff in order to increase their expertise in developing an appropriate curriculum to meet the needs of the *Desirable Learning Outcomes*.

This emphasis upon external evaluation, which clearly forces change, influences professional judgements made within the institution as to the training needs of the staff. The effect upon professional development is articulated in Vanessa Young's chapter in this book, where she draws analogies between accountability in school, target setting and measurable outcomes in relation to continuing professional development. The agenda set reflects government policy in a top-down model rather than using professional judgement to set one's own.

Focusing evaluation

As part of the inspection system, nursery providers are issued with copies of the DfEE revised version of the Self-Appraisal Schedule (DfEE 1998b). Here educators are urged to review their self-appraisal every six to twelve months as appropriate, depending upon staff turnover, changes made and the likely areas to be under the spotlight at the next inspection (as a result of what was highlighted by the last inspection). The headings given in the self-appraisal schedule are:

- general: setting's aims and objectives, etc.

- the setting's educational programme: who is responsible for planning, what sources of curriculum guidance are used, etc. areas of strength and areas for development (with reference to the Desirable Outcomes); how sessions are organised; assessment of children's learning;

- staff development: numbers employed, qualifications, training needs, etc.

- special educational needs: policy and provision, including monitoring of effectiveness;

- equal opportunities: policy and practice, monitoring that the policy is implemented;

- premises and equipment: strengths, areas for development, etc.

- children's welfare: how staff support children, procedures for promoting good behaviour, staff knowledge of child protection procedures, liaison with other agencies, effective monitoring of arrangements to ensure children's welfare;

- partnership with parents and carers: sharing information, learning from parents, assessing the effectiveness of partnership;

- quality assurance: steps taken to monitor quality (DfEE 1998b).

Such a document can be a helpful tool as part of a self-evaluation process. Here we give a further set of headings, which refer back to Figure 13.1 and to illustrate focuses, methods and the management of evaluation.

Children's needs

This is best addressed by group reflection and linked with discussion, consideration and confirmation of the school's policy and mission. As formative evaluation for development purposes, it is helpful to render the discussion 'data' by writing up key words and phrases which are expressions of individuals' values and evidence they present to support these values; this evidence is often not hard information but further values and this is entirely in order, since, as David and Powell point out in their chapter in *Young Children Learning*, each society constructs particular childhoods at particular times, depending on the underpinning, contemporary values. Such group reflections are sometimes aided by a recording format such as that in Figure 13.2 below which can be set out on a board or flipchart. Our ideas about what count as children's needs, our ideas about how they learn and develop should be contested concepts and to air these and argue about them is professionally valuable. For example, a number of research studies indicate the importance of children's self-esteem in relation to, for example, achievement in reading (Raban 1995), so one priority might be to ensure every child felt valued and was recognised for individual achievements – whether that be displaying kindness in sharing (by a child who had previously found this difficult) to singing a song for the group (by a child who was previously too shy to do so).

Main Priorities	Justification	Further Action

Fig. 13.2 Group reflection on children's needs

Conformance with national requirements

Checking this can most easily be accomplished by using an audit sheet, or *aide memoire*. This can list the activities, subject matter, etc., that should be covered and relate to a tick sheet upon which each class or the school as a whole can register whether the activity or content is covered or not.

Staff training and physical environment

Questionnaires can be very helpful and quick to gather perceptions of people about an activity or a context. Questionnaires can be produced quickly and simply. For staff training one could list the objectives and ask staff to record for each one whether it had been achieved, partly achieved or not achieved. For the physical environment one could list desirable attributes of the early childhood learning environment and use again the same response format for staff to register their judgement.

Curriculum appropriateness

This is best judged by the analysis of the school's documentation. In this there should be registered the learning experiences which it is expected children will have. A judgement can be reached as to whether it has, beyond conformance with National Curriculum requirements, the breadth, balance, colour, excitement and sparkle staff feel essential. In the chapter in this volume by Gill Bottle and Claire Alfrey on Mathematics in the early years, they relate how an assistant in a dress shop showed a child accompanying her mother how numbered tickets corresponded to the numbers on changing cubicles. Similarly, when some children in a reception class had been to a circus, the teacher encouraged them to arrange the chairs in a circle (like the seats around the circus ring), to number them and then to provide numbered tickets for other members of the class who would later find their own seats and watch a 'circus performance'. In both instances, the children's own interest has been captured to promote mathematical learning in particular (and other learning alongside that). The teaching and curriculum content were appropriate – and fun!

The teaching and learning process and equality of opportunity

Process is best observed. Choice of what to observe can be decided upon by staff bearing in mind their own mission and values about what counts as meeting children's needs. Peer observation is a very powerful tool for staff development as well as a manifestation of collegiality and mutual support. An instrument not unlike an audit sheet could be produced which asks if various things are happening and the judgement of the quality of that activity. Probably more useful is a less structured instrument which focuses on some of the children over a longish period of time perhaps intermittently. For equality of opportunity one could look at the activities of boys and girls to see that there is no undue bias and whether children with learning difficulties have suitable challenges and support. Similarly, staff should be reflecting on their relationships with children from different cultural, religious and linguistic backgrounds from their own, asking themsleves if they are ensuring social justice and fulfilling the requirements of the

Children Act 1989. Although the TTA (Teacher Training Agency) has been taken to task, and responded, over its omission of issues of social justice from Circular 4/98 and the initial teacher training curriculum (Millett 1998), teachers and educators can use other publications to help them question their own practices and policies, such as Siraj-Blatchford's *The Early Years: Laying the Foundations for Racial Equality* (1994).

Parental involvement

There is a whole range of ways in which feedback can be gathered about whether the school relates sufficiently well and sufficiently often with parents. Interviews with a sample are probably the most useful and penetrating way of gathering such perceptions. It is not necessary to interview many to achieve helpfully provocative feedback but it is useful to sample with care. Also, ask parents who are infrequent visitors to the school and whose interest in what is happening in the school may not appear strong. One can also ask staff about how they would like to relate to parents and whether they think sufficient information is exchanged and whether sufficient contact is maintained. At one first school, staff and parents went on a 'walk' to identify the first impression their school would give to a newcomer – they discussed how some new notices, a parents' room with coffee-making facilities would, among other improvements, help the school be more welcoming. The staff also discussed security and style of interaction with visitors – the first of these, though necessary nowadays, could be very off-putting to a 'new' parent, who perceived gaining entry to the building as intimidating; the other requires sensitivity on the part of all staff, with help from 'old' parents. In a similar way, school or nursery information, notices and letters to parents should be regularly reviewed, as well as the policy for ensuring parents who cannot read still have access to all the details.

Relationships

Relationships among children, between children and staff, and between parents and staff, governors/management committee and staff, etc. are the life-blood of every school and nursery. However, while these are the central relationships, there are others which are also important and need to be reflected upon. For example, one nursery head, on leaving to move to another post, decided to invite all those within and outside the school with whom she had worked during her term of office, to a 'tea party'. She drew up a list which began to look endless and it was only at this point she realised not only the breadth of experience the job had afforded her, but also that she should have held regular 'tea parties' throughout her headship, in order to enable the staff to be more involved in some of the liaisons. Her list included: health visitors, probation officers, social workers, librarians, education advisors, playgroup supervisors, childminders' coordinators, local education officers, tutors from further and higher education, members of the local police force, doctors, educational psychologists, physiotherapists, speech therapists, audiologists . . . and this is without the buildings inspector, the governors, the local vicar and priest . . . Thus the head or leader's personal philosophy and style can be very influential in setting the tone for so many relationships which have an impact on the smooth running of the school or group, and ultimately on the children and their learning.

Value for money and inspections

Ofsted inspections give a judgement on a value for money, a fairly ridiculous judgement since there is little one can do about expenditure to alter their judgement because it is based on the proportion of lessons judged to be sound or better. However, it is worthwhile judging whether the school, with the funding it receives, is allocating money in the most effective ways. Are there enough classroom helpers? Is enough spent on books and materials? Could there be re-allocations?

The Ofsted inspection process can be usefully hijacked by the school (see Parsons *et al.* 1990). One can devise one's own instrument from an examination of the Ofsted inspection guidelines and the Self-Appraisal Schedule (DfEE 1998b) and make judgements for oneself. The Ofsted inspection report can also be used to derive a fuller action plan than that required by the Key Issues For Action.

Assessment

Schools and nurseries should interrogate fully assessment data that is available to them. (See Beryl Webber's chapters in this volume and in *Young Children Learning*)

Joy

If the school is to be like a family it should have caring, happy attributes that should be recognisable and recordable by an observer. Looking round a room how many children look animated, interested, puzzled and challenged, exhilarated, concentrating? Is laughter a regular occurrence? Is learning challenging and fun?

Figure 13.3 gives a questionnaire which even the youngest children, given an oral presentation on it, can fill in.

Name..

1. When I come to school I feel
2. Doing number work makes me feel
3. Playtime makes me feel
4. PE makes me feel

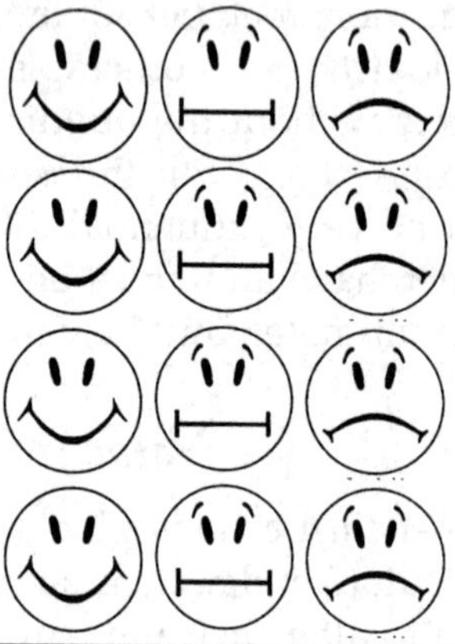

Fig. 13.3 Children's questionnaire

Making use of evaluation

Going back to the definition of evaluation and placing value on formative evaluation one would want to see the results of evaluation discussed by colleagues for there to be decisions which come out of the evaluation about who is to do what, by when, with what resources, and a commitment to monitor and review the impact that any changes make. The school or nursery which evaluates its work in a confident and efficient way is the one which is in charge of itself. A modicum of evaluation can reduce worries that arise at the prospect of someone else coming in carrying out an evaluation, or inspection. Evaluation should be a supportive collegial experience which celebrates and improves and empowers.

Issues

1. What can be done about the perceived 'home-school gap' and how could the education of children in the early years be organised to address such a problem?
2. What is the purpose of school mathematics? Is it purely for equipping children for everyday life or is it important that all children are given the opportunity to develop higher mathematical concepts?

3. It is widely recognised that there is a need to raise standards of achievement. Is there a danger, however, of dismissing all our current practice, even that which is good, in favour of a new and largely unresearched alternative?

References

Bartholomew, L. (1996) Working in a team, in S. Robson and S. Smedley (eds) *Education in early childhood* London: David Fulton/Roehampton Institute.

David, T. (1996) Nursery education and the National Curriculum, in T. Cox (ed) *The National Curriculum and the Early Years* London: Falmer Press.

DES (1990) *Starting with quality*. The Rumbold Report. London: HMSO.

DfEE (1998) *Early Years Development Partnerships and Plans* London: Department for Education and Employment.

DfEE (1998a) *Excellence in Schools* London: Department for Education and Employment.

DfEE (1998b) *Self-Appraisal Schedule* London: DfEE.

Drummond, M.J. and Nutbrown, K. (1996) 'Observing and Assessing Young Children', in Pugh, G. *Contemporary Issues in the Early Years: Working Collaboratively for Children* London: Paul Chapman/National Children's Bureau.

Long, P. (1996) Special educational needs, in S. Robson and S. Smedley (eds) *Education in early childhood* London: David Fulton/Roehampton Institute

Millett, A. (1998) Race to the fore. *Times Educational Supplement* No. 4280, 10 July, p. 17.

Ofsted (1995) *Guidance on the inspection of nursery and primary schools*. London: HMSO.

Ofsted (1997) *The Quality of Education in Nursery Voucher Settings* London: Office for Standards in Education.

Ofsted (1998) *School Evaluation Matters* London: Office for Standards in Education.

Ofsted (1998a) *The quality of education in institutions inspected under the nursery education funding arrangements* London: Ofsted.

Parsons, C., Howlett, K. and Corbett, F. (1994) *Institutional Development Planning: A Staff Development Manual for Primary and Secondary Schools and F. E. Colleges*, Lancaster: Framework Press.

Raban, B. (1995) *Early childhood years – problem or resource?* Inaugural lecture, Melbourne University Australia, 27 July.

SCAA (1996) *Desirable Outcomes for Children's Learning*, London: Department for Education and Employment and the School Curriculum and Assessment Authority.

Schweinhart, L.J., Barnes, H.V. and Weikart, D.P. (1993) *Significant benefits. The High/Scope Perry Preschool Study through age 27*. Monographs of the High/Scope Educational Research Foundation No. 10, Ypsilanti MI: High/Scope Press.

Siraj-Blatchford, I. (1994) *The early years: laying the foundations for racial equality* Stoke-on-Trent: Trentham Books.

Smedley, S. (1996) Working for equality and equity, in S. Robson and S. Smedley (eds) *Education in early childhood* London: David Fulton/ Roehampton Institute.

Index